Great World Religions: Islam

John L. Esposito, Ph.D.

THE
GREAT
COURSES®

PUBLISHED BY:

THE GREAT COURSES
Corporate Headquarters
4840 Westfields Boulevard, Suite 500
Chantilly, Virginia 20151-2299
Phone: 1-800-832-2412
Fax: 703-378-3819
www.thegreatcourses.com

John L. Esposito, Ph.D.

Professor, Religion and International Affairs,
Islamic Studies
Georgetown University

Professor John L. Esposito is University Professor, as well as Professor of Religion and International Affairs and of Islamic Studies at Georgetown University, Washington, D.C.

Professor Esposito earned his Ph.D. at Temple University, his M.A. at St. John's University, and his B.A. at St. Anthony College. At the College of the Holy Cross, he was Loyola Professor of Middle East Studies, Chair of the Department of Religious Studies, and Director of the Center for International Studies. Professor Esposito was also Founding Director of the Center for Muslim-Christian Understanding: History and International Affairs in the Walsh School of Foreign Service, Georgetown University. He has served as President of the Middle East Studies Association of North America and of the American Council for the Study of Islamic Societies, as well as a consultant to governments, multinational corporations, and the media worldwide.

Professor Esposito specializes in Islam, political Islam, and the impact of Islamic movements from North Africa to Southeast Asia. Editor-in-chief of *The Oxford Encyclopedia of the Modern Islamic World*, *The Oxford History of Islam*, and *The Oxford Dictionary of Islam*, his more than 25 books include: *Unholy War: Terror in the Name of Islam*, *What Everyone Needs to Know about Islam*, *The Islamic Threat: Myth or Reality?*, *Islam: The Straight Path*, *Islam and Politics*, *Islam and Democracy* and *Makers of Contemporary Islam* (with John Voll), *Political Islam: Radicalism, Revolution or Reform?*, *Iran at the Crossroads* (with R. K. Ramazani), *Islam, Gender and Social Change* (with Yvonne Haddad), and *Women in Muslim Family Law*. ∎

Table of Contents

Table of Contents

Great World Religions: Islam

Scope:

Islam today is the second largest and fastest-growing world religion, with majority populations in 56 countries spanning North Africa to Southeast Asia and significant minorities in Europe and the United States. Despite its more than 1.2 billion adherents, many in the West know little about the faith and are familiar only with the actions of a minority of radical extremists. Islam has had a significant impact on world affairs, both historically and in the contemporary era. Therefore, it is important to understand not only what it is that Muslims believe, but also how their beliefs are carried out both privately and publicly, both as individuals and as members of the Muslim community. We will see that Islam is not monolithic. Although Muslims share certain core beliefs, the practices, interpretations, images, and realities of Islam vary across time and space.

The focus of this course will be to better understand Islam's role as a religion and as a way of life. In 12 lectures, moving from Muhammad to the present, from the 7th to the 21st centuries, we will explore Muslim beliefs, practices, and history in the context of its significance and impact on Muslim life and society through the ages, as well as world events today. Thus, we will want to know the answers to many questions, including "What do Muslims believe?" "Who was Muhammad?" "How do Muslims view Judaism and Christianity and other faiths?" as well as "What is *jihad*?" "Does the Quran condone terrorism?" "Is Islam compatible with modernization, capitalism, and democracy?" and "Are women second-class citizens in Islam?"

As we see in Lectures 1 and 2, like Judaism and Christianity, Islam is one of the great monotheistic faiths that traces its ancestry to Abraham. We will discuss the similarities and differences in the three great Abrahamic faiths and explore more closely the core beliefs that serve as the common denominators that unite all Muslims throughout the world. We will also discuss the important and controversial concept of *jihad*, exploring the many roles *jihad* has played for Muslims historically and in contemporary times. Lecture 3 focuses on the Prophet Muhammad, a messenger from God who called for major reforms in the polytheistic, tribal Arabian society and served as the living model for all Muslims as their religious, political, and military leader. Lecture 4 will focus on the Quran, the Muslim scripture revealed to Muhammad over a 22-year period, which Muslims believe is the literal, eternal, uncreated Word of God. The Quran is believed to reflect and correct earlier revelations in the Torah and New Testament and to be the final revelation of God to humankind. We will see what the Quran says about God, the relationship between men and women, and dealings with other religions and communities, as well as the conduct of war and maintenance of peace.

Lecture 5 traces the stunning growth of the Muslim community, which within 100 years of Muhammad's death, became a vast, dynamic, and creative Islamic empire that stretched from North Africa to India. Islamic civilization flourished under the Umayyad and Abbasid empires, and Muslims made original contributions to art, architecture, mathematics, science, philosophy, law, and mysticism. Examining the history of Islamic civilization helps us to appreciate the remarkable achievements of its "Golden Age" and to understand the sources of sectarianism, religious extremism, and the conflict between Islam and Christianity, epitomized by the Crusades.

Lecture 6 takes a closer look at the historical development of two great Islamic institutions, Islamic law, the Shariah, and Islamic mysticism, Sufism. Islamic law has been seen as the ideal blueprint guiding Muslims' correct action, that is, what to do in their public and private lives in order to realize God's will. Sufism resulted from efforts to experience a more direct and personal sense of God. Both law, the *exterior path* to God, and mysticism, known as the *interior path*, developed as responses to what was perceived as the abuse of the enormous wealth and power in the Islamic empires.

Lectures 7 and 8 focus on the historical tradition of Islamic renewal and reform that developed to fight internal disintegration and upheaval in the Muslim world caused by outside forces from the 17th to the 20th centuries. We will examine the variety of religious sociopolitical movements that struggled to address weakness and decline in diverse Muslim societies through the ages, and we will discuss how and why these efforts continue to inspire Islamic modernists and contemporary movements in our time.

Lecture 9 looks at the worldwide "struggle for the soul of Islam" occurring today between conservatives and reformers, mainstream Muslims and extremists, on such contentious issues as the role of religion in state and society, the treatment of minorities, the compatibility of Islam and democracy, and the complex relations between Islam and the West. Among these issues, none is more fraught with controversy than the debates about women and Islam. Lecture 10 examines women and their changing roles in the modern world, a hotly contested topic, not only in the Muslim world but also in the West. We will discuss the diversity of dress, social status, education, and roles for women in the family throughout the world and will look at how women are fighting patriarchy and empowering themselves to forge new paths in the 21st century. Lecture 11 expands this human dimension to spotlight the ever-increasing reality of Muslims as our neighbors and colleagues in Europe and America. We will look at how and why Muslims came to Europe and America and the issues of faith and identity, integration and assimilation that face them in their new homelands and the multitude of ways they are grappling with these challenges in society and the workplace.

Lecture 12 concludes our study of Islam by reviewing the key questions that are raised about Muslims and Islam today. We also look at prospects for Islam *and* the West and Islam *in* the West in the 21st century. ∎

Islam Yesterday, Today, and Tomorrow
Lecture 1

The diversity of cultural and religious practices of Islam is reflected by the geographic expanse of the Muslim world.

Like Judaism and Christianity, Islam is one of the great monotheistic faiths that traces its ancestry to Abraham. Muslims share certain core beliefs, but the cultural practices, interpretations, and realities of Islam vary across time and space. Although Islam's more than 1 billion followers live in some 56 countries around the world, many in the West know little about the faith and are familiar only with the actions of a minority of radical extremists. Islam is the second largest and fastest growing of the world's religions, is part of the religious landscape of America and Europe, and has had a significant impact on world affairs.

The geographic, cultural, and religious diversity of Islam reflects its status as a world religion with a global presence and impact. Islam is the second largest and one of the fastest growing of the world's religions. Its followers can be found in some 56 countries and include many peoples, races, languages, ethnic groups, tribes, and cultures. Only 20 percent of the world's Muslims are Arab, the majority of Muslims live in Asian and African societies. Islam is a visible presence in the West as the second largest religion in Europe and soon to be the second largest in America. Despite the Islamic community's size, global presence, and significance, myths, stereotypes, and misinformation about Islam and Muslims abound.

The study of Islam today is often motivated by and cannot escape the threat that radical Islam—Muslim extremists and terrorists—have posed to their own societies and to the West. Significant interest in Islam in recent decades was not driven by Islam as the second largest and perhaps fastest growing world religion but by the challenge and threat of political Islam or Islamic fundamentalism. This is especially true after September 11, 2001, in the context of the war against global terrorism and, in particular, al-Qaeda.

Although all Muslims believe in God, the Quran, and the teachings of Muhammad, there is a rich diversity of interpretation and cultural practices. Understanding Islam requires a bridging of religion, history, politics, and culture. The word *islam* means "submission" or "surrender." A Muslim seeks to follow and actualize God's will in history, as an individual and a member of a worldwide faith community. The Muslim community (*ummah*) is a transnational community of believers, God ordained and guided, to spread an Islamic order to create a socially just society.

Like Judaism and Christianity, Islam is one of the great monotheistic faiths that traces its ancestry to Abraham.

Islam belongs to the family of great monotheistic faiths, the children of Abraham: Judaism, Christianity, and Islam. Jews and Christians trace their genealogy to Abraham through Sara and her son Isaac; Muslims represent the other branch of the family, which descends from Abraham's son Ismail and Sarah's handmaid, his mother, Hagar.

Although specific and significant differences exist among Judaism, Christianity, and Islam, all three faiths share a profound monotheism, belief in the one, transcendent God, who is creator, sustainer, and ruler of the universe. All believe in angels, Satan, prophets, revelation, moral accountability and responsibility, divine judgment, and eternal reward or punishment. Thus, for Muslims, Islam is the fulfillment and completion of earlier revelations.

Islam has a significant impact on world affairs. It is a dynamic religion that interfaces and, at times, competes with other faiths. In contrast to a separation of church and state, for many Muslims, religion and society, faith and power, are closely intertwined. From the creation of the first Muslim community in seventh-century Arabia to contemporary times, Muslims have debated and sought to implement God's will in their personal, as well as public lives; in their families, as well as states and societies. Thus, to be a Muslim was to live in an Islamic community-state, governed by Islamic law.

From the time of Muhammad to the present, Muslims have engaged in a continuous process of applying Islam to the realities of life. Islamic law, theology, and mysticism reflect this complex process. Religious doctrines, laws, and practices result not only from sacred texts but also from fallible interpreters, whose conclusions reflect their intelligence, political and social contexts, and customs, as well as power and privilege. The fact that interpreters of Islam were males living in patriarchal societies naturally affected the development of Islamic law and thought, especially its impact on women and the family.

Islamic doctrines and laws developed in response to political and social questions and issues. Thus, it is correct to say that there is one Islam, revealed in the Quran and the traditions of the Prophet, but Islamic tradition and heritage reveal many interpretations of Islam, some complementing each other, and others in conflict.

As Muslims today, like Jews and Christians, contend with the relationship of faith to the modern world, many questions arise. Should Islam be restricted to personal life or integral to the state, law, and society? Is Islam compatible with democracy, secularism, human rights, and the status of religious minorities, non-Muslims, and women? Muslims also face questions regarding the relationship of the Islamic world to the West. Christian-Muslim relations are often seen through the stereotype of *jihad* and extremism or a militant Judeo-Christian tradition of Crusades, Inquisition, European colonialism, and American neo-colonialism. Such perceptions lead both sides to foresee an impending clash of civilizations. In recent years, the questions of Islam *and* the West are joined to those of Islam *in* the West. Many issues are related to Muslim assimilation in non-Muslim countries. ∎

Suggested Reading

Akbar Ahmed, *Islam Today*, chapter 1.

John L. Esposito, *What Everyone Needs to Know about Islam*.

———, "The Many Faces of the Muslim Experience," *World Religions Today*, chapter 4.

1. What are some of the signs of the diversity of Islam today?

2. What are some of the questions that Muslims face in the modern world?

Islam—Yesterday, Today, and Tomorrow
Lecture 1—Transcript

The images and realities of Islam and the Muslims are multiple and diverse. This diversity is seen in a number of phenomena worldwide, in the many cultures in which Islam is to be found, from Africa to Southeast Asia, and from Europe to North America.

It is in the diversity of women's dress, their educational and professional opportunities, and their participation in mosques and societies. This element differs widely from country to country across the Muslim world. If women in some Muslim societies are fully covered in public, cannot drive cars, and are sexually segregated, women in many parts of the Muslim world wear a rich variety of clothing styles, drive cars, ride motorcycles, are among the top students in universities, serve in government, have been prime ministers or president of Turkey, Pakistan, Bangladesh and Indonesia, and are to be seen in the professions. We will discuss this further in our class on women.

The diversity is also seen in politics. In Turkey, Algeria, Jordan, Egypt, Kuwait, Yemen, Pakistan, and Malaysia, in all of these countries, we see Islamic activists peacefully pressing for the implementation of religion in state and society. Members of Islamic organizations have been elected to parliaments, served in cabinets, and been prime minister.

At the same time, extremist groups have engaged in acts of violence and terror. We see diversity in social action. Islamic organizations and associations provide a host of social services. They provide inexpensive and efficient educational, legal, and medical services in the slums, and in many lower-middle class neighborhoods of Cairo, Algiers, Beirut, Mindanao, and the West Bank, Gaza.

On the other hand, terrorists, in the name of Islam, hijacked commercial airliners and flew into New York's World Trade Center Towers and the Pentagon in Washington, resulting in the loss of some 3000 lives. The hijackers who committed this act reflected a religious radicalism that has threatened many governments and societies in the Muslim world, and as we've seen, also Europe and America.

The geographic, cultural, and religious diversity of Islam reflects its status as a world religion with a global presence and impact. Islam is the second-largest, and is among the fastest-growing of the world's religions. Some would argue that it is the fastest growing. The more than 1.2 billion followers can be found in some 56 Muslim countries, extending from North Africa to Southeast Asia, including minority communities from Europe and America to China, Thailand, and the Southern Philippines.

Muslims, then, include many peoples, races, languages, ethnic groups, tribes, and cultures. Only a little more than 20 percent of the world's Muslims are Arab, and yet most people equate Islam with the Arabs. The majority of Muslims live in Asia and Africa. The largest Muslim communities are in Indonesia, Pakistan, Bangladesh, India, and Nigeria; not one is an Arab country. Then, one could move on to talk about countries like Egypt or Iraq.

Islam is a visible presence in the West as the second largest religion in Europe; this is true particularly in France, Germany and England, as we'll discuss towards the end of this course, and is soon to be the second largest in America. It's currently third largest after Christianity and Judaism.

However, despite the size, global presence, and significance of the Islamic community, negative images, myths, stereotypes, and misinformation about Islam and Muslims continue to abound. As a Muslim writer titled his book years ago, many would agree that one can still say that Islam is "the misunderstood religion."

The focus of this course will be to better understand Islam's role as a religion and as a way of life for more than 1.2 billion Muslims globally. In only 12 lectures, we will be moving from Muhammad to the present, from the seventh to the 21st centuries. We will explore Muslim beliefs, practices, and history in the contexts of their significance and impact on Muslim life and society through the ages, as well as in relation to world events today.

Thus, we will want to know the answers to many questions, from: What do Muslims believe? Who was Muhammad? How do Muslims view Judaism, Christianity, and other faiths? to: What is *jihad*? Does the Quran condone violence and terrorism? Is Islam compatible with modernization, capitalism, democracy? Are women second-class citizens in Islam, and if so, why? The challenges we face are many.

As is obvious, in such a limited time we can never hope to do justice to Islam, nor any other faith for that matter. What we can do is provide information that can lead to a basic appreciation of Islam as a faith that has endured, prospered, and informed the lives of many, past and present. It is hoped that this discussion will motivate all who are interested to continue to study and learn in the future, to look to the bibliography that we've provided with the course and the materials.

One of the major problems with regard to the study of Islam today is that it is motivated by, and cannot escape the threat of, radical Islam. Radical Islam, Muslim extremists, and terrorists have posed threats to their own societies and to the West. It's easy for many of us to forget that the significant interest in, and awareness of, Islam in recent decades was not driven by recognition that Islam was the second largest and perhaps fastest-growing of the world's religions. Most people weren't even aware of that, but of the challenging threat of the Iranian Revolution, and of the impact of what is called "political Islam," or more popularly, called Islamic fundamentalism. Too often we've seen Islam, the religion of the majority of Muslims, through the lens of terrorism, the actions of a deadly minority. We don't do that with other faiths, and I'll talk about that in a short time. This problem is compounded by, and is especially true post-September 11, in the context of the war against global terrorism, and in particular al-Qaeda.

Thus, appreciation of the faith of the vast majority of Muslims has often been obscured by the tendency to view Islam and equate it with radical or revolutionary movements and their use of violence and terrorism.

We don't do this when we encounter the acts of violence and terror committed by Christians or Jews. Such acts have occurred in Northern Ireland and Serbia. They include those who blow up abortion clinics, and the extremists who killed Israel's Prime Minister Yitzhak Rabin; there is Dr. Baruch Goldstein, who slaughtered Muslims at prayer on the Hebron mosque in the 1990s.

The majority of us have been raised in the Judeo-Christian cultural society, and we are, or know, many Jews and Christians. We immediately and instinctively contextualize these acts as the acts of extremists, as aberrations, not representative of the mainstream.

Even when we use the word "extremist," we mean "extreme" as compared to mainstream Judaism and Christianity. We do not have a similar knowledge and experience of Islam and Muslims. Indeed, when we talk about extremist Muslims, it's not as if we instinctively then use the term "extreme," as compared to what norm?

It's hard for most of us to remember that until the late 1970s with the Iranian Revolution and the Soviet-Afghan war, Islam and Muslims were invisible. Neither is part of our cognitive nor our geographic landscapes. I can vividly recall the reaction of friends and family, when they learned that I intended to major in Islamic studies in the late 1960s. "You'll never get a job; why are you studying that abracadabra field?"

Having studied and taught Christian theology, and in the midst of graduate courses in Hinduism and Buddhism, my decision to study Islam seemed inexplicable; indeed, I was actually against doing it. What I knew of Arabs and Muslims, basically through a few movies or media, made me think, "Why would I want to study it?" I had to be pressured by the then-chair of the religion department at Temple University.

However, once I began to study Islam, I discovered a religious tradition with close affinities to Judaism and Christianity, with a rich religious, historical, and civilizational legacy that I had never been told about in high school or in university. For example, while all Muslims believe in God, the Quran, and the teachings of Muhammad, there is a rich diversity of interpretation in cultural practices. I knew neither about Islam, nor did I know about this richness of cultural practices. Indeed, that's true for many people today. They see the acts. It's like when you engage a new ethnic group; if you meet one Italian, and he tends to move his hands a lot, and seems emotional, and he's the only Italian you know, you think, "Well, all Italians are that way."

For many, the few Muslims that they see, the few actions, if they had just discovered Islam during the Iranian Revolution, and saw people shouting everyday "Death to America!" in the streets, the presumption would be that these people represented all Muslims.

Let's clarify several basic terms, as we begin this course. Like Hebrew, Arabic has a consonant-based root system. The Arabic root, "s-l-m," from which the word "islam" is derived, means "submission" and "peace." It yields three important terms among many: "Islam," "Muslim," and "salaam." Thus, the word "Islam" literally means "submission to God" and "peace," the peace that comes from following God's will, both to individuals and to a society. A "Muslim" is "one who submits," one who seeks to actualize or realize God's will in history, both as an individual and as a member of a worldwide faith community.

Finally, "salaam," whose root is similar to that of the Hebrew shalom or peace, is the common greeting that Muslims engage in: *salaam alaykum*, "peace be with you."

Muslims believe that God has given the Earth as a trust to humankind, and thus see themselves as God's representatives, God's vice-gerund. (Quran chapter 2, verse 30; chapter 6, verse 165) God's representative with a divinely mandated vocation to establish and spread God's religion, God's rule on Earth. It is on the basis of how God's will in history is realized that a person will be rewarded or punished.

Muslim's see their community, *ummah*, as a transnational community of believers that God ordained and guided, and which is to spread the faith and institutionalize an Islamic order, a "Pax Islamica," if you will. This is Islamic peace, just as the Romans had a "Pax Romana" to create a socially just society. As the Quran chapter 3, verse 110 says, "You are the best community ever brought forth for mankind, enjoining what is good and forbidding evil." Islam belongs to the family of great monotheistic faiths, the children of Abraham: Judaism, Christianity and Islam.

Again, when I was growing up, and for a good deal of my early career, one studied Judaism and Christianity here, and talked about a Judeo-Christian tradition; Islam was put with the other world religions. It was put with Hinduism, Buddhism, Confucianism; you name it. Very few talked about there being a Judeo-Christian Islamic tradition.

But, as many of you will recall from the Bible, Sara, the wife of Abraham, grown old and childless, told Abraham to have a child with Hagar, her handmaid or servant. Abraham and Hagar had a son, Ismail. Subsequently, to their astonishment, Sarah became pregnant and gave birth to Isaac. Fearing that her son Isaac would be overshadowed by Ismail, who was the first-born son, and that Ismail would receive, as it were, the inheritance, as the senior male of the family, the mantle of leadership, Sarah convinced Abraham to send Hagar and Ismail away. They made their way to Arabia. Jews and Christians traced their genealogy to Abraham through Sarah and her son Isaac.

Muslims represent the other branch of the Abrahamic family, the family that descends from Abraham's son, Ismail, and Sarah's handmaid, Ismail's mother, Hagar. While specific and significant differences exist, all the children of Abraham share a profound monotheism: Belief in the one transcending God, creator, sustainer, and ruler of the Universe. This belief provides answers to the ultimate existential questions, for example: "Who am I? Why am I here? What should I be doing? Why does it matter? Why does it matter whether I'm moral or immoral?"

All three faiths traditionally affirm the beliefs in angels, Satan, prophets, revelation, moral accountability and responsibility, divine judgment, reward and punishment, heaven and hell. Thus, for Muslims, Islam is the fulfillment and completion of God's earlier revelations to the biblical prophets of Judaism and Christianity. Indeed, Abraham, Moses, Jesus, and Mary are central in Muslim scripture, in popular piety and practice, and indeed in naming: Ibrahim, Abraham; Musi, Moses; Esa, Jesus; Maryam, Mary. One of my Muslim friends has two sons, Musa and Esa; Moses and Jesus, representing in his own family the Judeo-Christian Islamic family.

Islam has had also a significant impact on world affairs. It is a dynamic religion that interfaces, and at times competes, with other faiths. In contrast to belief in the separation of church and state, Islam, for many Muslims, represents a more comprehensive worldview, in which religion and society, faith and power are closely bound and intertwined. From the creation of the first Muslim community in seventh-century Arabia, to contemporary times, Muslims have debated and sought to implement God's will in their personal as well as public lives, in their families as well as in states and societies. Thus, to be a Muslim was not simply to belong to a faith community, or church, but to live in an Islamic community-state governed by Islamic law.

Many Muslims, then, see their religion as much more than a personal faith across time and space, and throughout Islamic history. Historically, Islam has significantly formed and informed Muslim politics and civilizations, giving rise, as we shall see later, to vast Islamic empires and states, as well as to a rich and dynamic Islamic civilization of arts, architecture, science, and medicine. In many ways, for example, in the fathers of algebra, and through major contributions to astronomy and optics. As we shall see later in this course, from the time of Muhammad to the present, Muslims have engaged in a continuous process of applying Islam to the realities of life. Islamic law, theology and mysticism reflect this complex process.

Religious doctrines, laws, and practices result, though, not only from sacred texts, but also from fallible, limited, human interpreters, whose conclusions reflect their intelligence, political and social context, and customs, as well as issues of power and privilege. In Islam, as in Judaism and Christianity, the Word of God has been mediated through the words of human beings. Religious traditions, beliefs, laws, and practices are the product of sacred text and human interpreters: Priests, monks, ministers, rabbis and *ulama*; that is, Muslim religious scholars.

The fact that interpreters and guardians of Islam were males living in patriarchal, male-dominated societies naturally affected the development of Islamic law and thought, especially its impact on women and the family. We'll have a lot to say about that.

While all Muslims believe in God, the Quran, and the teachings of Muhammad there is, then, a rich diversity of interpretation and cultural practice. Islamic doctrines and laws developed in response to political and social questions and issues: Who should succeed the Prophet? If somebody committed a major sin, a major negative act as a Muslim, if they assassinated the kala, for example, what did that mean in terms of their future in the next life? Religion and politics, the development of theology in politics closely intertwined. We'll see the same is true for the development of law and for the development of mysticism.

Thus, while in one sense it is correct to say that there is one Islam revealed in the Quran and in the traditions of the Prophet, as we shall now see, Islamic tradition and heritage reveal the extent to which there have many interpretations of Islam, some complementing each other, others in conflict.

Again, this shouldn't surprise us. We often say "Christianity," but there are in fact many Christianities: Catholics, Lutherans, Methodists, Unitarians. The same can be said with regard to Judaism. The result has been, within Islam, the development of two major branches of Islam, Sunni and Shii, as well as diverse schools of law, theology and mysticism, the revivalist and reform movements, as well as extremist groups and organizations.

As Muslims today, like Jews and Christians, contend with the relationship of their faith to modernity or post-modernity, from issues of faith and history, to politics, society, science and technology, many questions arise. I'll state some here that we'll be pursuing, but there'll be others in the course. Should Islam be restricted to personal life, or integral to state, law, and society? Is Islam compatible with modern notions of democracy, secularism, human rights, pluralism, and tolerance? Of particular concern are the status of religious minorities, non-Muslims, and women.

Muslims also face questions regarding the relationship of the Islamic world to the West. Christian-Muslim relations are often seen by non-Muslims through the stereotype of *jihad* and extremism. In contrast, many Muslims see too often in history, a militant Judeo-Christian tradition epitomized by the Crusades, Inquisition, European colonialism, Zionism, and what many call American neocolonialism. As you can see, at times there can be rather sharp and contrasting images of the other.

The fact is, however, and I should point out, that there are many Muslims and non-Muslims alike who cross those boundaries, who blur that distinction, and can see the acts of militancy of the past, not only in the other, but within their own tradition, and within their own heritage. Indeed, that is the challenge that we face in the 21st century, in an era of globalization; to have that level of self-criticism and, if you will, that level of global pluralist self-critical worldview.

Critics of the United States' actions in the Muslim world condemned support for authoritarian Arab and Muslim regimes during the Cold War and the post-Cold War, continuing down to the present. "Support by America and Europe," they would charge. Support today for Russia's occupation of Chechnya and its cleansing of Chechnya, and what many in the Arab and Muslim world charge is a bias or a tilt towards Israel in the Palestinian-Israeli conflict, and towards India and Indian rule over a Muslim majority population in Kashmir, in the current conflict in Kashmir.

Such perceptions often lead both sides to perceive an impending clash of civilizations. Indeed, many of us can recall, not only before, but certainly after September 11, many times when they asked the question, "Why?", their answer was: "It's us and them. They're against everything we stand for," or "They simply hate us." The answer wasn't that there may be causes for the spawning of terrorism; this is not to excuse terrorism, or those things that develop terrorism, but rather to emphasize almost a blind clash of civilizations.

In recent years, the questions of Islam and the West are joined to those of Islam in the West. Many issues are related to Muslim assimilation in non-Muslim countries. What does it mean to live in a country where Islamic law plays no role? American and European Muslims have to face this. How do Muslims cope with living in a secular America, or in Europe, which recognizes Christian and Jewish holidays, or holy days and customs, but has often been hesitant to accommodate Muslim Friday prayer, holy days, or the custom of women's headscarves.

Muslims have struggled to open mosques and schools, as well as faced harassment and hate crimes. This has particularly increased post-September 11. As we sit here in this part of the 21st century, it is very difficult, because we are on the one hand looking at Islam, a global religion, similar to the way in which we look at Judaism and Christianity, and as we are in this course,

Hinduism and Buddhism. Many of us who are non-Muslims will continue, until we learn more about what Islam and mainstream Islam and the vast majority of Muslims believe and stand for, to view Islam and Muslims through the lens of radicalism.

I recently did an online chat on a Muslim site, and I had questions from Muslims all over the world. Suddenly, though, I had a question from someone in the United States, a non-Muslim, who simply said, "Why are you in this conversation with all these terrorists?" There was nothing in the nature of the conversation, the questions or answers that was advocating violence or terror, et cetera; it was a sweeping assertion. I and others have seen these kinds of statements in the media. Many of you have seen statements made regrettably by some of our religious leaders, fortunately denounced by most, but people like Pat Robertson and Franklin Graham are using phrases like "Islamacy," not "extremecy," not drawing a line between extremists and mainstream, the very line they would want drawn when it comes to Christianity.

Muslims face the 21st century in their original homelands, that is, in Muslim countries, or in Europe and America, in a context in which finding answers within historical tradition is a time-honored strategy. As we shall see, like many other faiths, the tension between change and continuity with long held traditions often produces a struggle and a conflict between conservatives or traditionalists and reformers. Like the reformation and counter-reformation, with its struggle between Protestants and Catholics, the struggle for the soul of Islam today is not only one of lively and contentious theological debate, but, regrettably, can also spill over into violence and bloodshed.

As we turn to the heart of this course, we will seek to understand the faith and history of Islam, its ideals and realities, the inspiration and guidance that so many Muslims have found in their Islamic faith across time and space. At the same time, we will want to examine the challenges and diverse responses of Muslims to life in the 20th and now the 21st centuries. Thus, we shall address basic questions. What are the basic beliefs and practices that unify all Muslims? Who was the Prophet Muhammad, and what is the Quran? Why and how do they continue to be so influential in Muslim faith and life? How did the Muslim community grow and develop? What was the relationship of religion to politics and society? Why are Islamic law and mysticism so important for an understanding of Islam? How has religion affected Muslim women in the family, past and present? What is Islamic revivalism or fundamentalism? How have Muslims responded to modernity? What are the challenges that Islam and Muslims face in the 21st century?

The Five Pillars of Islam
Lecture 2

All Muslims accept and follow the Five Pillars of Islam: These pillars
are the core beliefs that unite all Muslims across time and space and are
the hallmarks that distinguish Islam from all other faiths.

Despite enormous religious, cultural, and political differences and
divisions, all practicing Muslims accept and follow these five
simple required observances, prescribed in the Quran. These *Pillars
of Islam* represent the core and common denominator that unite all Muslims
and distinguish Islam from other religions. Following the Pillars of Islam
involves a Muslim's mind, body, time, energy, and wealth. Meeting the
obligations required by the pillars reinforces an ongoing sense of God's
existence and presence and reminds Muslims of their membership in a
worldwide community of believers.

The first pillar is the declaration of faith. A Muslim is one who bears witness,
who testifies that "there is no god but God [Allah] and Muhammad is the
messenger of God." *Allah* is the Arabic word for "God," just as *Yahweh* is
the Hebrew for "God" used in the Old Testament. To become a Muslim,
one need only make this simple proclamation or confession of faith. This
proclamation affirms Islam's absolute monotheism, the uncompromising
belief in the oneness or unity of God (*tawhid*). Association of anything else
with God is idolatry and the one unforgivable sin.

The second part of the confession of faith asserts that Muhammad is not only
a prophet but also a messenger of God, one to whom God has sent a book for
a community.   For Muslims, Muhammad is the vehicle for the final and
complete revelation, the Quran. Like Jesus Christ, Muhammad serves as
the preeminent role model through his life example. The believer's effort
to follow Muhammad's example reflects the emphasis of Islam on practice
and action. This practical orientation is reflected in the remaining four Pillars
of Islam.

The second pillar of Islam is prayer (*salat*). Muslims pray (or, perhaps more correctly, worship) five times throughout the day: at daybreak, noon, mid-afternoon, sunset, and evening. In many Muslim countries, reminders to pray, or "calls to prayer," echo out across the rooftops. The prayers consist of recitations from the Quran in Arabic and glorification of God, accompanied by standing, bowing, kneeling, touching the ground with one's forehead, and sitting. Muslims can pray in any clean environment, alone or together, in a mosque or at home, at work or on the road, indoors or out. It is considered preferable and more meritorious to pray with others, demonstrating brotherhood, equality, and solidarity. When they pray, Muslims face Mecca, the holy city that houses the Kaaba (the house of God believed to have been built by Abraham and his son Ismail). Once a week on Friday, the Muslim equivalent of the Sabbath, the noon prayer is a congregational prayer at a mosque or Islamic center.

The third pillar of Islam is called the *zakat* or *tithe*, which means "purification." *Zakat* is both an individual and communal responsibility, expressing

The second pillar of Islam is prayer. Muslims worship five times throughout the day.

worship of and thanksgiving to God by supporting the poor. It requires an annual contribution of 2.5 percent of an individual's wealth and assets, not merely a percentage of annual income. *Zakat* is not viewed as "charity"; it is an obligation to respond to the needs of less fortunate members of the community. *Zakat* functions as a form of social security in a Muslim society.

Like Jesus Christ, Muhammad serves as the preeminent role model through his life and example.

The fourth pillar of Islam, the fast of Ramadan, occurs once each year during the month of Ramadan, the ninth month of the Islamic calendar in which the first revelation of the Quran came to Muhammad. During this month-long fast, Muslims whose health permits them to do so must abstain from food, drink, and sexual activity during the period from dawn to sunset. Fasting is not simply an act of self-denial. It is a discipline intended to stimulate religious reflection on human frailty and dependence on God. Many go to the mosque for the evening prayer, followed by special prayers recited only during Ramadan. Near the end of Ramadan (the 27th day) Muslims commemorate the "Night of Power" when Muhammad first received God's revelation. The month of Ramadan ends with one of the two major Islamic celebrations, the Feast of the Breaking of the Fast, called *Eid al-Fitr*, which resembles Christmas in its religious joyfulness, special celebrations, and gift-giving.

The fifth pillar is the "pilgrimage," or *hajj*, to Mecca in Saudi Arabia. At least once in his or her lifetime, every adult Muslim who is physically and financially able is required to make this pilgrimage, becoming a pilgrim totally at God's service. Every year, more than 2 million believers, representing a tremendous diversity of cultures and languages, travel from all over the world to the holy city of Mecca to form one community living their faith. Those who participate in the pilgrimage wear simple garments that symbolize purity, as well as the unity and equality of all believers. The second major Muslim celebration, the *Eid al-Adha*, or the Feast of the Sacrifice, occurs toward the end of the pilgrimage.

Jihad, "to strive or struggle," is sometimes referred to as the sixth pillar of Islam, although it has no such official status. In its most general meaning, *jihad* refers to the obligation incumbent on all Muslims, as individuals and as a community, to exert (*jihad*) themselves to realize God's will, to lead a virtuous life, to fulfill the universal mission of Islam, and to spread the Islamic community. More specifically, *jihad* also means the struggle for or defense of Islam, popularly referred to as "holy war." Despite the fact that *jihad* is not supposed to include aggressive, offensive warfare, as distinct from defensive warfare, this has occurred throughout history. As we shall see, the Five Pillars and the concept of *jihad* became integral parts of Islamic law and have remained central throughout Islamic history to what it means to be a Muslim. ■

Suggested Reading

Vincent J. Cornell, "The Fruit of the Tree," *The Oxford History of Islam*, chapter 2.

John L. Esposito, *Islam: The Straight Path*, chapter 3.

Michael Wolfe, *Hadj: An American's Pilgrimage to Mecca*.

Questions to Consider

1. How do the Five Pillars reflect Islam's emphasis on practice and action?

2. What are the multiple meanings of *jihad*?

The Five Pillars of Islam
Lecture 2—Transcript

When we look at Islam today, as in the past, we see unity and diversity. Whether rich or poor, educated or uneducated, "first world" or "third world," urban or rural, African, Asian, or American, however different, there is one thing that binds all Muslims together. Those are the Five Pillars of Islam. These are the essential observances or practices. Despite enormous religious, cultural, and political differences and divisions, all come together, whether it's to pray five times a day, to go on pilgrimage, or to offer the *zakat*, or the tithing.

These and others we'll be discussing today as we look at the Pillars of Islam. The Pillars of Islam are in fact the core and common denominators that unite. Not only do they unite all Muslims, but they distinguish Islam from other religions. As we'll see, they are actually very brief, and quite easy to understand, or get down. Meeting these obligations reinforces the ongoing sense of God's existence in Muslim life every day. It reminds Muslims of their membership in a worldwide community of believers.

The first Pillar of Islam is the declaration or confession of faith. There is no god but God, and Muhammad is the prophet of God. A Muslim, therefore, is one who bears witness and testifies: "There is no God but God (Allah the God,) and Muhammad is the messenger of God."

The *shahadah*, the bearing witness, will be pronounced and heard some 14 times each day by Muslims who pray five times a day, and in fact at many other times and occasions in a Muslim's life. *Allah*, literally, "the God," is the Arabic word for "god," very much as *Yahweh* is the Hebrew word for "God," to be found in the Hebrew Bible of the Old Testament. *Deus* is the Latin word for "God," used for centuries in the Roman Catholic Mass.

Who is this God? Allah is a God of might and majesty, of compassion and judgment. He is the Creator, Preserver, Sustainer, and Lord of the Universe. He is the Revealer and the Just Judge. As the Quran says, "He is Allah, there is no God but He. He is the knower of the invisible and the visible. He is the merciful and the compassionate. He is Allah, there is no God but He. He is the sovereign, the holy, the peaceable, the keeper of faith, the preserver, the mighty, the compeller, the sublime. Glorified be Allah, above all they associate with Him." Thus, to become a Muslim, one need only make this brief simple confession of faith. Again, "There is no God but God, and Muhammad is the messenger of God."

For those of us who are used to Christian creeds, in going to Christian services, one can appreciate the difference between what seems to be this simple sentence, however profound the beliefs behind it, and the rather lengthy variety of Christian creeds that we see in Christianity. The proclamation of this declaration affirms Islam's absolute monotheism, its uncompromising belief in the oneness of God. This is the doctrine of *tawhid*, of God's unity. There is the idea that associating anything with God is idolatry. To associate, not only other gods, but to associate other people, other values, is the one unforgivable sin for those who do not repent. Thus, for example, in Islamic art, religious art, Islamic art tends to rely upon the abstract. You will not see a presentation of God; you will not see a presentation of Muhammad. Indeed, the human form tends to be marginalized, although there are exceptions. Certainly, within Arab culture that has been the case. This is certainly true if one looks at the art and architecture of mosque.

The second part of the confession of faith asserts that Muhammad is not only a prophet, but also a messenger of God. This may take some of us a second to realize this distinction. In Islam, you have both prophets and messengers. Muhammad is not only coming as a prophet, as a warner, as a reformer, but he is a messenger. He is somebody who brings a revelation, who brings a book. For Muslims, Muhammad is the final prophet, the final vehicle. He brings the final and complete revelation of the Quran.

Like Jesus Christ, Muhammad serves as the preeminent role model through his life and example. Unlike Jesus, Muhammad is only a human being, although Muslims believe that he was a perfect man, or follower of God. Thus, the believer's effort is to follow Muhammad's example. He is the model; he is the paradigm. Many of the practices of the Prophet, what he said and did, came to be collected, as we'll discuss later, in a caucus of traditions or narrative stories, to which Muslims look. This practical orientation of Islam, then, is reflected in the remaining four Pillars of Islam. Again, note the emphasis throughout now on observance, on, if you will, "orthopraxy," right practice or observance, rather than, necessarily "orthodoxy."

The second Pillar of Islam is prayer or worship, *salat*. Muslims pray, or perhaps worship, more correctly, five times a day: daybreak, noon, mid-afternoon, sunset, and evening. In this way, the entire day is sanctified as they remember, worship, and find guidance in God. One experiences, in a sense, the presence of God. This is also to be found and captured in the Quran, where God says, "I am near. I answer the appeal of the prayerful one whenever he appeals to Me. Let them respond to Me and believe in Me, so they can be directed." This is from chapter 2, verse 185. In many Muslim countries, reminders to pray, or calls to prayer, echo out across the rooftops. The *muezzin* gives the "call to prayer." Indeed, modern technology's developed it's own novel ways of handling this, from audio and visual reminders to wristwatches, and clocks in the shape of mosques. Certainly this was true in the old days, I'm not sure about today, with most of them made in Japan; there are also computer programs.

Salat, or worship itself, consists of recitation from the Quran in Arabic, and the glorification of God. It's accompanied by standing, bowing, kneeling, touching the ground with one's forehead, and sitting. Muslims can pray in any clean environment. They can pray alone or together, in a mosque or at home, at work or on the road, indoors or outside. It is still not uncommon, while traveling in Muslim countries, to see people to stop on the street to pray, at a business meeting, or to see it as I have, on an airplane. Or most recently, in the British Air Executive Lounge in London, a Muslim quietly going aside to face Mecca and pray.

Wherever a Muslim prays, although not required, it is considered preferable and more meritorious to pray with others. This demonstrates and reinforces the common brotherhood, the sense of belonging to a common brotherhood, the sense of common equality and solidarity of that community.

When they pray, Muslims face Mecca. They face the holy city of Mecca that houses the Kaaba, the house of God, believed to have been built by Abraham and his son Ismail. Originally, Muslims faced Jerusalem. Muhammad had expected that the Jews of Medina would in time accept the message of

Islam. When it became clear that that wasn't the case, Muhammad received a revelation directing a change of the direction, or the *qibla*, the direction for prayer, from Jerusalem to Mecca.

In addition to prayer five times a day, which can be carried on by the individual, by his or herself, once each week, on Friday, the equivalent of the Sabbath, Muslims have a congregational prayer, the *juma* prayer. Here they go to mosque or to an Islamic center, again gathering every Friday. It doesn't necessarily mean that one ceases work on Friday, however. This varies from country to country.

What is held in common is this obligation to the common congregational prayer on Friday, and that this take place every week in a mosque. What is a mosque? A mosque, or *masjid*, literally means "a place of prostration." It's a building with a flat, open space for Muslims to assemble to pray. Mosques, like churches and synagogues the world over, can be small and simple, or they can be grand cathedral-like structures. Some of the largest ones occur, for example, in countries like Saudi Arabia, and more recently the new mosque in Morocco. On one of the walls is a niche, or a *mihrab*, that indicates the direction, the *qibla*, of Mecca. This is the orientation point for prayer. Nearby is a pulpit, or *minbar*, from which the sermon at the Friday congregational prayer is given.

In the courtyard, or the garden, there will be a place for the faithful to wash, to perform their ablutions, or ritual purification before prayer. Shoes are removed before entering the mosque. This is a sacred space, reminiscent of God's command in the Bible to Moses, as he approached the burning bush: "Take off your shoes, for the ground on which you stand is holy ground." At the end of formal, ritual prayer, individuals are free then to offer personal prayers, *dua*. These are prayers of petition or thanksgiving to God.

The third Pillar of Islam is *zakat*, the tithe, or almsgiving. *Zakat* literally means "purification." It's both an act of self-purification and a social obligation. Payment of this tithe purifies, therefore, not only a person's soul, but also what is given or distributed to people. It reminds Muslims, and this is the most important point, that their wealth is a gift from God, and that they have an obligation to share that wealth with others. We find, again, common variance on this in Judaism and Christianity, and their forms of tithing. *Zakat* and *salat* worship are often mentioned in the same Quranic verse, reinforcing its significance. Indeed, in early Muslim observe, it's almost a Muslim proverb, that "prayer carries us halfway to God; fasting brings us to the door of his praises; almsgiving procures for us admission."

Zakat, importantly, is both an individual and a communal responsibility. It's expressing worship of and thanksgiving to God by supporting the poor. It is paid during Ramadan, the Month of Fast. The *zakat* is constituted of a 2.5 percent tax on an individuals total wealth and assets, not merely on annual income. It's comprised of total wealth and assets. Thus, Islamic law stipulated very clearly and specifically those areas covered: silver and gold, animals, agricultural products. Today, modern forms of wealth, bank accounts, real estate, stocks, bonds are included. *Zakat* is not viewed as voluntary. It's not simply a voluntary charity. It is an obligation incumbent on all believers, for all who have received from God have an obligation to give back. It is a way of taking care of those who are poor, needy, or are debtors, as well as those who travel, those who are on pilgrimage, and those who seek religious knowledge.

Thus, *zakat* functions as an informal social security, at least in the past in Muslim society, and for some today. It is a way in which the poor in society, even today, can receive help from those who are in a better situation. There are religious taxes in Islam. In Shii Islam there is the *khums*. *Khums* means one-fifth. For Shii Muslims, they pay one-fifth, an obligatory tax to their religious leaders, who then redistribute it for a variety of purposes, from educational, to developing seminaries, to helping orphans. Then there are the more voluntary forms of almsgiving, called *sadaqah*. It is *zakat*, however, that is the obligatory form of almsgiving on all Muslims, whether they are Sunni, or Shii.

In early Islamic times, the *zakat* was collected by the government, held in a central treasury, and used to help the needy to build schools, hospitals, hostels, and to defray government expenses. In this way Muslims sought to fulfill the Quranic mandate. "The alms are for the poor, the needy, and those who collect and distribute them, and for redeeming slaves and captives, repaying debtors, and in the cause of God, and for travelers. Thus God commands. God is All-Knowing and Wise." Quran chapter 9, verse 60.

In modern times, *zakat* has been left to the conscience of individuals. Many people give it to poorer members of the family and those in their surrounding areas, as well as to others in more distant areas. However, some governments in recent decades, like Pakistan, have attempted to reintroduce the state collection and distribution of *zakat*. This has been highly contentious. The people worry about how the government will actually use their taxes, as it were. In addition, of course, those who really do not wish to pay all that they should be paying worry about a government that's going to go right into their bank accounts and take the money. Indeed, when it was first introduced in Pakistan, people woke up in the morning to an announcement on television, lest they suffer, I guess, undue anxiety.

The fourth Pillar of Islam, the "Fast of Ramadan," occurs once each year during the month of Ramadan, the ninth month of the Islamic lunar calendar. This, it's important to note, is the month in which the first revelation of the Quran came to Muhammad.

Ramadan is a time not only of physical discipline, but also spiritual reflection. During this month-long fast, Muslims whose health permits, and that's what's important, whose health permits, must abstain from dawn to sunset from food, drink and sexual activity. Those who are sick, pregnant, or weakened by old age are exempted. Muslims on a journey may postpone and make it up later.

Though rigorous, the Quran makes it crystal clear that the purpose of fasting is not to be excessively burdensome, but to foster spiritual growth. As the Quran says, "O, Believers, fasting is enjoined on you as it was on those before you, so that you might become righteous. Fast a fixed number of days, but if someone is ill or on a journey, then complete the number of days missed; and those who find it extremely difficult should, as a penance, feed a poor person…So whoever of you is at home, let him fast for a month. And let any who are sick or on a journey set aside an equal number of days at another time to fast. God wants things to be easy for you, and does not want any hardship for you, so complete the number and give glory to God for the guidance and be grateful." Chapter 2, verses 183-185.

It's important to note here, that for Muslims fasting is not a time of gloom. People welcome it. They look forward to it. Indeed, many Muslims who are not fully observant will fast during the Fast of Ramadan. So fasting is not simply an act of self-denial or asceticism. It is a discipline intended to stimulate religious reflection on our human frailty, on our dependence upon God, and to focus on our spiritual goals and values, our identity, and for Muslims to respond to the less fortunate in society. At dusk the fast is broken immediately with a quick, light meal. It is usually referred to as a "breakfast," breaking the fast. Families and friends share, in fact, a little bit later, a special evening meal that follows, which is often a very opulent meal in terms of the number of foods. Indeed, it has very many special sweets.

I can tell you as a Christian, particularly a Roman Catholic, who grew up with a different sense of fasting, this has amazed me that you had special sweets served during that time. I remember when I was in Cairo, even though I had studied Islam, I was jetlagged and a Muslim friend of mine picked me up, brought to the hotel, and said, "I'll see you at breakfast." Well, I went to sleep early and the next morning I got up and I waited for him. I waited all day. Finally, he called me in the middle of the afternoon. I said, "Where were you? I was waiting for you for breakfast." He said, "I was there last night!" I said, "Breakfast. Breakfast was this morning!" I completely disconnected that during Ramadan, breakfast means the breaking of the fast, and so is a much different time of the day.

Many, having broken the fast, go to the mosque for evening prayer, which is followed by special prayers recited only during Ramadan. Ramadan is also a special time to recite or listen to the recitation of the entire Quran. Properly, this is done by dividing the Quran into 30 sections or portions, to be recited each day of the month. You'll also see it on popular posters that are sold in many cities. Near the end of Ramadan, the 27th day, Muslims commemorate the "Night of Power," or the "Night of Power and Excellence." This is the night where Muhammad received the first of God's revelations.

The month of Ramadan ends with one of the two great Islamic feasts, or *eids,* the Feast of the Breaking of the Fast, the *Eid al-Fitr*. This celebration resembles Christmas or Hanukkah in its spirit of religious joyfulness, special celebrations, and gift giving. Muslims exchange cards, much the way others send Christmas cards, Hanukkah cards, and Easter cards.

The fifth Pillar, and probably the most well-known among non-Muslims, is the pilgrimage, or *hajj*, to Mecca in Saudi Arabia. It occurs approximately 60 days after the end of Ramadan. Every year, more than two million believers, representing a tremendous diversity of cultures and languages, more than 100 countries from all over the world, descend upon the holy city of Mecca, to form one community living out their faith, reenacting sacred events from the past. At least once in his or her lifetime, every adult Muslim who is physically and financially able is required to make this pilgrimage. They are putting themselves completely and totally at God's service. The ritual of the pilgrimage commemorates and reenacts events in the lives of Abraham, Hagar, and Ismail, as well as, as we shall see, the Prophet Muhammad.

For those who participate in this pilgrimage, men wear simple white, two pieces of white cloth, to symbolize purity, as well as the unity and equality of all believers. This is an equality that transcends class, wealth, privilege, power, nationality, race, and color. Whether poor or rich, you put aside your tattered clothes, or your Gucci wardrobe. The idea is that you can't see the difference. Women are to wear modest dress or modest clothes. Their bodies should be covered with the exception of their faces, hands, and feet.

Approaching Mecca, and throughout the pilgrimage, pilgrims will cry out, "I am here, O my God! You are without any associate. I am here! I am here! I am here!" Indeed, many, as they leave a city like Cairo or New York, will begin to say this on the plane in anticipation, and then as they approach Mecca. At the grand mosque of Mecca, and in the adjacent areas, pilgrims participate in rituals that symbolize key religious events.

Muslim tradition teaches that those who perform the *hajj* with great devotion and sincerity will be forgiven their sins. Thus, many of the elderly and sick will have as a hope that they will die on the *hajj*, having been cleansed of their sins, or shortly thereafter. Among the major rituals is the circumambulation seven times around the Kaaba, a cube-shaped building, the "house of God," that house believed to have been built by Abraham and Ismail. It symbolizes the believers' entry into the divine presence, reenacting, as it were, the movement of angels around the heavenly throne of God.

The Kaaba itself is about 40 feet long, 33 feet wide, 50 feet high, and it's covered with a black cloth with richly inlaid embroidered gold thread of Quranic verses. In its eastern corner is the Black Stone, about 12 inches in diameter, which tradition says came from heaven. It is a relic from the original Kaaba symbolizing God's covenant with humankind. Many pilgrims seek to touch or kiss it as they pass the Black Stone in their circular procession around the Kaaba.

Another ritual is walking or running between the nearby hills of Saffa and Marwah, commemorating Hagar's frantic search of the desert for water for her son Ismail. In the midst of her running back and forth, water sprang up, as it were, miraculously from the earth, producing the Well of Zamzan. Indeed, one of the rituals is drinking the water from Zamzan, and many will continue to drink water from Zamzan throughout. Many also, in small vials and bottles, bring samples of that water home to distribute to friends and family, commemorating the *hajj*.

According to Islamic tradition, both Hagar and Ismail are buried in an enclosed area next to the Kaaba. A ritual that some have seen, but not too many non-Muslims, unless you've seen recently some of the better programs that have shown many of the rituals of the *hajj* is the casting of seven pebbles; it's a symbolic stoning. Pebbles are cast at a stone pillar symbolizing Abraham's, or Ibrahim's, rejection of Satan's temptation that Abraham not follow God's command and sacrifice his son.

A climax to the pilgrimage is the assembling of these two million Muslims at the Plain of Arafat. This is where Muhammad delivered his farewell sermon. For as far as the eye can see, tents can be seen over valleys, and on the sides of mountains erected to house these pilgrims, who spend hours there reflecting on God, and reflecting on Muhammad's sermon, in which Muhammad said, "Here me, O people, for I know not if I ever shall meet with you in this place after this year…I have left among you that which, if you hold fast to it, shall preserve you from all error, a clear indication, the Book of God, and the word of His Prophet."

Then Muhammad recited to them the last revelation that he had just received. "This day the disbelievers despair of prevailing against your religion, so fear them not, but fear Me. This day have I perfected for you your religion, and fulfilled My favor unto you, and it has been my good pleasure to choose Islam for you as your religion." Indeed, Muslims will spend hours here at the Plain of Arafat talking, exchanging news and information, as well as reflecting religiously. On the *hajj* there is this exchange of information, as there always has been, both of news mundane, as well as sacred, and a certain amount of trading being done also.

The *hajj* ends with the *Eid al-Adha*, the feast that comes at the end of the *hajj*. It is celebrated not only by those on pilgrimage, but by Muslims around the world. This is the Feast of Sacrifice. It is a day for prayer, a day for sacrificing an animal, a sheep, or some other acceptable animal, commemorating again Abraham's ability to substitute an animal for the sacrifice of his son, Ismail. The excess meat will be distributed to the poor. Again, this feast is one of grand celebration, in which Muslim families come from far and wide, come home, as it were, to celebrate. Members come together, share meals, go to the mosques. In some societies it lasts for days, even weeks. Those who have made the *hajj* leave with the right to put a prefix before their names, to refer to themselves as "al-hajj," or "hajji," indicating that they are pilgrims, that they have made the pilgrimage.

Now we have the Five Pillars of Islam. At times, popularly, *jihad* has been referred to as the sixth Pillar of Islam. It's important to note that it is not the sixth Pillar of Islam in any formal sense. It has no such official status. We will be dealing with *jihad* more extensively later when we talk about the world view of the Quran. I think it important here, though, to speak briefly to the concept of *jihad*, because in many ways, *jihad* represents the entire vocation of the Muslim. *Jihad* and the Quran means, *jihad fi sabilillah Allah*: "To struggle in the path (or in the way) of God." The struggle to be a good Muslim as an individual and as a member of the community is encapsulated in the term *jihad*.

It is the struggle to realize God's will, to actualize God's will in history. It is the struggle to lead a virtuous life, to fulfill the universal mission of Islam, and to spread the Islamic community. Today, popularly, it can be used to describe a personal struggle, to keep the Fast of Ramadan, to be good, fulfill family responsibilities, to be good student, to clean up the neighborhood, to fight drugs, or to work for social justice.

More specifically, *jihad* can also mean the struggle for and defense of Islam. In this sense, it is sometimes referred to as a sacred struggle, or popularly, "holy war." Despite the fact that *jihad* is not supposed to include aggressive or offensive action, as distinct from defensive warfare, this has occurred throughout history. This is much as Christians develop a just war theory, but often with some of those wars, the justice all depends, as with beauty, on the eye of the beholder. Muslim rulers have used *jihad* to legitimate their imperial designs and expansion. In contemporary times, these have been religious extremists like the assassins of Anwar Sadat, the former president of Egypt. They include those like Osama bin Laden, and al-Qaeda, masterminds of terrorist attacks, carried out most recently on September 11, and subsequently also in Indonesia.

Those who engage in acts of global terrorism have often attempted to legitimate what they do by referring to them, these actions, as a *jihad*. As we shall see in our discussion, however, the Islamic tradition is quite specific in laying out rules and regulations, not just Islamic law, but the Quran itself, in terms of when and how the defense of the community is to take place. When is it legitimate to fight? When is violence legitimate? When is it illegitimate? Who can fight? Who may not fight? Who is exempted?

As we bring this lesson to a close, let's think then about the Five Pillars and their importance, because from the seventh century to today, however much Islamic faith has been subject to interpretation and reinterpretation, however much divisions have come up and differences among Muslims, however diverse culturally and politically, for all who claim to be Muslim, there are these five simple observances, the Five Pillars of Islam, that they share in common. There are these five simple things: the confession of faith, prayer, pilgrimage, fasting, and tithing or almsgiving. These five activities are what make an observant Muslim, a Muslim.

Muhammad—Prophet and Statesman
Lecture 3

> After 10 years of persecution and resistance in Mecca, Muhammad and the early Muslims moved to Medina, where Muhammad served as prophet, political ruler, military commander, chief judge, and lawgiver.

The birth of Muhammad (570–632 C.E.), prophet and statesman, and the rise of Islam has broad-based significance. The history of Muhammad and the emergence of the Muslim community have served as a paradigm to be remembered and emulated, as well as a sign that God's favor will be shown to those who carry out His will.

Muhammad is considered by Muslims to be both God's human instrument in receiving and reporting His revelation and the model or ideal for all believers, what some have called the "living Quran." Muhammad was a multifaceted personality who served as the religious, political, and military leader of a community-state. Muslims look to Muhammad's example for guidance in all aspects of life.

Information about Muhammad's life, deeds, and teachings is contained in the Quran, biographies, and the *hadith* ("tradition") literature. The religious message that Muhammad preached grew out of and responded to the realities of seventh-century Arabia. The success of Muhammad and the Muslim community was seen as a sign of God's favor to those who carry out His will. In contrast, such disasters as the fall of Baghdad in the 13th century or European colonial rule are seen by many as a sign of an errant Islamic community that had lost God's favor.

Religion in pre-Islamic Arabia was tribal in its religious, social, and political ideas and institutions and home to a variety of religious traditions and practices. Pre-Islamic Arabian religion was polytheistic, reflecting the tribal nature and social structure of society. Mecca, a rising commercial center, was the main site of a great annual pilgrimage to honor 360 different patron deities. The supreme god, Allah, was understood to be the creator and sustainer of life and the universe but was remote from everyday concerns. Tribal and family honor were central virtues. Pre-Islamic Arabian religion had little sense of cosmic moral purpose or of individual or communal moral responsibility or afterlife.

The message of Islam was revealed during and responded to a time of great socioeconomic transition in Arabia. Mecca was emerging as a major mercantile center at the heart of a new political, social, and economic order. New wealth and the rise of a new commercial class led to the greater division between social classes and a growing disparity between rich and poor.

Amidst this environment, Muhammad was born a member of the most prominent and powerful tribe in Mecca, the Quraysh. He was orphaned at an early age and raised by his uncle, Abu Talib, a well-respected and powerful tribal member who provided Muhammad and, later, his community with protection in Medina. Before becoming a prophet, Muhammad earned his living as a business manager for the caravans of a wealthy widow named Khadija, whom he married. Khadija was also the first person to believe in the revelation Muhammad received, making her the first Muslim convert. During the 24 years of their marriage, Khadija was Muhammad's only wife.

Muhammad was a man known for his integrity, trustworthiness, and reflective nature, who would regularly retreat to a hilltop in the desert to reflect on the meaning of life. In 610, on a night remembered in Muslim tradition as the Night of Power and Excellence, Muhammad, a Meccan businessman, was called to be a prophet of God and, later, religio-political leader of the Muslim community-state. He heard a voice commanding him to "recite"; this revelation was the first of what would be many revelations from God (Allah), communicated by an intermediary, the Angel Gabriel. Muhammad continued to receive revelations over a period of 22 years, until his death in 632 C.E. These would later be collected and compiled into the Quran.

Muhammad's reformist message posed an unwelcome challenge to the religious and political establishment, the priests, tribal leaders, and businessmen of the community. The new religious message that Muhammad preached, like that of Amos and other biblical prophets before him, denounced the status quo and called for social justice for the poor and the most vulnerable in society: women, children, and orphans. Muhammad's prophetic call summoned the people to strive and struggle (*jihad*) to reform their communities and to live a good life based on religious belief, not loyalty to their tribes. Muhammad's claim to be God's prophet and the divine revelation he proclaimed undermined traditional tribal political authority and sources of revenue (accrued during the annual pilgrimage and festival at the polytheistic shrine, Kaaba, in Mecca). The first 10 years of Muhammad's preaching in Mecca were marked by resistance and persecution and produced limited results.

Faced with ever-increasing threats and persecution, in 622 C.E., Muhammad and 200 of his followers emigrated to the town of Medina (approximately 250 miles away). This event, called the *hijra*, is centrally significant, as seen in the fact that the Muslim calendar begins with the year of the *hijra* and the creation of the Islamic community. This year also marks the transformation of Islam from being purely a religion to being a political system. While in Medina, the first Islamic community-state was founded and the fortunes of the Muslim community improved.

> **In Medina, Muhammad served as prophet, political ruler, military commander, chief judge, and lawgiver of the Muslim community, which was composed of Muslims and non-Muslims**

The experience of Muhammad's nascent community would provide the model for later generations. The twin ideals of *hijra* (which means to emigrate from a hostile, un-Islamic, *jahiliyya*, environment) and *jihad* were established. These concepts became the guides for responding to persecution and rejection and to threats to the faith, the security, and the survival of the community. Both mainstream and extremist movements and "holy warriors," such as Osama bin Laden, have selectively used the pattern of *hijra* and *jihad* for their own purposes.

In Medina, Muhammad served as prophet, political ruler, military commander, chief judge, and lawgiver of the Muslim community, which was composed of Muslims and non-Muslims—Arab polytheists, Muslims, Jews, and Christians. The Constitution or Charter of Medina established by Muhammad, which sets out the rights and duties of all citizens and the relationship of the Muslim community to other communities, reflects the diversity of its society. It recognized the People of the Book (Jews and Christians) as an allied community, entitled to coexist with Muslims and retain and practice their religions in return for loyalty and payment of a poll tax (*jizya*).

Having established his community at Medina, Muhammad and his followers continued to experience bitter conflict with Mecca. Several key battles occurred, which are remembered as a source of inspiration and guidance. These battles culminated in the Battle of the Ditch (627 C.E.), which resulted in a shift of the balance of power in favor of Muhammad. It also marked the onset of a particular deterioration in Muslim-Jewish relations.

Muhammad had anticipated the acceptance and eventual conversion of the Jewish tribes to Islam. However, the Jews did not recognize Muhammad's prophethood, and in the Battle of the Ditch, some of the more powerful Jewish tribes fought against him. He ultimately crushed them, executing the men and capturing the women and children.

Muhammad's treatment of these Jewish tribes in Medina has been seen as anti-Semitic, but it is important to note that the tensions and ultimate violence between Muslims and Jews were more political than theological or racial. The Muslims of Medina continued to coexist with smaller Jewish tribes who honored the covenant and would go on doing so in later centuries in Islamic empires from Andalusia to the Ottoman Empire.

Finally, in 628 C.E., a truce was struck between the Meccans and the Muslims in Hudaybiyah, granting the Muslims the right to make the pilgrimage to Mecca. After establishing his leadership in Medina, Muhammad and his followers subdued Mecca and consolidated Muslim rule over the rest of Arabia through a combination of diplomatic and military means. ■

Karen Armstrong, *Muhammad*.

John L. Esposito, *Islam: The Straight Path*, chapter 1.

Questions to Consider

1. In what ways is Muhammad the model for Muslim life?

2. To what extent was Muhammad a religious reformer?

Muhammad—Prophet and Statesman
Lecture 3—Transcript

Last class, we talked about the Five Pillars of Islam, and in particular focused on, in a sense, the foundation stones as are revealed in the confession of faith, God and the Prophet Muhammad. Today, we'll spend some time looking at the Prophet Muhammad and his role in Islam.

The origins of Islam and its Prophet, like those of Judaism and Christianity, would've seemed improbable to many who were forecasting at the time. In many ways, just as some could've never thought that a slave, Moses, and a carpenter's son, Jesus, would play a major role in developing or generating two major world religious traditions, how much more improbable would it have seemed that an often illiterate caravan manager, in many ways in the wilds of Arabia, in a country being torn by tribal strife, would in fact receive the revelation from God and become the great Prophet of the second largest of the world's religions, a religion that has had a global religious, political, and cultural presence and impact throughout history?

The birth of Muhammad, and the fact that he was both a prophet receiving and reciting God's message, as well as a statesman responsible for guiding the development of a totally new community, its military protection, politics, and social development, have had a major impact on history. It's affected the history of religions as well as international politics for Muslims and non-Muslims alike, for more than 14 centuries.

Information about Muhammad's life, his deeds, and teachings can be found in the Quran, early biographies and the *hadith*, or tradition literature—narrative reports of what the Prophet said and did. Muhammad is considered by Muslims to be God's human instrument, His messenger, and prophet in receiving and reporting His Revelation. The story of Muhammad's life and the emergence of the Muslim community have provided a paradigm to be remembered and emulated.

Thus, Muhammad's words and deeds represent the model, the ideal for all believers, what some have called the living Quran. As the Quran says, "You have in the messenger of God an excellent exemplar, for him who looks to God in the Last Day and remembers God often." Quran Chapter 32, verse 21.

Muslims look to Muhammad's example for guidance in all aspects of life, including how to treat friends and enemies, marital and family relationships, personal hygiene, dress, diplomacy, warfare, how to carry out religious duties, how to pray, and when to pray.

Muhammad was a multifaceted personality who served as religious, political, and military leader of a community state. Muhammad in Muslim tradition can best be described or characterized as a remarkable personality who inspired confidence and commitment. Despite persecution and oppression, he was a shrewd military strategist, and a pious, righteous, trustworthy, compassionate, and honest man.

He was also, and is also, portrayed as a caring husband and father, who through his teachings and actions sought to improve the status of all women. Let's look at the context in which Muhammad and Islam emerged.

The religious message that Muhammad preached grew out of and responded to the realities of seventh-century Arabia. Like all religions, Islam did not appear in a vacuum, but was influenced by and responded to the political and social conditions, as well as other religious traditions.

The world in which Islam emerged seventh-century Arabia, was a rough neighborhood where war was the natural state of affairs. The broader Near East in which Arabia was located was divided, itself, between two warring superpowers of the day: There was the Byzantine Eastern Roman Empire, on the one hand, and the Sasanian Persian Empire on the other. Each had competed with the other for world dominion.

Seventh-century Arabia was critically located along profitable trade routes of the Orient. As a result, it was subject to the rivalry and interventions of its powerful imperial neighbors.

The rising spread of Islam was caught, though, in both local politics and fighting in Arabia, as well as the imperial warfare. Muhammad's preaching would add to this mix and would itself become a source of conflict, as the Meccans resisted, as well as conflict resolution.

Arabia and the city of Mecca, in which Muhammad lived and received God's revelation, was beset by tribal raids and cycles of vengeance and vendetta. Raiding was an integral part of tribal life in society. It was the way things ran. It had established regulations and customs. Raids were undertaken to increase property and goods, such as camels, cattle, jewelry, and slaves. Bloodshed was to be avoided if at all possible, lest it lead to retaliation and vendetta, the existing primitive form of justice.

Pre-Islamic Arabia was tribal in its religious, social, and political ideas, its practices, and its institutions, but it was also a multi-religious environment. It was home to a variety of religious traditions and practices from the prevailing tribal polytheism to Judaism, Christianity, and Zoroastrianism. Pre-Islamic Arabian religion was predominantly polytheistic, reflecting this tribal nature and social structure. A variety of gods and goddesses served as the protectors of tribes. Their spirits were associated with sacred objects, trees, rocks, springs, and wells. These gods and goddesses were feared and respected rather than loved, the object of cultic rituals and supplication at local shrines.

Tribal and family honor were central virtues: manliness, courage in battle, chivalry, and upholding tribal and family honor were major virtues celebrated by all the poets of the time. Pre-Islamic Arabian religion had little sense of cosmic moral purpose or individual communal moral responsibility. There was no belief in the afterlife. Justice was obtained and carried out through vengeance and retaliation.

Mecca, a rising commercial center, was the main site of a great annual pilgrimage to its central shrine, the Kaaba, the cube-shaped structure that housed at this time representations of some 360 different tribal gods and goddesses. Muhammad would later conclude, having received God's revelation that the Kaaba was the original home built by Abraham and Ismail, that the identity had been lost as polytheism had overtaken the area and had in effect overtaken the Kaaba.

At the head of the shrine's pantheon was a supreme god called Allah, creator and sustainer of life and of the Universe, but remote from everyday concerns. This pilgrimage, sponsored by the Meccans, was a very profitable endeavor, bringing money as worshippers of the many different gods from far and wide came to this center in Mecca, where money was exchanged, and where trade took place.

Judaism and Christianity existed within Arabia, alongside pre-Islamic Arabian polytheism. There were then monotheistic communities present before the rise of Islam. Muhammad would encounter them also in his travels as a merchant and caravan manager.

In addition to belief in a single all-powerful God, as we'll see, again, Islam shared with Christianity and Judaism many common beliefs, from prophets and revelation, to notions of eternal reward and punishment. The message of Islam was revealed at, and responded then, to a time of great socioeconomic transition in Arabia. Cities, more precisely oasis towns, most importantly Mecca and Medina, were attracting many nomads to a more sedentary lifestyle. Mecca was emerging as a major mercantile center at the heart of new political alliances, a new social and economic order. New wealth in the rise of new commercial classes led to a greater division between classes, and a growing disparity between rich and poor.

Amidst this environment, Muhammad was born, a member of the most prominent tribe, the Quarysh. His father, and then his mother, died. At a very early age, Muhammad was orphaned, and was raised by his uncle Abu Talib, a well-respected and powerful member of the Quraysh, who provided protection to Muhammad both in his early years, as well as to Muhammad in the community later on. In a society that marginalized women often, Muhammad would remain sensitive to their plight as well as to the plight of widows like his mother throughout his life.

Prior to becoming a prophet, Muhammad earned a living as a business manager for caravans. He worked for a widow named Khadija. She was 15 years older than Muhammad. They eventually married, and interestingly enough tradition tells us that Khadija was the one who approached him in an offer of marriage. There was a 15-year gap between their ages; Muhammad was 25, Khadija, 40. Tradition records that they had two sons who died in infancy, and four daughters who survived.

Khadija was, in fact, the first person to believe in the revelation of Muhammad, and in many ways the first Muslim convert. As we'll see, she played a pivotal role in Muhammad's life. During their 24 years of marriage, Khadija was Muhammad's only wife. As we'll discuss later, after Khadija's death, Muhammad married a number of women. Most were widows as was the custom of the time; others were to forge alliances, political alliances. Muhammad was a man known for his integrity, his trustworthiness, and his reflective nature. He would regularly retreat to a cave on a hilltop.

In 610, on a night remembered in Muslim tradition as the "Night of Power" or the "Night of Power and Excellence," Muhammad, born in 570 and who died in 632 at the age of 40, this businessman, this caravan manager was called to be a prophet of God. As we shall see, he would later become the religio-political leader of a Muslim community-state, or prophet and state.

Muhammad heard a voice commanding him, "Recite!" Muhammad replied warily that he had nothing to recite. Twice more the angel repeated this, and commanded, "Recite!"

Muhammad, frightened and bewildered, pleaded that he didn't know what to say. Finally, the words came to him: "Recite in the name of your Lord, who has created, created man out of a germ cell. Recite for your Lord as the Most Generous One, who has taught by the pen, Taught man what he did not know." This was the first of what would be many revelations from God. They were communicated by an intermediary, the Angel Gabriel, over a 22-year period.

Like the biblical prophets before him, Amos, Jeremiah, and others, Muhammad's initial reaction was consternation, surprise, fear, and reluctance. Remember that prophets weren't exactly treated very well by those in their society, because they came and basically said to the society, "There's something wrong here." They were calling them back to God from what was seen as their wandering from God's path.

Muhammad also feared that he might be losing his mind, or that others would dismiss him as a madman. As in so many situations, he turned to his wife, Khadija, who reassured him that he wasn't crazy, that he indeed received God's revelation.

They also turned to Khadija's cousin, a Christian, Waraqa. Waraqa said to Muhammad, "Surely by Him in whose hand is Waraqa's soul, you are the Prophet of the people. The Angel Gabriel who came to Moses, has come to you."

Waraqa warned Muhammad, however: "Like the Hebrew prophets, you will be called a liar, and they will treat you contemptuously, cast you out and fight you." Muhammad continued to receive his revelations, then, for the rest of his life, for 22 years, until he died in 632. They were preserved verbatim orally, and then written down by scribes, and would later be collected and compiled into the Quran.

Muhammad's reformist message posed, though, an unwelcome challenge to the religious and political establishment, including the priest, the tribal leaders, the businessmen of the community. For indeed, like all prophets, he was a warner. The new religious message that Muhammad preached, like that of Amos and other biblical prophets, denounced the status quo, called for social justice for the poor, for the oppressed, the most vulnerable in society, for women, children, and orphans.

Muhammad, in the Quran, condemned Arabian polytheism and put a spotlight on Meccan society's unbridled materialism, its avarice, its corruption, characterized as a condition of pre-Islamic Arabia's pagan, *jahiliyya* society. That is a society that was ignorant of Islam. The term *jahiliyya* originally referred to pre-Islamic Arabia. However, it becomes a very important term today, rich in meaning, re-appropriated and reinterpreted by fundamentalists, and by others within the Muslim community, to describe the condition of modern society. Extremists will use the term *jahiliyya* to describe modern societies, their own as well as Western societies, as un-Islamic or anti-Islamic.

Muhammad was also a reformer, as all the great biblical prophets were. He brought a prophetic message that summoned people to strive, to struggle, *jihad*, to reform their communities, to live a good life based on religious belief and not loyalty to the tribe.

This insistence, that each person was personally accountable, not to primary tribal customary law, but to an overriding divine law, shook the very foundations of Arabian society and custom. Muhammad's newly-claimed status of authority as God's messenger, and his entreaties to believers to take action against social corruption in society, was in fact a direct threat to the powerful elites of Mecca. Muhammad proclaimed a sweeping program of religious and social reform that affected religious life and practice, business contracts, gender relations, and family relations.

Most importantly, the Quran rejected Arabian polytheism and insisted that there was only one true God. The oneness or unity of God, the absolute monotheism of Islam, would become the foundation stone of Muslim faith and belief. The Quran denounced corrupt practices, the practices of many merchants, and the exploitation of orphans and their inheritance rights. It condemned infanticide, spoke of the religious equality of men and women, and expanded the marriage and inheritance rights of women. To uphold this deeply challenging message and mission, Muhammad and his followers would not only have to preach their message in an increasing hostile environment, but also fight to wage a sacred struggle, to wage a *jihad* to stay alive.

Muhammad's claim to be God's prophet, and the divine revelation he proclaimed, undermined traditional tribal political authority and sources of revenue, mainly the revenues accrued during the annual pilgrimage, the festival to this polytheistic shrine.

The first 10 years of Muhammad's preaching in Mecca, as a result, were marked by resistance, and produced very limited results. The community was small and under constant pressure, suffering derision, verbal attacks, and later, active persecution. The life and livelihood of the community was eventually threatened by sanctions that prevented them from doing business, and were literally starving them out.

The hardship may well have contributed to the death of Khadija. It certainly contributed to the bankruptcy of Muhammad's protector, Abu Talib.

Muhammad was now, most likely, a target for assassination, with no longer the protection of his uncle.

It was at this very low point in Muhammad's life that an incredible mystical experience occurred, the "Night Journey" or "Ascension." One night, while sleeping near the Kaaba, Muhammad was awakened by the Angel Gabriel. Muhammad mounted a mystical steed, who flew him from Mecca to Jerusalem. Jerusalem referred to in the Quran as *al-masjid al-aqsa*, the "Further Mosque, the site of the Temple Mount.

Here, Muhammad climbed a ladder leading to the Throne of God. Along the way, he met the great patriarchs and prophets: Abraham, Moses, Jesus, John the Baptist, Joseph, as well as other prophets. During his meeting with God, Muhammad received guidance. Among the guidance received was the fixing of the prayers, the daily prayers at five. The Night Journey made Jerusalem, for Muslims, the third holiest city, after Mecca and Medina, in Islam, and affirmed continuity and affinity of Islam with Judaism and Christianity, that Jerusalem connection, a continuity that has theological significance, but also regrettably has also influenced conflict down through the ages.

Faced with ever-increasing threats and persecution, in 622 Muhammad accepted an invitation from the warring clans of the city of Yathrib, which would later be renamed Medina. This was a city where people were locked in a cycle of vendetta and destruction. To find some way out, they looked for an arbiter, and Muhammad had that reputation; I referred to him before as being an honest man and a good arbiter.

He was invited to the settlement to be a binding arbitrator amidst these diverse groups. It was a testimony to his established reputation. Muhammad began sending his followers to Yathrib, which is approximately 250 miles north of Mecca.

He followed a short time later himself, escaping the plot to kill him, and made his way with Abu Bakr, his companion, and the man who would later become his first successor, or caliph. Yathrib itself would later be named Medina, Medinat al-Nabi, the "city of the Prophet."

The year 622, when this migration, or *hijra*, to Medina took place is essentially significant. It underscores the importance of the notion of community in Islam. The Muslim calendar begins with the year of the *hijra*, the creation of the Islamic community, rather than, let's say, with the year the prophet was born, the year the prophet died, or the year that he first received the revelation.

It is also this year that marks the transformation of Islam from being purely a religion of individuals, to a religion that would inform state and society. In Medina, the fortunes of the Muslim community improved and thrived, resulting in the establishment of the first community-state. The experience and example of Muhammad's nascent community would provide the model for later generations, both then and now.

In times of danger, the twin ideals of *hijra* and *jihad*—*hijra*, to emigrate from a hostile anti-Islamic environment, and *jihad*, to resist and fight against depression and injustice—were established. Again, these are twin ideals that have endured throughout history. These concepts became guiding principles for responding to persecution and rejection, to threats to the faith, and to the security and survival of the community.

In the midst of persecution or resistance to aggression, Quranic verses revealed shortly after the *hijra* to Medina provided guidance concerning armed struggle and *jihad*. As the Quran says, "Leave is given to those who fight because they were wronged—surely God is able to help them—who were expelled from their homes wrongfully, for saying, 'Our Lord is God'." Quran chapter 22, verse 39.

The defensive nature of this struggle, or *jihad*, is reinforced in the second chapter of the Quran, verse 190, which commands fighting against aggression and against aggressors, but warns against aggression itself: "And fight in the way of God with those who fight you, but aggress not: God loves not the aggressors."

Both mainstream and extremist movements, and self-proclaimed "holy warriors" like Osama bin Laden have used the pattern of *hijra* and *jihad* for their own purposes. We'll discuss this in later lessons. In Medina, Muhammad therefore was both prophet and head of state, leader of a multi-religious community comprised of Muslims and non-Muslims. The constitution, or charter, of Medina, established by Muhammad sets out the rights and duties of all citizens, and the relationship of the Muslim community to other communities. It reflects this religious diversity. It recognized People of the Book; so Jews and Christians who have received God's revelation through their prophets were seen as allied and allies of the communities. These People of the Book were entitled to live in coexistence with Muslims, and retain and practice their religion in return for loyalty and payment of the head tax, or a poll tax.

Having established this community at Medina, the bitter conflict between Mecca and Muhammad and his followers continued, for Muhammad threatened the economic power and political authority of the Meccan leaders. He did that with a series of raids against Meccan caravans. In addition to this, several key battles occurred in this ongoing conflict between the powerful Meccans and the Muslims. These are remembered by Muslim tradition as a source of inspiration and guidance. Let's take a brief look at some of them, first and foremost Badr.

The Battle of Badr took place in 624. Muslim forces, although greatly outnumbered, defeated the Meccan Army in the Battle of Badr, when they were aided, as the Quran in chapter three, verse 20 says, "Aided by thousands of angels who assisted them." This battle has special significance for Muslims, because it represents the victory of monotheism over polytheism, good over evil, the army of God over the army of ignorance and unbelief. Badr remains an important symbol for contemporary Muslims. For example, Egypt, when it launched the 1973 Arab-Israeli war under Anwar Sadat, declared a *jihad*, and its code name was "Operation Badr."

A second and important battle was the Battle of Uhud, fought in 625. This was a major setback for the Muslims, however. They were overwhelmed by the Meccans, were soundly defeated, and Muhammad himself was wounded. In 627 the Meccans decided to finish the job, and mounted a battle that came to be remembered as the Battle of the Ditch. They put the Muslims under siege.

However, the Battle of the Ditch or the Battle of the Trench proved a major turning point. Muslims dug a trench to protect themselves from the Meccan cavalry. From within their enclave, the Muslims doggedly resisted the Meccan siege, and in the end the Meccans were forced to withdraw. The Meccan loss led to the ascendancy of Muhammad to a position of recognized influence and independence. It began the shift of the balance of power in favor of the Muslims.

Here we have to deal with a very important and contentious point, Muslim/Jewish relations during that battle and shortly after, which particularly deteriorated as a result of the Battle of the Ditch. Muhammad, as you'll recall anticipated the acceptance and eventual conversion of Jewish tribes. Thus, he had had the early community pray facing Jerusalem. However, the Jews did not recognize his prophethood. In addition, politically powerful tribes, some like the Banu Qurayza, kept up their relations with the Quraysh, Muhammad's and the Muslims' enemy.

During the Battle of the Ditch, the Quraysh encouraged the Banu Qurayza to attack Muhammad from the rear. Muhammad accused them of treason, conspiring with the enemy, and breaking their agreement under the constitution or charter of Medina. He moved decisively to crush them. After a 25 day siege they surrendered. Their men were executed, and the women and children taken captive.

Although there are many passages in the Quran that speak of Jews as People of the Book, recognizing God's revelation to Moses, Muhammad's treatment of these Jewish tribes in Medina has been cited by those who charge that he was anti-Semitic, as well as by Muslim extremists like Osama bin Laden to support their anti-Semitism.

However, it's important to note that the tensions and ultimate violence between Muslims and Jews at that time were more political than they were theological or racial. Muhammad regarded them as traitors, guilty of treason, a political threat to Medina, and an obstacle to the consolidation of Muslim dominance in ruling Arabia. He responded in accordance with the customs in Arabia and in many societies of his day. Remember that this was a rough area, a rough time.

Indeed, Muhammad's use of warfare was comparable to the warfare that we see at times in the Old Testament under Joshua, David, and Saul, in which God sanctioned battle with God's enemies. The Muslims of Medina continued to coexist with other smaller Jewish tribes, living side by side with those who honored the covenant. They would continue to do so in later centuries, in Islamic empires from Andalusia to North Africa, and to the Ottoman Empire. It's important to recall that when Jews were driven out of Andalusia, out of Spain, they fled to North Africa, and to the Ottoman Empire, where they were welcomed and able to continue to live and survive.

Finally, in 628 a truce was struck between the Meccans and the Muslims in Hudaybiyah, allowing Muslims the right to make the pilgrimage the following year, but requiring that Muhammad end his raids with their attempt at an economic blockade of Mecca. At the same time, the truce signaled the political legitimacy of Muhammad.

In 630, the feud between Mecca and Medina came to an end. After client tribes in Mecca and Medina clashed, Muhammad declared the truce broken and moved against Mecca with a large force. The Quraysh capitulated. The Meccans converted to Islam, and the Pax Islamica or Islamic Order was created.

In victory, Muhammad proved magnanimous and strategic, using diplomacy rather than force. Avoiding vengeance and plunder, he offered amnesty to his enemies. Regarding the Kaaba as the original house of the true religion, of true monotheism, he cleansed it of its 360 idols. The Meccans, formerly many of his oldest enemies, now joined him, converting to Islam, with some becoming leaders in the community.

The conquest of Mecca established Muhammad's paramount political leadership. He continued to employ his religious message, diplomatic skills, and when necessary, used force to establish Muslim rule in Arabia.

Consolidation of Arabia took place in the final two years before his death. When he died in 632, all of Arabia was united under the banner of Islam. Within a matter of decades, Muhammad had initiated a major religious and historical transformation that began in Arabia, but would become a global religious and political movement. He created a community based upon a common religious bond, way of life, and monotheistic vision, and brought a religious synthesis that recognized and incorporated Jewish and Christian prophets and revelations, and a universal mission to spread God's word and rule. It is this life, an example of the prophet that will continue to inspire the life and development of the community, as we'll see in our remaining lessons.

God's Word—the Quranic Worldview
Lecture 4

> **Muslims believe that the Quran is the literal, eternal, uncreated Word of God sent down from heaven to the Prophet Muhammad as a guide for humankind (Q 2:185).**

The Quran confirms the Torah and the New Testament (Gospel) as revelation from God, but revelation that became corrupted over time. Thus, the Quran was sent as a correction, rather than a nullification or abrogation, of the Torah and the Gospel. Muslims believe, therefore, that Islam is the oldest of the monotheistic faiths, because it represents both the original and the final revelation of God.

The Quran was revealed in stages over a 22-year period, first to Muhammad in Mecca (610–622 C.E.) and, later, in Medina (622–632 C.E.). The Quran was preserved in both oral and written form during the lifetime of Muhammad but was not collected and compiled into its current format until the reign of the third caliph, Uthman ibn Affan (r. 644–656 C.E.).

The Quran's 114 chapters and 6,000 verses (shorter in length than the New Testament) were collected, rather than edited or organized thematically or chronologically. Longer chapters (Medinan) come first, with the shortest chapter (Meccan) at the end. Arabic, Muslims believe, as the sacred language of Islam, is the language of God. All Muslims, regardless of their mother tongue or country of origin, memorize and recite the Quran in Arabic. Quranic passages are central to Muslim prayer five times each day. The Quran was central to the development of Arabic linguistics, grammar, vocabulary, and syntax. One popular activity in the Muslim world is Quran recitation competitions. Quran reciters and chanters are held in great esteem in the Muslim world.

God (*Allah*, Arabic for "The God and Creator") is central to the Quranic universe. The word *Allah* appears in the Quran more than 2,500 times. Allah is identified as the transcendent, all-powerful, and all-knowing creator, sustainer, ordainer, and judge of the universe. Although transcendent and, thus, unknowable, God's nature is revealed in creation; His will, in revelation; and His actions, in history.

The Quran declares an absolute monotheism, that there is no god but The God (Allah). Thus, Muslims do not believe in the Christian doctrine of the Trinity. Muslims recognize Jesus as a prophet, not as God's son. Concerns about idolatry have led historically to a general ban on artistic representations of human beings; most Islamic art is based on the use of Arabic script in calligraphy or of arabesque (geometric and floral) designs. Although God is all-powerful and is the ultimate judge of humankind, at the same time, the Quran emphasizes that God is also merciful and compassionate.

The Quranic universe consists of three realms—heaven, earth, and hell—in which there are two types of beings—humans and spirits. All beings are called to obedience to God. Spirits include angels, *jinns*, and devils. Human beings enjoy a special status because God breathed His spirit into the first human being, Adam. Humans were created by God to be His representatives on earth. The Quran teaches that God gave the earth to human beings as a trust so that they can implement His will. Although Muslims believe in the Fall of Adam and Eve in the Garden of Eden, there is no doctrine of an inherited Original Sin in Islam. Consequently, in contrast to Christianity, there is no belief in a vicarious suffering or atonement for all of humankind. Islam emphasizes the need for sinners to repent by returning to the straight path of God. There is no emphasis on shame, disgrace, or guilt in Islam. There is an emphasis on the ongoing human struggle—*jihad*—to do what is right and just.

The obligation of Muslims to be God's servants and to spread God's message is both an individual and a community obligation. All believers are equal before God in Islam.

Poverty and social justice are prominent themes in the Quran, and Quranic reforms presented a significant threat to the tribal power structure in place. Throughout all its declarations, the Quran emphasizes the responsibility of the rich toward the poor and dispossessed. The new moral and social order called for by the Quran reflected the idea that the purpose of all actions is the fulfillment of God's will to create a socially just society, not following the desires of tribes, nations, or the self. By asserting that all believers belong to a single universal community (*ummah*), the Quran sought to break the bonds of tribalism and create a sense of a broader Islamic identity.

Another major message in the Quran is that men and women are equal and complementary. Quranic revelations raised women's status in marriage, divorce, and inheritance. Men and women are equal in the eyes of God; man and woman were created to be equal parts of a pair (51:49). Men and women are equally responsible for promoting a moral order and adhering to the Five Pillars of Islam. (9:71–72).

The Quran frequently stresses pluralism and tolerance, that God has created not one but many nations and peoples.

The Quran frequently stresses pluralism and tolerance, that God has created not one but many nations and peoples. Many passages underscore the diversity of humankind. Despite the example of the Taliban in Afghanistan and sporadic conflicts between Muslims and Christians in Sudan, Nigeria, Pakistan, and Indonesia, theologically (and historically) Islam has a record of comparative tolerance. The Quran clearly and strongly states that "there is to be no compulsion in religion" (2:256). Jews and Christians are regarded as People of the Book, people who have also received a revelation and a scripture from God (the Torah for Jews and the Gospels for Christians). Historically, although the early expansion and conquests spread Muslim rule, in general, Muslims did not try to impose their religion on others or force them to convert.

From Egypt to Indonesia and Europe to America, Muslim reformers today work to reexamine their faith in light of the changing realities of their societies. Like Jews and Christians before them, they seek to reinterpret the sources of their faith to produce new religious understandings that speak to the realities of religious pluralism in the modern world. Many Muslims challenge the exclusivist religious claims and intolerance of Islamic groups who believe that they alone possess the "true" interpretation of Islam and attempt to impose it on other Muslims and non-Muslims alike.

The use of *jihad* in the Quran helps us to explain the term's varied use throughout history. The two broad meanings of *jihad*, nonviolent and violent, are found in the Quran and expressly contrasted in a well-known prophetic tradition. This tradition reports that when Muhammad returned from battle, he told his followers, "We return from the lesser *jihad* ["warfare"] to the greater *jihad*." The greater *jihad* is the more difficult and more important struggle against one's ego, selfishness, greed, and evil.

In its most general meaning, *jihad* refers to the obligation to follow and realize God's will: to lead a virtuous life and to extend the Islamic community through preaching, education, example, writing, and so on. *Jihad* also includes the right, indeed the obligation, to defend Islam and the community from aggression. The earliest Quranic verses dealing with the right to engage in a "defensive" *jihad*, or "struggle," were revealed shortly after the *hijra* ("emigration") of Muhammad and his followers to Medina in flight from their persecution in Mecca.

As the Muslim community grew, questions quickly emerged as to what was proper behavior during times of war, providing detailed guidelines on who is to fight, when war should end, and how prisoners should be treated. However, Quranic verses also underscore that peace, not violence and warfare, is the norm. Permission and commands to fight the enemy are balanced by a strong mandate for making peace.

Today, we frequently hear the question "Does the Quran condone terrorism?" This is the kind of question no one asks of his or her own scripture and religion; we save it for others! Historically, some Muslims have engaged in terrorism and used the Quran and Islam to justify their actions. The Quran does not advocate or condone terrorism. Throughout the Quran, in many contexts, Muslims are reminded to be merciful and just. However, Islam does permit, indeed at times, requires, Muslims to defend themselves and their families, religion, and community from aggression.

Like all scriptures, Islamic sacred texts must be read within the social and political contexts in which they were revealed. It is not surprising that the Quran, like the Hebrew scriptures or Old Testament, has verses that address fighting and the conduct of war. The Quran emphasized that warfare and the response to violence and aggression must be proportional: "Whoever transgresses against you, respond in kind." The Quran also underscored that peace, not violence, is the norm. From the earliest times, it was forbidden in Islam to kill noncombatants, as well as women, children, monks, and rabbis, who were given the promise of immunity unless they took part in the fighting.

Throughout history, past and present, the Quran, like the scriptures of Judaism and Christianity, has been the sacred sourcebook to which believers in every age look for inspiration and guidance. As we shall see throughout this course, because it is interpreted by human beings in diverse historical and social contexts, the Word of God has yielded multiple and diverse meanings, doctrines, and practices. ■

Suggested Reading

Akbar Ahmed, *Islam Today*, chapter 2.

John Alden Williams, *The Word of Islam*, chapter 1.

Questions to Consider

1. What Quranic beliefs and values are similar to those found in other religions, notably Judaism and Christianity?

2. Why do Muslims believe that their faith requires action in the public sphere?

God's Word—the Quranic Worldview
Lecture 4—Transcript

We've talked about the cornerstones, or the foundation stones for Islam, the Quran and the Prophet Muhammad. In our last class, we talked about Muhammad and his role, his reception of the revelation and the way in which he then served as prophet statesmen. However, central and pivotal and most foundational is the Quran itself. Thus, today we'll talk about God's word, the Quranic worldview.

Muslims believe that the Quran is the literal, eternal, uncreated Word of God, sent down from heaven to the Prophet Muhammad as a guide for humankind. Sacred scriptures exist because, throughout history, God has sent His guidance to prophets so that His will may be known. For Muslims, in terms of their worldview, and recognition, and certainly the Quran itself, this is especially true with regard to the great prophets of Judaism and Christianity— Moses and Jesus, and the revelations that they brought, the Torah and the Gospels.

The Quran confirms the Torah and the Gospel as revelations from God, but revelations that became corrupted over time. Muslims believe that, after the deaths of the prophets, extraneous, non-Biblical beliefs infiltrated the Torah and the Gospel, altering the original pure revelation. For example, Christian doctrines such as the elevation of Jesus from the great prophet to the Son of God, his death on the cross, and the Trinity are seen as human fabrications that distort and contradict God's original revelation and its monotheistic message.

Thus, the Quran was sent as a correction, rather than a nullification or abrogation, of the Torah and the Gospel. Muslims, therefore, believe that Islam is the oldest of the monotheistic faiths, since it represents both the original and final revelation of God. From a historical point of view, we might say that Islam is the youngest of faiths, dating Islam in terms of the creation of the Islamic community in the seventh century. For Muslims, Islam is the religion of God, is the religion that can be traced back through the prophets to Abraham and to God himself. The Quran has that and embodies that original revelation. Therefore, Islam is the oldest, if you will, of religions. The Muslim scripture, the Quran, is believed to be, then, the final and complete Word of God. The Quran and the example of the Prophet, his Sunnah, Muhammad's sayings and deeds, preserved, as we said before, in narrative traditions or *hadith*, are what Muslims have as their guide for daily life. They represent the foundation stones of not only Islamic faith but also Islamic civilization.

As we have seen, the Quran was revealed to Muhammad in stages over a 22-year period, first in Mecca from 610 to 622, and later in the Medina, 622 to 632. The Quran was preserved in both oral and written form, during the lifetime of Muhammad. That is, each of these revelations was preserved as it came. It then was collected and eventually compiled in its current format during the reign of the third caliph, Uthman, who reigned from 644 to 656.

The Quran's 114 chapters and 6000 verses, shorter in length than the New Testament, were collected rather than edited thematically or chronologically. The longer chapters, the Medinan, come first, with the shortest of the chapters or the shorter chapters, the early Meccan revelations, at the end.

As we have said, the verses are organized in two broad categories. These are the early revelations, which were those Muhammad received in Mecca, and the later ones, those in Medina.

The revelations to Muhammad at Mecca tend to be more concerned with religious belief and practice, while the later Medinan verses reflect the life, problems, and issues of the Islamic community-state at Medina. The Quran was revealed in Arabic and, therefore, Arabic is the sacred language of Islam. All Muslims, regardless of their mother tongue or country of origin, memorize and recite the Quran in Arabic and pray in Arabic. Quranic passages are central to Muslim prayer five times each day.

Translations of the Quran are typically accompanied by an Arabic text, not all the time, but often. Until relatively recently, translations of the Quran into local languages were resisted, even forbidden, for fear that the original text and meaning would be corrupted. Muslims believe that the Quran is a miraculous text whose divinely inspired and revealed ideas, language, or style cannot be imitated or duplicated. There are many stories about the great poets of the time who were non-believers, attempting to create poetry that would compete with the poetry of the Quran, or even being challenged to do so and failing. At the same time, there are many examples of people, both in the past and today, who, hearing the Quran recited, converted to Islam.

I can remember a member of the military who taught at a college that I was at; he was raised a Roman Catholic, educated in some of the best schools, and was a convert to Islam, telling my class how he had been walking through a small street in Thailand and heard the Quran recited in a mosque, having known nothing about Islam. It was that very recitation that drew him to the mosque, and that drew him to study Islam, and eventually to convert to Islam. For many Muslims, therefore, the Quran is the only miracle brought by Muhammad.

The Quran has played a major role in the development of Arabic language and literature. It's been a central force in the development of Arabic linguistics, grammar, vocabulary, and syntax. Quran reciters and chanters are held in great esteem in the Muslim world. Quran recitation competitions are a popular and widespread activity. It's much like going to the opera. Stadiums are filled as people come to hear the recitation of the Quran and the stature of reciters is significant. Audios and videos are sold in airports and in major stores and parts of town. While it used to be that native Arabic speakers seemed to have the inside track, in fact, in recent years, some of these competitions have tended to be won by people from Asia and Africa, from Nigeria, Pakistan, and Malaysia.

Let's turn to the Quranic Universe. Quranic Universe, at its center, is God and Creation. This means God, Allah the God, and Creation. The word "Allah" appears in the Quran more than 2500 times. Allah is identified as the transcendent, all-powerful, all-knowing, Creator, Sustainer, Ruler, and Judge of the Universe.

Although transcendent and thus unknowable, God's nature is revealed in creation, His will in revelation, and He acts in history. Thus, the Quran does not reveal God per se, but God's will or law for all of creation. The Quran declares, in absolute monotheism, that there is no god but The God. Thus, Muslims do not believe, as I noted before, in the doctrine of the Trinity, one

God in three persons, which most find impossible; they fail to understand how one can have that belief and still be holding onto absolute monotheism.

There is a similar basis for the rejection of the notion that Jesus, the prophet, was raised to the status of "son of God." Associating anyone or anything with God, remember, is the unforgivable sin of idolatry or associationism.

Although God is all-powerful and is the ultimate Judge of humankind, God is also Merciful and Compassionate. Every recitation of the Quran begins with the phrase, "In the name of God, the Merciful and Compassionate...." The Muslim vision of God is a God who forgives, sustains, protects, judges, rewards, and punishes. God's mercy, therefore, is believed to permeate the entire life and milieu of the believer, as we'll see now. The proclamation of God's mercy and compassion is made in the opening verse of the Quran, *Bismallah al-Rahan al-Rahim....*—"In the name of God, the Merciful and the Compassionate...." This phrase is used by pious Muslims at the beginning of letters, speeches, and the like if they're to give the kind of lecture I'm giving today; I would as well, if I were a Muslim.

A Muslim will say, *Bismallah al-Rahan al-Rahim....*, or just, *Bismallah al-Rahan* when they drive a car, begin a meal, begin a task. God's mercy, though, exists in dialectical tension with God's role as ultimate judge. Although justice can be tempered by mercy for the repentant, justice requires punishment for those who disobey God's will. On Judgment Day, all human beings will be judged according to their deeds, and will be either punished or be rewarded on the basis of their obedience or disobedience.

It's also believed that the Quranic Universe has three realms: Heaven, earth and hell. There are two types of beings residing in these places, humans and spirits.

Spirits include angels, *jinns*, and devils. All beings are called to obedience to God.

Angels serve as a link between God and human beings. Created from light, they are immortal and sexless. They function as guardians, guardian angels, and recorders and messengers, such as the Angel Gabriel who brought the revelation from God.

Jinn are between angels and humans. Although invisible by nature, they can assume visible form, and can be either good or bad. They, like human beings, will be rewarded or punished in the afterlife. Jinn are often portrayed as magical beings, and are popularly known in the west as genies. One can think of the story of Aladdin and his lamp, or the former television series, "I Dream of Jeannie."

Devils are fallen angels and jinn that tempt human beings in their earthly moral struggle. The leader of the devils is Satan, "Shaytan," who is also known as "Iblis." Satan represents evil, which is defined as disobedience to God. Satan's fall was caused by his refusal to prostrate himself before Adam upon God's command. The fall led to the struggle of human beings, who were torn between the forces of good and the forces of evil.

Human beings enjoy a special status, because God breathed His spirit into the first human being, Adam. They are to be obedient to God. Created by God to be His representatives on earth, as the Quran notes, God gave the earth to human beings as a trust. It is the job of human beings to carry out God's will. Although Muslims believe in the Fall of Adam and Eve, and the Garden of Eden, in contrast to Christianity, for example, there is no doctrine of an inherited Original Sin in Islam. Consequently, in contrast to Christianity, there is no belief in vicarious suffering or atonement for all of humankind. The punishment of Adam and Eve is due to their own personal act of disobedience. Each person, each human being, is held responsible for his or her own actions.

Human beings are mortal due to their human condition, therefore, not to the sin or the Fall of Adam and Eve. It is their mortality that makes them, and that follows from their humanity. The sin is the result of an act of disobedience, rather than a state of being.

Islam emphasizes the need to repent by returning to the straight path of God. This is the meaning of repentance, to return to the straight path of God. There is no emphasis on shame, disgrace, or guilt in the Quran. There is an emphasis on the ongoing human struggle, *jihad*, "to do what is right and just." The obligation of Muslims to be God's servants, and to spread God's message, is both an individual and a community obligation. Remember that the community is bound together by their common faith, not by tribal or family ties.

This common faith is not just a matter of belief and knowledge, but is to be acted out and implemented. The Muslim community, according to the Quran, and according to Islam, has a mandate mission to create a moral social order. Historically, this mission has provided a rationale for political and moral activism, spawning Islamic activists and revivalist movements, both mainstream and extremist. The requirement to implement a just society is reflected in a number of prominent themes emphasized by the Quran.

Obviously, among the most prominent of these is social justice. One of the most striking and controversial elements of the Quran at the time when it was revealed was its firm commitment to social justice, which was a significant threat to the tribal power structure. Rather than accepting the principle that the strongest are the most powerful, the Quran emphasized the responsibility of Muslims to care for and protect each other, regardless of socioeconomic status. Social justice was institutionalized by the Quran in decrees requiring the payment of an alms tax, *zakat*, a voluntary charity for the poor, stipulations for fixed shares of inheritance for women and children, along with other regulations for the just treatment of the dispossessed.

In addition, usury, the collection of interest, exploitation, was forbidden because it served as a means of exploiting the poor. False contracts were also condemned. Moreover, the Quran and Sunnah, the example of the Prophet, teach that Muslims should make every effort, struggle, *jihad*, to promote justice. This includes, therefore, the right to engage in armed defense. *Jihad* is present for the rights of the downtrodden, in particular, women and children, as we see in the fourth chapter of the Quran, verses 74 to 76, and in the defense of victims of oppression and injustice, such as those Muslims who had been driven out of their homes unjustly by the Meccans.

Throughout all of its declarations, the Quran emphasizes the responsibility of the rich toward the poor and the dispossessed. The new moral and social order called for by the Quran reflected the fact that the purpose of all actions is the fulfillment of God's will, not following the desires of tribes, nations, or self.

Another major message and theme of the Quran is that men and women are equal and complementary. The revelation of Islam raised the status of women in a number of ways: It prohibited female infanticide, abolished women's status as property, established women's legal capacity, and allowed women to retain control over their property. It changed marriage from a proprietary to a contractual relationship, granting women the right to receive their own dowry, and also granting women financial maintenance from their husbands in divorce, for example. It also prescribed a set of conditions to limit the husband's free ability to divorce at will.

Men and women are equally responsible for promoting a moral order and adhering to the Five Pillars of Islam, as the Quran in the ninth chapter, verses 71 to 72 states: "The Believers, men and women, are protectors of one another; they enjoin what is just, and forbid what is evil; they observe regular prayers, pay *zakat*, and obey God and His Messenger. On them will God pour His mercy: for God is exalted in Power, Wise. God has promised to believers, men and women, gardens under which rivers flow to dwell therein." This verse draws added significance from the fact that it was the last Quran verse to be revealed that addressed relations between men and women. Some Muslim scholars, certainly not all, argue on the basis of both content and chronology that this verse outlines the ideal vision of the relationship between men and women in Islam, one of equality and complementarity.

Related to this are the themes of love, justice, and family relationships, emphasizing that it is love and justice, not cruelty, which is promoted by the Quran. Quran, chapter 30, verse 21, states: "And among His signs in this, that He created for you, mates from among yourselves, that you may dwell in tranquility with them, and He has put love and mercy between your hearts: behold, verily in that are signs for those who reflect." Quran 4:19 further commands: "O, you who believe! You are forbidden to inherit women against their will. Nor should you treat them with harshness. On the contrary, live with them on a footing of kindness and equity. If you take a dislike to them, it may be that you dislike a thing through which God brings about a great deal of good." Likewise, the *hadith* or prophetic traditions note Muhammad's respect and protection of women. Indeed, Muhammad is said to have said, "The best of you is he who is best to his wife."

A major theme in the Quran that has been relevant, not only in the past but the present, is that of religious tolerance. The Quran clearly and strongly stresses, chapter 2, verse 256: "There is to be no compulsion in religion," and also that God has created not one, but many nations and peoples.

Many passages underscore the diversity of humankind. The Quran teaches that God deliberately created a world of diversity. Chapter 49:13 tells us, "O, humankind, we have created you, male and female, and made you nations and tribes, so that you might come to know one another."

Muslims, like Christians and Jews before them, believe they have been called to a special, therefore, covenant relationship with God, constituting a community of believers intended to serve as an example to other nations, so diversity is in-built. We see this in the second chapter of the Quran, verse 143, "...and in establishing a just social order." Jews and Christians are regarded as People of the Book, people who have also received a revelation. The Quran and Islam recognize that followers of the three great Abrahamic religions, the children of Abraham, share a common belief in the one God, and all share a common hope and promise of eternal reward. As the Quran says, "Surely the believers and the Jews, Christians, and Sabians, whoever believes in God and the Last Day, and whoever does right, shall have his reward with his Lord, and will neither have fear nor regret." Quran, chapter 2, verse 62.

Historically, as we shall discuss, while the early expansion and conquest spread Islamic rule, Muslims did not try to impose their religion on others or force them to convert. As People of the Book, Jews and Christians were regarded as protected, *dhimmi*, protected people, permitted to retain and practice their religion, be led by their own religious leaders, be guided by their own religious laws and customs. For this protection, they paid a poll or a head tax.

While, by modern standards, this treatment amounted to second-class citizenship in a modern nation-state, in pre-modern times, as compared to Christianity, for example, it was very advanced. Of course, this position is contended today and, indeed, some Islamic reformers, from Egypt to Indonesia, from Europe to America, attempt to work to reexamine their faith in light of the changing realities of societies. Like Jews and Christians before them, they seek to reinterpret the sources of their faith, and to produce new religious understandings that speak to religious pluralism in the modern world.

Many challenge the exclusivist religious claims and intolerance of ultra-conservative, fundamentalists, and extremist Islamic leaders and groups, who believe that they alone possess the true interpretation of Islam, and attempt to impose it on other Muslims and on non-Muslims alike, what I call a "theology of hate." The use of *jihad* in the Quran helps us to explain the term's varied use and misuse throughout history, and why it is such a central and, in a sense, comprehensive term.

Jihad's importance, *jihad* as exertion or struggle, is rooted, as we talked about in an earlier lesson, in the Quran's command to struggle, the literal meaning of the word *jihad*, in the path of God, and in the example of the Prophet Muhammad and his early community, his companions. *Jihad* as struggle refers to the difficulty and complexity of living a good life, struggling against the evil in ourselves, to be virtuous, moral, making a serious effort to do good works, and to help reform society.

Depending on the circumstances in which one lives, it also can mean the right, indeed the duty, to fight injustice and oppression, to spread and defend Islam, to create a just society through preaching, teaching and, if necessary, sacred struggle or holy war. The two broad meanings of *jihad*, both nonviolent and violent, are found in the Quran and expressly contrasted in a well-known prophetic tradition that reports that, when Muhammad returned from battle, he said to his followers, "We return from the lesser *jihad* [warfare] to the greater *jihad*." The greater *jihad*, of course, is the more difficult and more important struggle against one's ego, of selfishness, greed, and evil.

Throughout history, the call to *jihad* has rallied Muslims to the defense of Islam. In recent years, it has been used in wars of liberation and wars of independence, as well as wars of terror. We can see it in the decade-long Afghan *jihad* against Soviet occupation, in Palestine, Israel, Bosnia, Kosovo, Kashmir, and Chechnya, as well as its use by terrorists like Osama bin Laden and al-Qaeda.

Let's take a closer look, now, at *jihad* in the Quran, its violent and nonviolent uses. The earliest Quranic verses dealing with the right to engage in a defense of *jihad* or struggle were revealed shortly after the *hijra*, the emigration of Muhammad and his followers to Medina, in flight from their persecution in Mecca. At a time when they were forced to fight for their lives, Muhammad is told, "Leave is given to those who fight because they were wronged—surely God is able to help them—who were expelled from their homes wrongfully for saying, 'Our Lord is God'." Chapter 22, verses 39 to 40.

The defensive nature of *jihad* is clearly emphasized and underscored in chapter 2, verse 190, "And fight in the way of God with those who fight you, but aggress not: God loves not the aggressors." At critical points throughout history, Muhammad received revelations from God that provided guidelines for the *jihad*. As the Muslim community grew, questions quickly emerged as to what was proper behavior during times of war. The Quran provided detailed guidelines and regulations regarding the conduct of war: Who is to fight and who is exempted. When hostilities must cease. How prisoners should be treated. Most important, verses such as chapter 2, verse 294, emphasize that in warfare, the response to violence and aggression must be proportional. As the Quran says, "Whoever transgresses against you, respond in kind." In kind.

However, Quranic verses also underscore that peace, not violence and warfare, is the norm. Permission to fight the enemy is balanced by a strong mandate for making peace. "If your enemy inclines toward peace, then you too should seek peace and put your trust in God." Chapter 8, verse 61. Another example is: "Had Allah wished, He would have made them dominate you, and so if they leave you alone and do not fight you and offer you peace, then Allah allows you no way against them." Chapter 4, verse 90.

From the earliest times, it was forbidden, in Islam, to kill non-combatants, to kill women, children, monks, and rabbis, who were given the promise of immunity unless they took part in the fighting. Now, though, let us deal with a very contentious issue, and indeed, one that is raised today, the so-called "sword verses."

What are these verses, sometimes referred to as the "sword verses" that call for the killing of unbelievers? An example is: "When the sacred months have passed, slay the idolaters wherever you find them, and take them and confine them, and lie in wait for them at every place and ambush." This is from chapter 9, verse 5, and it was aimed at the Meccans that the Muslims were fighting. This is one of a number of Quranic verses that are cited by critics to demonstrate the inherently violent nature of Islam and its scripture.

These same verses have also been selectively used or abused by religious extremists, to develop a theology of hate and intolerance, and to legitimate unconditional warfare against unbelievers. By "unbelievers," they mean other Muslims who don't believe the way they do, as well as non-Muslims.

During the period of imperial Islam, of expansion and conquest, many of the *ulama*, the religious scholars, enjoying royal patronage, provided a rational for caliphs to pursue their imperial dreams and extend the boundaries of their empires. As a result, they maintained that the "sword verses," these later verses, abrogated or overrode the earlier Quranic verses that limited *jihad* to defensive war. In fact, however, the full intent of these verses is better understood when we read the subsequent verse. "When the sacred months have passed, slay the idolaters wherever you find them…" is missed or distorted when quoted in isolation, for it is followed and qualified by, "… but if they repent and fulfill their devotional obligations and pay the *zakat*" the charitable tax or alms tax, "…then let them go their way. God is forgiving and kind." Chapter 9, verse 5.

The same is true of another often-quoted verse today. "Fight those who believe not in God nor the Last Day, nor hold that forbidden which hath been forbidden by God and his Apostle, nor hold the religion of truth [even if they are] of the People of the Book." This is often quoted, recited, without the line that follows, which is, "Until they pay the tax with willing submission." Chapter 9, verse 29.

Throughout history, past and present, the Quran, like the scriptures of Judaism and Christianity, has been the sacred sourcebook to which believers in every age look for inspiration and guidance. As we shall see throughout this course, because it is interpreted by human beings in diverse historical and social context, the Word of God has yielded multiple and diverse meanings, doctrines and practices. We shall see, in later classes, dealing particularly with the rise of Islamic revivalism, the resurgence of Islam, the extent to which there is, indeed, today a struggle, in many ways, a struggle for the soul of Islam over the interpretation and application of Islam in contemporary society and politics.

The Muslim Community—Faith and Politics
Lecture 5

For many who observed the development of Islam, particularly in early Islamic history, they are struck by the extent to which the Prophet Muhammad was both a prophet and a statesman.

The original community-state founded in Medina established the example of Islam as both a faith and a political order. Religion informed the institutions of the Islamic empire that spread to North Africa and Southeast Asia: the political system, the law, education, the military and social services. Islam split into two branches, a Sunni majority and Shii minority, over issues of leadership. These differing religious and political views led to different interpretations of history. The development of Islam and Muslim history from the period of Muhammad and the "Rightly-Guided Caliphs" to that of the Umayyad and Abbasid empires enables us to appreciate the remarkable political and cultural achievements of the "Golden Age" of Islamic civilization and to understand the sources of sectarianism, religious extremism, and conflict between Islam and Christianity, epitomized by the Crusades.

The history of Islam demonstrates the extent to which religion is integrally related to politics and society. Faith, power, civilization, and culture are intertwined. The relationship of faith and a political order were embodied in the existence and spread of the original community-state at Medina. Within a century after Muhammad's death, Islam as a faith and as an Islamic empire stretched from North Africa to South Asia. Islam informed state institutions, including the caliphate, law, education, the military, and social services.

The development of the Caliphate began with the traumatic event of Muhammad's death in 632 C.E., marking the end of direct guidance from the Prophet. The majority of Muslims, who came to be called Sunnis, or followers of the Sunnah ("example") of the Prophet (Sunni Muslims today make up 85 percent of the world's Muslims), selected Abu Bakr, Muhammad's close companion and trusted advisor, as well as his father-in-law, to be the *caliph* ("successor, deputy"). Sunni Muslims adopted the belief that leadership should pass to the most qualified person, not through hereditary succession. As caliph, Abu Bakr became the political and military leader of the community.

A minority of the Muslim community, the Shiis, or "Party of Ali," opposed the selection of Abu Bakr as caliph, believing that succession should be hereditary within the Prophet's family and that Ali, Muhammad's first cousin and closest living male relative, should be the leader (called *imam*) of the Islamic community. Ali was passed over for the position of caliph three times, finally gaining his place after 35 years, only to be assassinated a few years later. Ali's charismatic son Hussein, along with his small band of followers, was overwhelmed and massacred by the army of the Sunni Caliph Yazid. This tragedy of Karbala and "martyrdom of Hussein" became a paradigmatic event, remembered and reenacted ritually in a passion play every year.

Muslims point out that the differences between Sunnis and Shiis do not have to do with dogma but, rather, are political, concerning the qualifications for the head of the Muslim community. Their shared belief and practice notwithstanding, however, they also developed different views about the meaning of history. Sunnis claim a "Golden Age," when they were a great world power and civilization, which they believe is evidence of God's favor upon them and a historic validation of Muslim beliefs. Shiis, as an oppressed and disinherited minority, see in these same developments the illegitimate usurpation of power by Sunni rulers at the expense of a just society.

The original Muslim state was expanded by Muhammad to extend and consolidate Muslim authority over Arabia through a combination of force and diplomacy. The most striking aspect of the early expansion of Islam was its rapidity and success. Within 100 years after the death of the Prophet, the Muslim empire and rule extended from North Africa to South Asia, an empire greater than Rome at its zenith. The new order of Islam was to be a community of believers who acknowledged the sovereignty of God, lived according to Islamic law, and dedicated their lives to spreading God's law and rule.

The Muslim expansion was marked by building (adoption and adaptation of existing political institutions and sciences), rather than destruction, and motivated by religious fervor, as well as the desire for economic rewards. Although the indigenous rulers and armies of the conquered countries were replaced, much of their government, bureaucracy, and culture was preserved. Muslim rule was often more flexible and tolerant than that of the Byzantine or Persian empires. These early conquests sought to spread Muslim rule, rather than to gain converts to Islam. The inhabitants of newly conquered areas were given three options: (1) convert to Islam, (2) accept *dhimmi* ("protected") status and pay a poll tax, or (3) face battle or the sword, if they rejected the first two options.

The period of Muhammad and the Rightly-Guided Caliphs (632–661 C.E.) is regarded as the normative period of Sunni Islam and serves as the idealized past to which Muslims look for inspiration and guidance. The Rightly-Guided Caliphs were the first four successors to Muhammad. All of them were Muhammad's companions and were chosen by a process of consultation, followed by an oath of allegiance.

Sectarianism and extremism in the Muslim empire were born with two civil wars following the succession of the fourth caliph, Ali; both were sparked by Ali's failure to find and punish the murderers of the third caliph, Uthman. Following Ali's assassination in 661 C.E. by a splinter group, the Kharijites ("those who leave or secede"), the caliphate was seized by Muawiyah, who moved the capital to Damascus. Muawiyah founded the Umayyad Dynasty, ending what later generations would call the "Golden Age" of Muhammad and the Rightly-Guided Caliphs and turning the caliphate into an absolute, hereditary monarchy dominated by an Arab military aristocracy.

From the eighth to the 12th centuries, Islam and Muslim political power expanded exponentially under the Umayyad and Abbasid caliphates. The Umayyad Dynasty (661–750 C.E.), centered in Damascus, completed the conquest of the entire Persian and half of the Roman (Byzantine) empires. The Umayyads were successful in acquiring power and wealth, symbolized by the lifestyle of the flourishing, cosmopolitan capital in Damascus and the growth of new cities. But these strengths were considered by some to be innovations that undermined the older Arab way of life and sowed the seeds of destruction.

The Umayyads met with considerable opposition. One opposing group was a splinter group, the Kharijites, the earliest example of radical dissent in Islam, who combined rigorous puritanism with religious fundamentalism and exclusivist egalitarianism. The Kharijites continue to inspire religious extremist groups today. The Shii (shiat al-Ali, or "Party of Ali") opposed the Umayyads because of their refusal to submit to Ali's authority and their illegitimate usurpation of the caliphate. The Umayyad caliphate came to an end in 750 C.E., after a revolt led by an Abbasid slave that led to the foundation of the Abbasid caliphate.

Under Abbasid rule (750–1258 C.E.), the Islamic community became an empire of wealth, political power, and cultural accomplishments. The Abbasid caliphate ushered in an era of strong centralized government, great economic prosperity, and a remarkable civilization. They aligned their government with Islam and became patrons of the emerging class of *ulama* ("religious scholars"). They also supported the development of Islamic scholarship and disciplines, built mosques, and established schools. Abbasid success was based on trade, commerce, industry, and agriculture, rather than conquest.

Enormous wealth enabled the Abbasid caliphs to become great patrons of art and culture, resulting in the florescence of Islamic civilization. Muslims made original creative contributions in law, theology, philosophy, literature, medicine, algebra, geometry, science, art, and architecture. Islamic philosophy grew out of and extended the teachings and insights of Greek philosophy but in an Islamic context and worldview. The cultural traffic pattern was again reversed when Europeans, emerging from the Dark Ages, turned to Muslim centers of learning to regain their lost heritage and to learn from Muslim advances. Through Islamic philosophy, Greek philosophy was re-transmitted to Europe. Many of the great medieval Christian philosophers and theologians acknowledged their intellectual debt to their Muslim predecessors.

Muslims regard the time of the Abbasid caliphate as the sign of God's favor upon Muslims and the validation of both Islam's message and the Muslim community's universal mission. Abbasid patronage included the Arabization of the empire, so that Arabic became the language of literature and public discourse. Centers were created for the translation of manuscripts from Sanskrit, Greek, Latin, Syriac, Coptic, and Persian into Arabic. The Arabization and Islamization of new ideas was a process of change, assimilation, and acculturation characterized by continuity with the faith and practice of Muhammad and controlled by Muslims. The Golden Age of Islamic civilization ironically paralleled the progressive political fragmentation of the universal caliphate, as internal and external opposition arose, particularly from the Fatimid Dynasty and the Crusades.

The Crusades established a paradigm of confrontation between Islam and Christianity and Islam and the West.

The Crusades (1095–1453) established a paradigm of confrontation between Islam and Christianity and Islam and the West, the legacy of which continues to affect Muslim-Christian relations and relations between the Muslim world and the West. The Christian West experienced the spread of Islam as both a religious and a political threat. Challenged both theologically and politically, Christian Europeans responded. Muhammad was vilified as the anti-Christ and Islam, as a religion of the sword. Europe engaged in the *Reconquista*, a struggle to reconquer territories in Spain, Italy, and Sicily, and a holy war, the Crusades. The Crusades ended in 1453 when Constantinople, the Byzantine capital, fell to the Turks and was renamed Istanbul. Istanbul became the seat of the Ottoman Empire.

The Abbasid caliphate was replaced by a variety and series of sultanates. They extended from Africa to Southeast Asia as Islam penetrated Africa, Central and Southeast Asia, and Eastern Europe, largely through the missionary work of traders and Sufi brotherhoods. Three imperial sultanates emerged: the Turkish Ottoman Empire (1281–1924), the Persian Safavid Empire (1501–1722), and the Indian Mughal Empire (1520–1857), all of which experienced political power and cultural florescence. By the turn of the 18th century, the power and prosperity of the sultanates were in serious decline. This decline coincided with the Industrial Revolution and modernization in the West, leading to clashes in the era of European colonialism. ■

Suggested Reading

Akbar Ahmed, *Islam Today*, chapter 5.

Jonathan Bloom and Sheila Blair, *Islam: A Thousand Years of Faith and Power*, chapters 5 and 8.

Fred M. Donner, "Muhammad and the Caliphate" and "Science, Medicine, and Technology," *The Oxford History of Islam*, chapters 1 and 4.

John L. Esposito, *Islam: The Straight Path*, chapter 2.

Questions to Consider

1. How did Islam influence the development of Muslim empires, from political institutions to social structures?

2. What were some of the major achievements of Islamic civilization?

The Muslim Community—Faith and Politics
Lecture 5—Transcript

For many who observed the development of Islam, particularly in early Islamic history, they are struck by the extent to which the Prophet Muhammad was both a prophet and a statesman. In earlier lessons, we've explored the initial relationship of religion to state and society, certainly as it became articulated within the first community at Medina. Today, we'll look at the development of faith and politics throughout history down to the contemporary period.

The history of Islam demonstrates the extent to which religion is integrally related to politics in society. Faith, power, civilization, and culture were intertwined in regard to the development of Islam from the period of Muhammad to the "Rightly-Guided Caliphs," the first four successors following Muhammad, to the development of early Islamic empires. First, there were the Umayyad from 661 to 750, then the Abbasid from 750 to 1258. These empires reveal the remarkable achievements that culminated in what some call the "Golden Age" of Islamic civilization. They also help us to understand the sources of sectarianism, religious extremism, and conflict between Islam and Christianity, epitomized by the Crusades. Many of these have an influence on today's realities as well.

The relationship of religion to a political order begins with the birth and the spread of Muhammad's original community, his community state at Medina. Within a century after Muhammad's death, Islam as a faith and as an Islamic empire stretched from North Africa to South Asia. Islam informed state institutions, including the Caliphate, on notions of citizenship, war and peace, law, taxation, education and social services.

Previously, we discussed that first Islamic community under Muhammad. The development of the Caliphate began with the traumatic event, though, of Muhammad's death in 632, marking the end of direct guidance from the Prophet, the period of Muhammad and the Rightly-Guided Caliphs.

The Rightly-Guided Caliphs, the first four, ruled from 632 to 661; this period is regarded as the normative period of Sunni Islam, and provides the ideal past to which Muslims look for inspiration and guidance today. The Rightly-Guided Caliphs were the first four successors to Muhammad. All of them were Muhammad's companions and were chosen by a process of consultation.

Today, we hear the words "Sunni" and "Shii" Muslims, the two major branches of the community. The Sunni comprise 85 percent of the world's Muslims, and Shii approximately 15 percent. The division stems from an early disagreement and conflict over who should lead the community.

The majority of Muslims who came to be called Sunni, or Sunnis, followers of the Sunnah example of the Prophet, selected Abu Bakr, Muhammad's close companion and trusted advisor, to be Caliph, the successor. But his successor as political leader, not as Prophet; he was the political leader of the community. Sunni Muslims adopted the belief that leadership should pass to the most qualified person, not through hereditary succession. As Caliph, Abu Bakr became the political and military leader of the community.

Although he was not a Prophet, as the Quran had declared Muhammad to be the last of the Prophets, the Caliph had religious prestige as the head of the community of believers, the *ummah*. A minority of the Muslim community, who would later come to be called "Shiis," or the "party of Ali," opposed the selection of Abu Bakr as Caliph, believing that succession should be hereditary, staying within the Prophet's family. Thus, they maintained that Ali, Muhammad's closest living male relative, should be the leader, *imam*, of the Islamic community.

Ali was Muhammad's first cousin, the husband to Muhammad's daughter, Fatima. She believed that the *imam*, although not a prophet, is divinely inspired, sinless and infallible. Consequently, in contrast to the Sunni caliph, for Shii, the *imam* is both a religious and a political leader, and serves as the final authoritative interpreter of God's will as formulated in Islamic law. However, the majority, the Sunni opinion, prevailed. Ali was passed over for the position of Caliph three times. Finally gaining his place after 35 years, he was assassinated only a few years later. At his death, Muawiyah, a general and governor of Damascus who had challenged Ali's leadership, asserted his power and established the Umayyad Dynasty.

Ali's followers remained disaffected. Shii opposition to Umayyad rule came to a head in 680 when Ali's son and Muhammad's grandson, Hussein, led a rebellion in an attempt to recover the leadership of the Muslim community. When popular support failed to materialize, Hussein and his followers were slaughtered by the overwhelming forces of the Umayyad army at Karbala in modern day Iraq. The memory of this tragedy, called the "martyrdom of Hussein," created a paradigm of suffering and protest that has guided and inspired Shii ever since. Thus, the "martyrdom of Hussein" proved an effective symbol for protest and mobilization during the Iranian Revolution of 1978-79, as well as the Iran-Iraq war and the Lebanese civil war.

Although Sunni and Shii share many fundamental beliefs and practices, their differences regarding who should succeed Muhammad and lead the community, and their struggles for power resulted in contrasting views of the meaning of history. The Sunni majority remembers a golden age of faith in empire, marked by Islam's spread and expansion globally as a faith world power in civilization. Thus, success, power, and wealth are seen as evidence of God's favor and historic validation of Islam.

The Shii minority, on the other hand, who had failed in their opposition to Sunni, saw themselves as victims of the illegitimate usurpation of power by Sunni rulers at the expense of a just society. For Shii, history serves as the theater for the struggle of an oppressed and disinherited minority community, to restore God's rule on Earth over the entire Muslim community, under the leadership of the *imam*. Realization of this just social order remained a frustrated hope and expectation for Shii across the centuries.

In time, though, Shii did enjoy political power, creating the Fatimid Dynasty in Egypt, which reigned from 909 to 1171, and the Safavid Empire in Iran from 1501 to 1722. Indeed, the Shii have remained as the dominant religion down to today in Iran.

Shii Branches had come to exist within a decade after the creation of Shiism. Over time, disagreement within the community over succession led to three major divisions within Shiism itself, depending on how many *imams* or leaders each community recognized. The three divisions are the "Fivers," also known as the Zaydis, the "Seveners," represented today in large part by the Ismailis, who are followers of the Agha Khan, and the "Twelvers," also known as the Ithna Asharis.

The Twelvers are the most populous of the Shii. They're found as the overwhelming majority in Iran, where it remains the official religion, but also in countries like Iraq and Bahrain and elsewhere. Shii believe that the last *imam* went into hiding or occultation, creating the doctrine of the Hidden Imam.

The Hidden Imam is expected to return as a *Mahdi*, a messianic figure who will come at the end of time to restore the community to its rightful place, and usher in a perfect Islamic society in which truth and justice will prevail. During the Hidden Imam's absence, the community is to be guided by religious experts, capable of interpreting Islamic law, so-called *mujtahids*.

The most striking aspect of the early expansion of Islam and of early Islamic history was the rapidity and the success of this political expansion. Within 100 years after the death of the Prophet, Muslim empire and rule extended from North Africa to South Asia, an empire greater than Rome at her zenith. For many believers, it was proof of God's guidance and reward for their faithfulness.

The Muslim expansion was marked by building, adoption, and adaptation of existing political institutions and sciences, rather than by destruction. It was motivated by religious fervor, but also by the desire for economic rewards of conquest, plunder, and booty. Although the indigenous rulers and armies of conquered countries were replaced, much of their government, bureaucracy, and culture were preserved. The inhabitants of newly conquered areas were given three options: One could convert to Islam, become protected, a *dhimmi* minority; protected people able to practice their religion, and be protected from other invaders in exchange for payment of the head tax or poll tax; if one chose to resist, then the option was battle or the sword.

Muslim rule often proved to be more flexible and tolerant than that of rule under the Byzantine or Persian Empires. Thus, some Christian communities, in fact, did convert. There was broader tolerance, and often the tax system was far, far less than under Christian rule. These early conquests sought primarily to extend Muslim rule, and to gain territory and tax revenue, rather than to gain converts to Islam. Religious minorities were able to exist, as I said earlier, and practice their faith. From the eighth to the twelfth centuries, Islam and Muslim political power, then, expanded exponentially under the Umayyads and, subsequently, the Abbasid Caliphates.

The Umayyad Dynasty, which reigned from 661 to 750, ended what later generations would call the "Golden Age" of Muhammad and the Rightly-Guided Caliphs. It turned the Caliphate into a hereditary monarchy dominated by an Arab military aristocracy.

Centered in Damascus, the Umayyads completed the conquest of the Persian and Byzantine Empires. The Umayyads were successful in acquiring power and wealth, symbolized by the lifestyle of the flourishing cosmopolitan capital in Damascus. Remember, now, the movement from Medina to Damascus and the growth of new cities. They established a strong, centralized dynastic kingdom and empire. Although they used Islam to legitimate and rationalize their conquests, the Umayyads adopted and adapted the advanced government institutions and bureaucracy of the Byzantine Empire.

The Umayyads met, though, with considerable opposition. Their new dynastic ambitions, imperial court, lifestyle, and materialism were considered by their critics to be innovations that undermined the older, pristine, Arab Islamic way of life of the Prophet, and of the early community at Medina. Their strengths sowed the seeds of dissent and violence. One early opposition group was a splinter group, the Kharijites, "those who secede or leave," the earliest example of radical descent in Islam.

The worldview of the Kharijites, who combined the rigorous Puritanism with a militant religious fundamentalism and exclusivism, continued to inform contemporary religious extremist groups, from the assassins of Egypt's former President Anwar Sadat, to Osama bin Laden and al-Qaeda today. They believe in literal and absolute interpretation of the Quran and the Sunnah, the example of the Prophet. They regarded anyone who deviated from their interpretation of Islam, a nonbeliever, and subject, therefore, to excommunication, warfare and death. As we'll see later, this is precisely the position that Osama takes.

The Shii were another opposition group, the followers of Ali. They also opposed the Umayyads, because of their refusal to submit to Ali's authority, and their illegitimate usurpation of the Caliphate. In the 1970s, Shii would liken the Shah of Iran's authoritarian rule to that of Yazid, the son of Muawiyyah, the founder of the Umayyads. In addition, it was Ali's army, remember, that defeated Hussein at Karbala in that slaughter that came to be remembered as the martyrdom.

The Umayyad Dynasty came to an end, though, in 750, after a revolt that led to the establishment of the Abbasid Caliphate. Under the Abbasids, who ruled from 750 to 1258, with their new capital in Baghdad, modern day Iraq, the Islamic community peaked as an empire of wealth, political power, and cultural accomplishments. The Abbasid Caliphate ushered in an era of strong centralized government, at least in its early centuries, with great economic prosperity and a remarkable civilization. Jews and Christians, as well as Muslims, served in the Abbasid bureaucracy.

Abbasid success was based upon trade, commerce, industry and agriculture, rather than conquests. The Abbasids aligned their government with Islam and became patrons of the emerging class, this new class of *ulama*, religious scholars, supporting the development of Islamic scholarship and disciplines, and building mosques and schools, or *madrasas*.

Enormous wealth enabled the Abbasid Caliphs to become great patrons of art, architecture, and culture, resulting in the florescence of Islamic civilization. Great urban cultural centers were founded in Cordoba, in modern day Spain, Baghdad, Iraq, Cairo, Egypt, Nishapur, Iran, and Palermo, Italy, eclipsing Christian Europe.

From the seventh to the ninth centuries, manuscripts were obtained from the far reaches of the empire, and translated from Sanskrit, Greek, Latin, Syria, Coptic, and Persian into Arabic. The best works of philosophy, science, and literature from other cultures were appropriated, such as those from Aristotle, Plato, Galen, Hippocrates, Euclid, and Ptolemy.

This age of translation was followed by a period of great creativity as a new generation of educated Muslim thinkers and scientists made their own contributions to learning in philosophy, medicine, chemistry, astronomy, optics, art, architecture, and algebra, which takes its name from "Arabic."

At the same time, Islamic sciences, in particular law, theology, and *hadith* studies, that is, study of the prophetic traditions, flourished. Intellectual giants of the time included al-Farabi, Ibn Sina, known in the West as Avicenna, Ibn Rushd known in the West as Averroes, and al-Ghazali, who we'll talk about shortly.

These masters were true "Renaissance men," multi-talented geniuses who often mastered the major disciplines of philosophy, medicine, mathematics, and astronomy. A prime example is Avicenna, who is remembered as "the great commentator" on Aristotle. Here he describes his remarkable accomplishments at an amazingly early age. He was young man, talented, with a strong ego. "I busied myself with the study of Fusus al-Hikam (this is a treatise by Al-Farabi) and other commentaries on physics and mathematics, and the doors of knowledge opened before me. Then I took up medicine... Medicine is not one of the difficult sciences, and in a short time I undoubtedly excelled at it, so that physicians of merit studied under me. ...At the same time, I carried on debates with and controversies in jurisprudence (law.) At this point, I was 16 years old."

He was definitely on the fast track. He continued: "Then for a year and a half, I devoted myself to study. I resumed the study of logic and all parts of philosophy. During this time, I never slept the whole night, and did nothing but study all day long. Thus, I mastered logic, physics, and mathematics. When I reached the age of 18, I had completed the study of all these sciences. At that point, my memory was better, whereas today my learning is riper." This is good news for all of us who see ourselves as senior citizens or fast approaching it.

The cultural traffic pattern was again reversed later, when Europeans emerging from the Dark Ages turned to these Muslim centers, to the products of these Renaissance men, to these centers of learning, to regain their lost heritage and to learn from Muslim advances. Through Islamic philosophy, Greek philosophy was re-transmitted to Europe. Many of the great medieval Christian philosophers and theologians such as Albert the Great, Thomas Aquinas, Abelard, Roger Bacon and Duns Scotus have acknowledged their debt to their Muslim predecessors.

The failures and reforms of Muslim societies today, as in the recent past, are often measured against this history, at times romanticized of an earlier period of brilliant success. Many Muslims regard the time of the Abbasid Caliphate as the sign of God's favor upon Muslims, and the validation of both Islam's message and the Muslim community's universal mission.

The Golden Age of Islamic civilization ironically, though, paralleled the progressive political fragmentation of the Abbasid Caliphate. This occurred as internal and external opposition arose from the growing independence of generals, to Shii inspired revolts, to external threats like the Christian Crusades, a Christian Crusade that has had a significant impact, both then and now.

Let us look at the Crusades. The Crusades, which were in fact a series of Crusades, stretched from 1095 to 1453, and established a paradigm of confrontation between Islam and Christianity, a legacy that continues to impact Muslim-Christian relations and relations between the Muslim world and the West. The Christian West had viewed the spread of Islam as both a religious and a political threat. Islam, remember, claimed to supercede Christianity, much as Christianity claimed originally to supercede Judaism, and challenged Christian religious claims and authority.

The Quran was the final revelation. Muhammad was the final prophet. Muslim armies overran the East and Roman Empires, Spain and the Mediterranean from Cicely to Anatolia. Many Christians living under Muslim rule converted to Islam. Christian fears became a reality as Islam became a world power in civilization, while Christianity, in contrast, staggered and stagnated in the Dark Ages.

Two myths pervade in terms of popular Western perceptions of the Crusades. The first is that the Crusades were simply motivated by a religious desire to liberate Jerusalem. The second is that Christendom ultimately triumphed. The contrast between these myths and reality can be seen in the following. Admittedly, here, I'm being selective, but it's to address this kind of contrast.

After Jerusalem fell to the Muslims in 638, both Christians and Jews were allowed to live in and make pilgrimages to Jerusalem under Muslim rule. This peaceful coexistence lasted for 500 years. The Crusades were the result of a combination of political events and an imperial papal power play, in which Christendom was pitted against Islam, leaving a legacy of misunderstanding and distrust.

The Crusades were called for by Pope Urban II following the defeat of the Byzantine army by the Abbasids. The Byzantine emperor responded by calling upon fellow Christian rulers for help, and called upon the Pope to come to the aid of Christianity to free Jerusalem and its environs from the Muslims.

The Pope saw an opportunity to gain recognition for papal authority, and its role in legitimating the action of temporal rulers, of emperors. Christian rulers, knights, and merchants participated, not only out of piety, although many did out of piety, but also due to political and military ambitions, and the promise of economic and commercial trade and banking rewards that were expected to accompany the establishment of a Latin kingdom in the Middle East.

The appeal to religion captured the popular mind and support of many Christians, who responded enthusiastically to its battle cry, "God wills it!" As with all wars, both sides had their heroes and villains. In recent years, the Crusades have often been portrayed as the defense of Christianity against barbaric Muslim warriors. The overly romanticized image in the West sharply contrasts with Muslim memories, as well as the record of history.

When the Christian Crusaders stormed Jerusalem and established Christian sovereignty over the Holy Land in 1099, they left neither Muslim nor Jewish survivors. Women and children were massacred, and Jerusalem's holy sites were desecrated.

By contrast, the Muslim army, led by Salah al-Din (Saladin) recaptured Jerusalem in 1187. The Muslim army spared civilians, and left churches and shrines largely untouched. Saladin was faithful to his word, and compassionate towards noncombatants. Muslim memories of Christian heroes like Richard the Lionhearted are decidedly more negative than in the West.

Having accepted the surrender of Acre, Richard proceeded to slaughter all of its inhabitants, including women and children, despite his promises to the contrary. The Crusades ended in 1453 when Constantinople, the Byzantine capital, fell to the Turks and was renamed Istanbul, the seat of the Ottoman Empire.

Now let us shift to the Sultanate Period. The Abbasid Empire, its Caliphate, fell in 1258, overrun by the Mongols. However, within a short period of time, it was replaced by a string of smaller Muslim states, or governments, called sultanates. They extended from Senegal in Africa to the Philippines in Southeast Asia, as Islam penetrated Africa, Central and Southeast Asia and Eastern Europe, largely through the missionary work of traders and Sufi brotherhoods.

Three imperial sultanates emerged: The Turkish Ottoman Empire, from 1281 to 1924, the Persian Safavid Empire from 1501 to 1722, and the Indian Mughal Empire in the Indian subcontinent, 1520 to 1857, all of which experienced political power and a cultural florescence.

All of the imperial sultanates demonstrated a common outlook and approach to state organizational support and use of Islam, although they were different in many other ways. The rulers were generally called "sultan," "the one with power," or in Iran, "shah," king.

Rule was based upon a combination of military strength and religious legitimacy. The ruler served, for example, as the protector and defender of the faith. Islamic law was the official law of the state, even though rulers might also make their own regulations or laws in addition to that. Religion both supported, and was supported by, the state. The *ulama* played an important role in the state, assisting in the centralization and control of the educational, legal, and social systems, educating the military, the bureaucracy, and religious elites. They supervised and guided the application and interpretation of Islamic law, and oversaw the disbursement of funds from religious endowments, called *waqf*, for educational and social services.

The imperial sultanates peaked in the 16th century. By the turn of the 18th century, their power and prosperity were in serious decline. This decline coincided with the Industrial Revolution and modernization in the West, leading to the era of European colonialism, and its profound impact on Islam in the Muslim world, as we shall see later in this course.

It's very important to think about what was happening, and what the results were and their impact on, if you will, both Muslim history and the Muslim psyche. Islam had begun, remember, in Arabia, in an area torn by tribal strife, an area with tremendous division, an area that was positioned between two empires that were fighting each other and squeezing the center, as it were. The Prophet Muhammad somehow comes and, in the mind of most Muslims, in a very ingenious way, guided by God, unites Arabia, and creates a prophet-led religio-political state, existing under the banner of Islam.

In subsequent centuries we see the expansion of Islam, as a religion becoming global, and we discussed that today, but also that Islam is part of the state. Thus, we can talk about imperial Islam, the creation of the Umayyad Empire, the Abbasid Empire, and then, even when the Mongols overran the Abbasids and it looked like this is a major turn in history, the reemergence of Islam came, not only as faith, but again, as state and empire, with this vast set of sultanates from literally Timbuktu in Africa to Mindanao in Southeast Asia.

Despite the ups and downs of history, with its record of failure and success, Islamic history is generally remembered by many Muslims as a time in which Islam then spread as both faith and empire. Thus, from the time of the Prophet, the seventh century, to European imperialism, roughly the 18th century, to be a Muslim was to live in a Muslim society and belong to a transnational community, and in a sense, to have a sense of belonging to, in a sense, a kind of interconnected transnational empire. One could feel as a Muslim that you were traveling protected, as it were, under Muslim rule from one part of the world to the next, and many did that.

This vision and ideal has been challenged in recent centuries by the decline of Muslim fortunes, and the subordination of much of the Muslim world to outside powers, and one does not want to underestimate that impact, going from European colonialism and the Cold War, the super power rivalry, to the powerful influence of America and the West today.

Muslims have struggled, and continue to struggle, with these formidable challenges to their faith and governance. This will continue to be seen throughout the rest of the course. Shortly, we are going to look at the playing out of Islam in modern history, and see how the impact of the West becomes a dominant theme from the 18th century down to today, a dominant theme affecting Muslim perceptions of the West, and affecting relationships between the Muslim world and the West.

Before we do that, however, we want to turn and take a look at the development of two institutions: Islamic law and Sufism. As it were, we want to look at the two major, if you will, paths that Muslims chose to define and pursue as they sought to follow the Quranically mandated straight path of Islam.

Paths to God—Islamic Law and Mysticism
Lecture 6

Piety, as well as the desire for reform, resulted in the development of Islamic law and Islamic mysticism.

Islamic law reflects Islam's emphasis on *orthopraxy* ("correct practice"), rather than *orthodoxy* ("correct belief"). Islamic law applies to both the private and public realms and is concerned with human interactions with God (worship) and with each other (social relations). Sufism, as the "interior path," has emphasized personal spirituality and devotion and has played an important role in the spread of Islam through missionary activities.

Dissatisfaction with abuses of power and corruption in Umayyad rule gave rise to the development of two Islamic movements or institutions: Islamic law, the Shariah, and Sufism, or Islamic mysticism. Islamic law was a response to real religious, political, and social concerns and issues. Piety and politics were intertwined. Those who turned to law during the Umayyad Dynasty in the eighth and ninth centuries did so to limit the autonomy and power of rulers, by standardizing the law and taking its control out of the hands of the caliph or his appointed judges. Many centers or schools of thought were established, but four major Sunni law schools have endured: the Hanafi, Maliki, Shafii, and Hanbali. The development of law flourished during the 10th century under the Abbasid Dynasty in the hands of a new class of scholars—the *ulama* ("learned ones").

Islamic law springs from the basic meaning and requirement of Islam, submission to and realization of God's will. The Quran teaches that Muslims must strive or struggle (*jihad*) in the path (Shariah) of God to implement God's will on earth, expand and defend their community, and establish a just society. Like Judaism, and in contrast to Christianity, which emphasizes *orthodoxy* ("correct belief"), Islam emphasizes *orthopraxy* ("correct action").

Though they overlap, the distinction between Shariah and *fiqh* is critical to understanding the meaning and dynamic nature of Islamic law and its possibilities for reinterpretation and reform today. Shariah in the Quran and in Islam refers specifically to divine law, for God is the only lawgiver. Islamic law is a broader category that encompasses the divine law and human understanding (*fiqh*) and interpretation of God's law. The development of Islamic law was the work of religious scholars (*ulama*), rather than judges, courts, or governments.

The two main divisions of law concern: A Muslim's duties to God, obligatory practices or essential observances, such as the Five Pillars. A Muslim's duties to others, social transactions or relations, which include regulations governing public life, from contract and international law to family laws governing marriage, divorce, and inheritance.

> **The two main divisions of law concern a Muslim's duties to God, obligatory practices or essential observances, such as the Five Pillars, [and] a Muslim's duties to others.**

Sunni Muslims recognize four official sources of Islamic law: The bulk of the Quran consists of broad, general moral directives or principles. Approximately 80 prescriptions in the Quran rank as legal prescriptions; most come from the Medinan period when Muhammad was establishing the first Islamic community state. The second source is the Sunnah ("example") of the Prophet, what he said and did, which was believed to be preserved in narrative stories or reports known as "traditions of the Prophet" (*hadith*). The third source is analogical reasoning (or *qiyas*), a technique used when no clear text of the Quran or Sunnah directly relevant to a legal question exists. Jurists then use their independent judgment or reasoning (called *ijtihad*) to examine similar situations with principles that could be applied to the new situation. This led to a great deal of diversity of opinion. The fourth source is the consensus (*ijm*a) of the community, which in practice meant the consensus of the majority of scholars (*ulama*) who were the guardians and interpreters of the law. This source originated from a tradition of the Prophet that said, "My community will never agree on an error."

Shii Muslims have a somewhat different set of legal sources. They accept the Quran and Sunnah, as well as their own collections of the traditions of Ali and other *imams* or preeminent leaders, whom they regard as supreme authorities and legal interpreters.

Islamic law is a source of both unity and of difference and diversity. Different law schools reflect individual reasoning and social customs of diverse geographic, social, historical, and cultural contexts. Reformers reclaim the right to *ijtihad* ("independent reasoning") to reinterpret Islam to address the new contingencies and needs of modern society. A considerable variance is found in the diversity of legal opinions or interpretations (*fatwas*) rendered by legal experts (*muftis*) who advise judges and litigants. Because of the centrality of the community in Islam, the Muslim family as the basic unit of society enjoyed pride of place in the development and implementation of Islamic law. The formulation of Muslim family law (marriage, divorce, and inheritance) has been subject to reform and widespread debate and revision since the 20th century. Although the Quran introduced a number of reforms that enhanced the status of women, these reforms were often compromised by social realities and circumvented. Much of the traditional pre-Islamic patriarchal social structure is incorporated into Islamic law. Legal reform remains a contested issue in many Muslim countries today. Fundamentalist voices reject reforms as un-Islamic. Few governments have been willing to replace Islamic law and be accused of abrogating "God's law."

Like Islamic law, Sufism—or Islamic mysticism—began as a reform movement in response to the growing materialism and wealth of Muslim society that accompanied the expansion and growing power of the Islamic Empire. Early Sufis found the emphasis on laws, rules, duties, and rights to be spiritually lacking. Instead, they emphasized the "interior path," seeking the purity and simplicity of the time of Muhammad as the route to direct and personal experience of God. They pursued an ascetic lifestyle that emphasized detachment from the material word, repentance for sins, and the Last Judgment.

Sufis have often played an important role in the political life of Muslims, spearheading Islamic revivalist waves that regenerated societies, creating Islamic states, and fighting off colonial powers.

The Sufi orders also played an important role in the spread of Islam through missionary work because of their tendency to adopt and adapt to local non-Islamic customs and practices in new places, along with their strong devotional and emotional practices. Because of Sufism's adoption of external, "un-Islamic" influences, Sufis conflicted with the more legal-oriented *ulama* over authority and power. These religious divergences were synthesized and reconciled and Islam was revived through the teachings of Abu Hamid al-Ghazali (1058–1111), called the Renewer of Islam.

By the 13th century, Sufi brotherhoods had created international networks of lodges or monasteries that transformed Sufism into a mass movement. Sufi leaders enjoyed great influence, both spiritual and material. Many of Sufism's characteristics find similar experiences in Christianity and other faiths, such as monasteries, distinctive garb, ascetic practices, litanies, and saints. The Whirling Dervishes represent Sufism's most famous use of music and dance to induce states of mystic communication.

Today, Sufism remains a strong spiritual presence and force in Muslim societies, in both private and public life, and enjoys a wide following in Europe and America, attracting many converts to Islam. ∎

Suggested Reading

John L. Esposito, *Islam: The Straight Path*, chapters 2–3.

Mohammad Hashim Kamali, "Law and Society," *The Oxford History of Islam*, chapter 3.

Martin Lings, *What Is Sufism?*

Questions to Consider

1. What are the sources of Islamic law?

2. What is Sufism and what role did it play in the spread of Islam?

Paths to God—Islamic Law and Mysticism
Lecture 6—Transcript

The rapid expansion of Islam brought the rise of new centers of power and wealth, as we saw last class, an influx of "foreign ways" and greater social stratification. The contrast between the idealized community of the Prophet, the realities of the Umayyad life, and its dissatisfaction with abuses of power and corruption gave rise not only to revolutionary groups like the Kharijites, whom we discussed last class, but also to two major non-revolutionary reform movements or institutions, Islamic law and Sufism, or Islamic mysticism.

Historically, from the seventh to the 10th centuries, Muslim scholars formulated Islamic law. Many of the earliest scholars were, in fact, pious Muslims who had their jobs, their day jobs as it were, as merchants and traders, but also were serious students of the Quran and the traditions of the Prophet. It would only be later that they would develop into a separate professional class, the *ulama*, literally the "learned ones," the religious scholars. These early scholars developed the science of law or jurisprudence: *fiqh*, meaning understanding, understanding in order to ascertain, interpret and apply God's guidance, the Shariah, as found in the Quran, and the Sunnah of the Prophet, the example of the Prophet.

Based, then, upon both divinely revealed prescriptions, the Quran an example of the Prophet, and their own human interpretation, they attempted to delineate a comprehensive blueprint for Muslim life and society, what we often refer to as Islamic law or Shariah.

Islamic law, then, was a response to real religious political and social concerns, and issues. Piety and politics were intertwined. Those who turned to law during the Umayyad Dynasty in the eighth and ninth centuries did so to limit the autonomy and power of rulers by standardizing the law, and taking its control out of the hands of the Caliph or his appointed judges. They both wanted to delineate what it meant to be a good Muslim, as well as limit the power of rulers.

Centers, or schools, of thought sprang up in Medina and Damascus, in Baghdad, in Kufa and in Basra, across the then-existing Muslim world.

While many schools were established, four schools came to be the major Sunni law schools, the Hanafi, Maliki, Shafii, and Hanbali law schools. These have endured to modern times.

Based, then, both upon revelation and human interpretation, which is called *ijtihad*, a very central concept which we'll talk about a lot during the course, scholars attempted to delineate a comprehensive blueprint for Muslim life in society, what it meant to be a good Muslim. Although there was general agreement on many matters, significant differences also existed, reflecting differences of interpretation, as well as the diverse geographic, social, and cultural context in which the jurists were writing. It made a difference whether you lived in a more conservative, or, if you will, a more open society.

The development of law flourished, in particular, during the 10th century under the Abbasid Dynasty. Remember that the Abbasids enjoyed great wealth and became patrons of religious leaders, of the sciences and the arts.

The Abbasid caliphs, having led a rebellion that overthrew the Umayyads, sought to justify their revolution and legitimate their rule in the name of Islam, and so became the patrons of Islam. The study of Islamic sources, and the development of Islamic studies in the Quran, the prophetic traditions, or *hadith,* and law excelled in the hands of a new class of scholars, and here we see this class emerge.

The *ulama* take their name from *alim*, the Arabic singular which means "a learned one." The *ulama* are the learned ones. They become as it were, a religious class. Islamic law developed then, as the ideal social blueprint for the believer, responding to the questions: "What should I do, if I am to be a Muslim and realize God's will?" "What does that mean concretely?" "How should I live my life?"

Islamic law springs from the basic meaning and requirement of Islam, submission to and realization of God's will. The Quran, remember, teaches that Muslims must strive or struggle, *jihad*, in the path, Shariah, of God, to implement God's will on Earth, to expand and defend their community, and to establish a just society.

Like Judaism, and in contrast to Christianity's emphasis on doctrine, on "correct belief," on *orthodoxy*, Islam emphasizes "correct action, observance," or *orthopraxy*. Thus, in Islam as in Judaism, law rather than theology enjoys pride of place as the central expression of the faith. One defines oneself in terms of whether one is an observant Muslim, just as one talks about an observant Jew. In Christianity, the tendency was to tilt towards doctrine.

Though they overlap the distinction between Shariah, God's law, and *fiqh*, human understanding and interpretation of law is critical to understanding the meaning and dynamic nature of Islamic law, and its possibilities for modern reinterpretation and reform today. Many say: "Is Islam, and is Islamic law, capable of change and reform?" We'll see the importance of these terms.

Shariah in the Quran and in Islam, refers specifically to divine law, for God is the only lawgiver. Islamic law, in many ways, is a broader category that encompasses the divine law, and human understanding or interpretation, *fiqh*; it's an interpretation of God's law. Too often, though, Shariah is simply equated with the term "Islamic law," obscuring the degree to which human interpretation influenced the final product, so that the final product is actually a combination of that which is immutable, and that which is mutable or changeable due to human interpretation.

The development of Islamic law was the work, then of religious scholars, the *ulama*, rather than judges, courts or governments. They primarily laid out the law that we find in the law books. The main divisions of law concern two broad areas. First, a Muslim's duty is to God. Obligatory practices are essential observances, here, primarily those involved with worship. Think concretely of the Five Pillars of Islam; these are unchangeable.

Second, a Muslim's duty is to others, to social transactions or relations. These would include regulations governing public life, from contract and international law, to family laws governing marriage, divorce, and inheritance. Sunni Muslims recognize four official sources of Islamic law. The bulk of the Quran consists of broad, general, moral directives or principles, and this is the first source of law. Remember that the Quran is the book of God, the Revelation. Approximately 80 prescriptions in the Quran rank as legal prescriptions in the very narrowest sense or definition of law. In other senses you're talking about legal principles and values, and most of these come from the Medinan period, when Muhammad was establishing the first Islamic community state.

The second source of law is Sunnah, the "example of the Prophet." Remember, we talked about how the Quran, and Sunnah the Prophet, are the foundation stones. It is the Prophet Sunnah, and what he said and did, which were believed to be preserved in the narrative stories and reports known as "traditions of the Prophet," *hadith*.

The third source is analogical reasoning, or *qiyas*. It's a technique used when no clear text of the Quran or the Sunnah is directly relevant to a legal question. When there's no clear text that exists, then jurists are free to use their independent judgment or reasoning, called *ijtihad*, to examine similar situations whose principles could be applied to this new situation. This, of course, led to a great deal of diversity of opinion.

The fourth source of law is the consensus, the *ijma*, of the community. In practice, it came to be understood as the consensus of the majority of scholars, religious scholars, the *ulama*, who were the guardians and interpreters of the law, in many ways the self-proclaimed guardians and interpreters. This source originated from a tradition of the Prophet that said, "My community will never agree on an error."

While that tradition of the Prophet was referring to the *ummah*, the community in general, as I said, over time it came to be understood as the *ulama*, as speaking for representatives of the community, because they were the knowledgeable ones, and they knew the religious sources.

Concern for justice led to the development of other subsidiary legal principles. Among them were equity, which permits exceptions to a strict or literal legal reasoning in favor of public interest, another source, public interest or human welfare, the general welfare, assuring a flexibility that enabled judges to arrive at just and equitable decisions.

Shii Muslims have a somewhat different set of legal sources and, most importantly, within this context, we need to note that they accept, yes, the Quran and the Sunnah, but also their own collections of the traditions of Ali and his successors as *imam*. Remember in Shiism the importance of Ali and the *imams*, whom they regard as supreme authorities and legal interpreters.

While there is an overall unity within Islamic law, it's important to note that there's also a diversity. Islamic law is both a source of unity, as well as difference and diversity. While the four schools of law agree in their essentials, they differ in a number of particulars, reflecting the role of individual reasoning and social custom; there'll be differences about the qualifications in terms of who you can marry, or areas that have to do with the maintenance of a wife: How much maintenance and for how long? This will vary from school to school.

Individual jurists differed in their interpretation of text. They, after all, were using their human reason, their personal opinions, and their notions of equity and public welfare. So too, the diverse social backgrounds and cultural context of legal scholars. The technical term for legal scholars here is *faqih*, the plural *fuqaha*, to refer to the jurist or the legal scholar.

That also affected their judgments and informed their interpretations. What was their social context? What was the cultural context? Thus, law schools differed about the grounds on which a woman could sue for divorce, or an amount to be paid for maintenance.

The differences in local customs of the more cosmopolitan and class-conscious city of Kufa, a Hanifi center, versus the more conservative Medina, where the Malachi law school developed, can be seen in the varying regulations of these law schools. A similar diversity is illustrated by the official legal opinions or interpretations, what are called *fatwas*. A *fatwa* is a legal opinion rendered by an expert, a consultant, a *mufti*, and we see these terms emerging more in our media. The *mufti* is one who advises judges and advises litigants. It's a bit like in a law case today where either the plaintiff/ the defendant might go to a prominent legal scholar at a major law school to get an opinion, and then bring that to court and then use that before the court.

We see these differences among *muftis*, or legal scholars, and differences, therefore, in their *fatwas*. In recent times, when *muftis* have provided contrasting opinions, or *fatwas*, in the Salman Rushdie case, for example, and in the Gulf War of 1991, the Ayatollah Khomeini's *fatwa* found Salman Rushdie, the author of *The Satanic Verses* guilty of blasphemy and he was condemned to death. That resulted, as many of you will recall, in his going into hiding.

Other *muftis*, while deploring the book, called for his trial by Islamic law, and illustrates that difference in approach. In the Gulf War, *mufti's* opinions varied in providing, on the one hand, supporting positions for Iraq, or on the other, support for the U.S. led armada that included Arab and Muslim countries, like Egypt and Saudi Arabia. Similar differences of opinion have been seen more recently regarding the issue of suicide bombing and martyrdom, most particularly in Palestine, in Israel today, and in that conflict.

A major area of Islamic law, and one that we need to mention both here and later on when we have the class on women, is Muslim family law. Because of the centrality of the community in Islam, the Muslim family as the basic unit of society enjoyed pride of place in the development and implementation of Islamic law.

Muslim family law includes three major areas: marriage, divorce, and inheritance. While rulers in early Islam and today might limit, circumvent, or replace other areas of law, such as penal and commercial laws. Muslim family law has generally remained in force. The formulation of Muslim family law has been subject to reform, widespread debate, and revision since the 20th century, and we certainly see it today in the 21st century. The place of women in family law reform remains, therefore, an important, extremely sensitive, and hotly-contested issue in Islam and in Muslim societies.

The status of women and the family in Islamic law was the product of Arab culture, Quranic reforms, and foreign ideas and values assimilated from conquered people. The Quran introduced substantial reforms, providing new regulations and modifying local custom and practice.

At the same time, in much of the traditional pre-Islamic social structure, with its extended family and the paramount position of males in a patriarchal society, I want to underscore that the importance of patriarchal society, was incorporated. Marriage and family life are the expected norm in Islam.

In contrast to Christianity, in Islam, marriage is not a sacrament, but a contract between a man and a woman, or perhaps more accurately, between their families. In the traditional practice of arranged marriages the families or guardians, not the bride and groom, are the two primary actors.

The Quran introduced a number of reforms that enhanced the status of women. It recognized, for example, a woman's right to contract her own marriage, and receive the dower from her husband, in chapter 4, verse 4. Thus, she became a party to the contract, not just an object for sale.

In a society where no limitations on polygamy existed, the Quran sought to control and regulate polygamy, stipulating that a man could marry up to four wives, provided he could support and treat them equally. It's important to note here, that the Quran did not require that a man marry four wives, but limited him to that number.

The relationship between a husband and a wife in Islamic law is viewed as complementary, reflecting their differing characteristics, capacities and dispositions, as well as the traditional roles of men and women, again, in the patriarchal family. The primary arena for the man is the public sphere; he's to support and protect the family. Women's primary roles are those of wives and mothers, managing the households, and supervising the upbringing and religious training of their children.

While both are equal before God and equally required to lead virtuous lives. In family matters and in society, women were subordinate, because of their more sheltered and protected lives, and because of their dependency on men, who had greater economic responsibilities in the extended family.

While divorce is permissible, both the Quran and the prophetic traditions underscore its seriousness. The Prophet Muhammad is reported to have said, "Of all the permitted things, divorce is the most abominable with God." An authoritative legal manual describes divorce as a "dangerous and disapproved procedure" as it dissolves marriage. In Arab society, men could divorce at will and on whim, while women had no grounds for divorce.

The Quran and Islamic law introduced guidelines based on greater equity and responsibility, to constrain a man's unbridled right to divorce, and to establish a woman's right to a judicial court divorce. However, these laws were often compromised by social realities and circumvented. Thus, for example, a husband was required by law to pronounce the formula for divorce, "I divorce you," three times, once each month, for a period of three months, during which a time for reconciliation was to be pursued.

In fact, some men bypassed the Quranically mandated three-month waiting period, which is found in the Quran chapter 65, verse 1, by saying, "I divorce you, I divorce you, I divorce you," three times, all at one time. While Islamic law considered such an act unapproved or deviant, it was nevertheless legally valid.

The force of patriarchy was especially evident in the requirement that women, in contrast to men, go before a court and present grounds to obtain a divorce. Patriarchy also governed the rules of inheritance in pre-Islamic Arabia, according to which all property passed to the nearest male relative of the deceased.

In contrast, the Quran gave rights to wives, daughters, sisters and grandmothers of the deceased, guaranteeing them a fixed share before the remainder of the inheritance could pass to the senior male. Men still inherited more than women, a fact that reflected gender relations in a male dominated society, as well as a male's greater economic responsibilities.

In practice, however, Quranic and legal reforms were often circumvented by families whose women were either ignorant of their rights or intimidated into not pursuing them. With the creation of modern nation-states in the 20th century, many Muslim governments implemented Western-inspired legal codes. However, family law was subject to reform rather than replacement. Among the key areas of concern were marriage, polygamy and child marriages, divorce and inheritance.

This process of reform often set in motion a struggle between governments and their Western-oriented elite, who legislated or imposed change from above, and the *ulama,* religious scholars, who saw themselves as the defenders of the tradition of Islam and as the only qualified interpreters.

Reforms raised the minimum age for marriage, requiring that men obtain permission from a court to take a second wife or to divorce, and expanded the grounds for women to obtain a divorce. Faced with resistance to legal reforms, governments did not pursue systematic reform and compromises were made. Often the penalties, fines, and imprisonment for failure to comply with the law were minimal. The force of religious tradition could be seen in the fact that failure to comply with reform laws rendered an act illegal but not invalid, since few governments were willing to replace Islamic law and be accused of abrogating Shariah or God's law.

Thus, if a man took another wife, his second marriage would be illegal, and his progeny illegitimate in the eyes of the law, but not invalid in the eyes of God, according to many Islamic jurists. The tenuousness of family law reforms have become evident in Muslim countries such as Iran and Pakistan in recent decades, as conservative *ulama* and Islamic movements pressed for their repeal.

More fundamentalist and conservative voices reject reforms as un-Islamic and motivated by Western-oriented elites. They continue to pose a major obstacle to substantive reform. However, the momentum today for greater gender equality, and the growing empowerment of women, have increased pressure for a debate over substantive reform in many Muslim societies.

Now we move or shift from the exterior path to the interior path, Sufism or mysticism. Like Islamic law, Sufism, or Islamic mysticism, began as a reform movement in the Umayyad Empire. Sufis found the emphasis on this life, in contrast to the next, on power and wealth, and on Islam as a system of laws and rules, to be spiritually lacking. In contrast to the exterior path of law and duty, they emphasize the more interior path of piety and devotional love. These early Sufis or mystics were motivated by a desire to return to what they regarded as the purity and simplicity of the time of Muhammad that led them to seek direct and personal experience, now, of God in this world.

They pursued an ascetic lifestyle that emphasized detachment from the material world, repentance for sins, and focus on the Last Judgment. This ascetic lifestyle was symbolized by their wearing of a simple, coarse woolen garment. Early Sufis dedicated themselves to a life of prayer, fasting, meditation on the Quran, an imitation of Muhammad.

The early mystics typify the concerns and spirit of Sufism. Hasan al-Basari, who lived from 643 to 728, an eminent scholar, typifies the ascetic reaction to the extravagances, what he considered to be the decadence of imperial Islam. Thus, he declared, "The lower material world is a house whose inmates labor for loss, and only abstention from it makes one happy in it. He who befriends it in desire and love for it will be made wretched by it, and his portion with God will be laid waste. For this world has neither worth nor weight with God, so slight it is."

Both men and women participated in Sufism. Emphasis on ascetic detachment, or renunciation of dependence on the material world, was complemented by the contribution of Rabia al-Adawiyya, who died in 801. She fused asceticism with an undying devotional love of God. This combination of the ascetic with the ecstatic would permanently influence the future development of Sufism.

An attractive and desirable woman, she declined all offers of marriage, not permitting anyone or anything to distract her from total dedication and commitment to God. The following words attributed to Rabia capture her selfless love and devotion: "O my Lord, if I worship you out of fear of hell, and if I worship you in hope of paradise, exclude me from it. But if I worship you for your own sake, then withhold not from me your eternal beauty."

The spread of Sufism led to the absorption of outside influences from the new areas to which Sufism spread, from Africa to Southeast Asia. Sufism adopted and adapted a variety of mystical doctrines, ranging from the sober to the intoxicated.

Because of its adoption of external un-Islamic influences, Sufis came to be in conflict, often, with the more orthodox, legal-oriented, legal-minded *ulama*, or religious scholars. Their conflicts revolved around issues of authority and power.

The *ulama* typically sought to apply the letter of law, while Sufis were more concerned with the spirit of the law. The majority of the *ulama* dismissed Sufi doctrine and practice as heretical deviation from orthodoxy. Many Sufis were persecuted, and even executed, as a result.

A prominent theologian emerged to save the day, Abu Hamid al-Ghazali, who died in 1111. He synthesized and reconciled these diverse religious and philosophical currents of his day. Trained in law, theology, and philosophy, he responded to the major theological and philosophical challenges of his time. However, his brilliant career was cut short by a spiritual and psychological breakdown.

In the midst of this spiritual crisis, al-Ghazali turned to Sufism, tempering reason and law with Sufism's emphasis on religious experience and love of God. The results were captured in what many considered to be his greatest work, *The Revivification of the Religious Sciences*, which synthesized law, theology, and mysticism. Law and theology were presented in terms that were acceptable to the *ulama*, but were grounded in direct religious experience and interior devotion. Al-Ghazali's work led to his recognition as one of Islam's greatest scholars, and earned him the title of the "Renewer of Islam," a title which is reserved for one individual in each century, for their work in revitalizing Islam.

Sufi orders emerged also around the 12th century, and it is the 12th century which proved to be a turning point, both because of al-Ghazali's legitimization of Sufism and the emergence of these orders or brotherhoods that transform Sufism into a popular mass movement, cutting across social classes and educational backgrounds. Sufism grew, now, beyond its more urban elite roots. Its loose voluntary groups or associations that had met in mosques or private homes were replaced now by organized brotherhoods or religious orders, *tariqas*, with their own distinctive institutions and international networks.

By the 13th century, brotherhoods had created international networks of centers or monasteries, *zawiyyas*, that transformed Sufism into a mass movement, whose preachers were the great missionaries of Islam. Mystics, not the military, spread the faith from Africa to Southeast Asia. Sufism became integral and pervasive to popular religious practice and spirituality in Islam. Sufi spiritual leaders or masters, *shaykhs* or *pirs*, enjoyed great religious influence, authority, and power, both spiritual and material.

Sufi monasteries or compounds served as spiritual, social, educational and cultural centers. Their buildings and services included the master's residence, living quarters, a mosque, school, hospice, soup kitchen to feed the poor, and a clinic to care for the sick.

Many of the characteristics, though, of Sufism find similar experiences in Christianity and other faiths. Sufi orders or brotherhoods formed with centers or monasteries. The investiture of initiates or disciples included distinctive garb of the order, and a discipline of body and mind. Sufis recited a litany of God's names and attributes, counting them on a string of beads similar to a rosary.

The founders of Sufi orders often came to be venerated as saints. Their tombs became sites for pilgrimage, and even miracles, their births or deaths commemorated and celebrated. In contrast to the more austere interpretations of Islam, some Sufis used music and song, as well as dance and bodily movements. The followers of the great Sufi mystic, Jalal al-Din Rumi, who died in 1273, the "whirling dervishes" are a prime example, and they exist down to today.

Popular Sufism, at times, did slip into magic and superstition, as well as withdrawal from the world. Some of the major Islamic revival or reform movements of the 18th, 19th, and 20th centuries sought to eliminate these superstitious practices. It indeed is these practices, and the reactions to them, that we will look at when we turn to the rise of Islamic revivalist movements in the 17th and 18th centuries. We will also look at Islamic modernist movements in the 19th and 20th centuries, and indeed other reform movements existing down to the 21st century.

Islamic Revivalism—Renewal and Reform
Lecture 7

From the 17th to the 20th centuries, the Muslim world experienced both internal disintegration and upheaval and the external aggression of the European colonial era. A variety of religious sociopolitical movements arose throughout the Muslim world in response.

The Islamic world experienced a major transition as the power, prosperity, and dynamic expansionism of imperial Islam gave way to political disintegration and social and moral decline, followed by the advent of European colonialism throughout much of the Muslim world. Pre-modern revivalist movements of the 17th and 18th centuries addressed social and moral problems and provided inspiration to late 19th- and 20th-century Islamic modernist movements that offered Islamic responses to the challenges of European colonialism and modernization. Islam possesses a long history and tradition of religious revival and reform in response to perceived compromises in faith and practice. Islamic concepts of renewal (*tajdid*) and reform (*islah*) are based in the Quran and Sunnah, and both call for a return to these sources. Renewal and reform are carried out by practicing *ijtihad*, or "personal interpretation" of the Quran and Sunnah. Great revivalists throughout Islamic history have claimed the right to function as *mujtahids* in order to purify and revitalize their societies.

A wave of religio-political revivalism in the 17th and 18th centuries spread across the Islamic world from the Sudan to Sumatra, with some of the most important events occurring in Arabia, Africa, and India. The ideological worldviews of revivalists shared several points in common: The purpose of pre-modernist revivalists was not to reinterpret Islam to yield new solutions but to return to the pure and pristine vision of Islam, preserved in the Quran and Sunnah, and to reestablish an authentic Islamic community modeled on the Prophet and his early companions. For this reason, these types of revivals have been referred to as fundamentalist movements. The process involved the creation of a socio-moral reform movement governed by Islamic law, a religious community-state of "true believers," in contrast to existing societies that were no longer truly Islamic. Removal of foreign un-Islamic practices that had infiltrated and corrupted the community was necessary. Struggle (*jihad*), whether through moral self-discipline or armed conflict, was required to reassert the rightful place of Islam in society. Muslims who resisted these measures were no longer regarded as Muslims, but were to be numbered among the enemies of God.

A series of revivalist movements led to the establishment of several Islamic states: the Wahhabi in Arabia and Africa, the Fulani in Nigeria, the Sanusi in Libya, and the Mahdi in the Sudan. In contrast to the Wahhabi, who were anti-Sufi, African movements were distinguished by their Sufi leadership—reformist, militant, and politically oriented charismatic heads of Sufi orders. The Wahhabi movement in Saudi Arabia and the Mahdi in the Sudan are perhaps the most well known of pre-modern Islamic movements. Each has had a formative influence on modern Muslim states and, although similar in some respects, each represents contrasting styles of leadership and reform. The Wahhabi movement (founded by Muhammad ibn Abd al-Wahhab, 1703–1792) chose to completely suppress rather than merely reform Sufism, including destroying the tombs of the Prophet and Husayn. This act influenced Ayatollah Khomeini's call for the overthrow of the House of Saud and had an impact on the conflict between the Sunni majority and Shii minority in Saudi Arabia. Some have claimed Wahhabi influence in the Taliban's destruction of Buddhist monuments in Afghanistan.

In contrast to the Wahhabi movement, the Mahdi of the Sudan (Muhammad Ahmad, 1848–1885, founder of the Mahdiyya Order) claimed to be a divinely appointed representative of God. He justified holy war against other Muslims by pronouncing them blasphemers. His movement reformed Sufism; alcohol, prostitution, gambling, and music were outlawed as foreign (Ottoman Egyptian), un-Islamic practices that had corrupted society.

Islamic modernism of the 19th and 20th centuries was a response both to continued internal weaknesses and to the external political and religio-cultural threat of European colonialism. The result of Western imperialism for Muslims was a period of self-criticism and reflection on the causes of decline. Secularists blamed an outmoded tradition in Islam and advocated the separation of religion and politics and the establishment of the Western model of modern nation-state building. Conservative religious leaders advocated non-cooperation or rejection of the West, believing that accommodation of Western culture was tantamount to betrayal and surrender. Some even advocated armed struggle (*jihad*) or emigration to Islamic territory.

Islamic modernists sought to reinterpret Islam to demonstrate its compatibility with modern Western science and thought and to meet the changing circumstances of Muslim life through legal, educational, political, and social reforms. In the Middle East, Jamal al-Din al-Afghani (1838–1897) called for religious, scientific, and political reforms in order to defend Islam, strengthen the Muslim community, and ultimately, regain independence from the West. His disciples or protégés, Muhammad Abduh (1849–1905) and Rashid Rida (1865–1935), were the great religious reformers of modern Islam. They founded the Salafiyyah movement, whose influence extended from North Africa to Southeast Asia.

Islamic modernists sought to reinterpret Islam to demonstrate its compatibility with modern Western science and thought and to meet the changing circumstances of Muslim life through legal, educational, political, and social reforms.

In the Indian subcontinent, Sir Sayyid Ahmad Khan (1817–1898) called for a modern, rational reinterpretation of Islam based on the acceptance of the best that Western thought had to offer. He was especially supportive of educational reforms that would allow for the development of a new generation of Muslim leaders equipped to face the challenges and demands of modernity and the West.

Muhammad Iqbal (1875–1938), the most important Indian reformer and poet of the 20th century, educated in Britain and Germany, emphasized the dynamism and creativity of Islam, arguing for a reconstruction of religious thought in Islam. He was especially important for his Islamization of Western concepts, such as democracy and parliamentary government. He emphasized the ideal of an Islamic community that transcended ethnic, racial, and national ties.

Although Islamic modernism existed in different places and contexts, Islamic modernists shared some common teachings and understandings. Modernists rejected an unquestioned return to past solutions in favor of accepting and incorporating change and proclaimed Islam the religion of reason, science, and nature. They reclaimed the progressive, creative past of Islam, whose political and cultural florescence demonstrated Islam's ability to produce great empires and civilizations.   They stressed that stagnation and decline were caused by blind imitation of the past (*taqlid*); the continued survival and revitalization of the Muslim community required a bold reinterpretation (*ijtihad*) of Islam's religious tradition. They criticized the popular religious practices of Sufism as responsible for un-Islamic and even superstitious practices that were a major source of decline.

Islamic modernism had both positive and negative results. It appealed to only an elite group of intellectuals and never developed into a popular mass movement that could implement change at a national or regional level. Modernists did not provide a systematic, comprehensive theology or program for legal reform or establish effective organizations to continue and implement ideas once the original charismatic leaders were gone. Modernists, however, emphasized pride in an Islamic heritage and the dynamic, progressive, rational character of Islam, helping new Muslim generations to see change as an opportunity, rather than a threat, and providing the vocabulary for a new Islamic discourse for change. Modernists inspired educational reforms and nationalist independence movements rooted in religion that harnessed Islam for mass mobilization. Islamic modernism produced a legacy of reinterpretation that often resulted in a synthesis of traditional concepts and modern thought to relate Muslim faith and religious tradition to modern realities. The holistic approach of modernists viewed Islam as a comprehensive guide for both public and private life, making Islam an alternative ideology for both modern state and society.

Some Muslims rejected conservative and modernist positions in favor of Islamic organizations that combined religious activism and ideology. The Muslim Brotherhood in Egypt and the Jamaat-i Islami (Islamic Society) of the Indian subcontinent are prominent examples of modern neo-revivalist Islamic organizations that linked religion to activism. Both movements emerged in the shadow of British colonialism in societies where anticolonial national independence movements were active. The leaders, Hasan al-Banna and Mawlana Abu al-Ala Mawdudi, respectively, were pious, committed Muslims whose upbringing exposed them to Islamic education, Islamic modernist thought, and Western learning. Both leaders combined religious reform with social activism. Both leaders formed ideological fraternities in which members were trained and reinforced in their faith and commitment to create a more Islamically oriented state and society. They supported religious instruction, youth work, schools, hospitals, religious publications, and social welfare projects.

The actual means of carrying out their visions differed. The Muslim Brotherhood grew rapidly as a mass movement, expanding to include members of the lower and middle classes in both rural and urban areas. The Jamaat remained a more elitist group, particularly focused on developing a new core of well-educated and Islamically committed leaders. The Muslim Brotherhood's dissatisfaction with the Egyptian government's failure to establish an Islamic state escalated into violence and the assassination of al-Banna, culminating in the repression of the Brotherhood and a long series of confrontations, imprisonments, proscriptions, and executions. The Jamaat served as an opposition party within the system, working through elections and political action, although some of its leaders, including Mawdudi, were imprisoned.

Both the Brotherhood and the Jamaat became models that sparked similar movements across the Muslim world. Both gained popular support when they addressed issues that directly concerned a cross-section of society: colonialism, dependence on the West, religious identity, poverty, illiteracy, economic exploitation, education, and health care. Involvement with the material world and the pursuit of social justice, political and social activism, were critical components of the neo-revivalist message. They did not simply propagate religion but called on Muslims to become better and more involved in society. ■

John L. Esposito, *Islam: The Straight Path*, chapter 4.

———, *The Islamic Threat: Myth or Reality?*, chapter 3.

John O. Voll, "Foundations for Renewal and Reform," *The Oxford History of Islam*, chapter 12.

Questions to Consider

1. What were the causes for and responses of revival/reform movements?

2. What were the major achievements and failures of Islamic modernists?

3. How have 20th-century Islamic movements built on past movements and what new ideas and methods have they implemented?

Islamic Revivalism—Renewal and Reform
Lecture 7—Transcript

The Islamic world experienced a major transition from the 17th to the 20th centuries as the power, prosperity, and dynamic expansionism of imperial Islam gave way to political disintegration. It was a traumatic period. Social and moral decline spread, followed by the advent of European colonialism throughout much of the Muslim world. Islam possesses a long history and tradition of religious revival and reform in response to perceived compromises in faith and practice.

Historical examples of incidents covered in previous lectures that led to the calls for religious revival and reform include the Kharijites secession during the early Islamic period, and Shii revolts, as well as the development of Islamic law and Sufism.

Islamic concepts of reform, *islah*, and renewal, *tajdid*, are based in the Quran and in the Sunnah, and both call for return to these sources. *Islah*, or reform, is a Quranic term found in chapters 7, 11, and 28, for example, that describes the vocation and activities of prophets. As in Judaism and Christianity, in Islam prophets are messengers or warners, reformers who call upon a wayward or sinful community to return to God's path. Thus, Muslim reform has called for the realignment of individual and community life with the norms of the Shariah.

This Quranic mandate, coupled with God's command to enjoin good and prohibit evil provides the time-honored rationale for Islamic reformism. Renewal, or *tajdid*, proclaims the belief that an individual, a renewer of Islam, is sent by God at the beginning of each century to restore true Islamic practice and regenerate the Muslim community by returning it to the straight path of Islam. This tradition of renewal, *tajdid*, is based on a saying of the Prophet: That "God will send to this *ummah*, (Muslim community,) at the head of each century those who will renew its faith for it." It was expressed in a number of popular religious forms or beliefs.

The most prominent was the idea of the *mahdi*, the "divinely guided one," in contrast to other reformers or revivalist leaders who simply claim to be qualified to interpret or reinterpret Islam. A *mahdi*, though not a prophet, asserted that he was a divinely appointed and inspired representative of God. While Islamic revival has claimed to simply return to the original teachings of the Quran and the Prophet Muhammad, in fact, they produce new religious interpretations and cultural syntheses to guide their age.

Practicing *ijtihad*, or "personal interpretation" of the Quran and Sunnah, great revivalists in the Middle East and South Asia, like Muhammad Al-Ghazali, Ibn Taymiyya, Muhammad ibn Abd al- Wahhab, whom we'll shortly discussed, and Shah Wali Allah, claimed the right to function as interpreters or re-interpreters, *mujtahids*, in order to purify and revitalize their societies.

Implicit was the belief that the righteous community of Muhammad at Medina has set the norm that all Muslims are to follow. Pre-modern revivalist movements spread across the Islamic world in the 17th and 18th centuries, from Sudan to Sumatra, from Africa to Southeast Asia. The ideological worldviews of revivalist shared common points.

The purpose of pre-modern revivalists was not to reinterpret Islam to yield new solutions, but to return to the fundamental sources of Islam, the Quran and the Sunnah, and to establish or reestablish in authentic communities, such as the community of the Prophet. For this reason they are often popularly referred to as "fundamentalist" movements, those that return to the fundamentals. The process involved the creation of a sociomoral reform movement governed by Islamic law, a religious community state of "true believers," in contrast to existing societies that were no longer seen as truly Islamic.

Removal of foreign un-Islamic practices that had infiltrated and corrupted the community was necessary. This included a critique of the *ulama*, the religious scholars, reform of Sufism, a rejection of *taqlid*, the following of tradition, here seen as the blind following of the scholars of the past, and a return, therefore, to the original teachings of the Quran and Sunnah. Struggle, *jihad*, whether through both moral self-discipline or armed struggle, was required to reassert the rightful place of Islamic society. Muslims who resisted these measures were no longer regarded as Muslims, but would be numbered among the enemies of God.

A series of *jihad* revivalist movements in the late 18ᵗʰ and 19ᵗʰ centuries led in time to the establishment of several Islamic states, the Wahhabi in Saudi Arabia, and in Africa the Fulani, in what is modern-day Nigeria, the Sanusi in Libya, and the Mahdi in the Sudan. The Wahhabi movement in Arabia and the Mahdi in Africa are perhaps the best known of pre-modern Islamic movements. Each has been a formative influence on modern Muslim states. Although similar in some respects, each represents contrasting styles of leadership and reform.

A religious leader, Muhammad ibn Abd al-Wahhab, who lived from 1703 to 1792, and a local tribal chief or prince, Muhammad ibn Saud, who died in 1765, joined forces to create a united religiopolitical movement that would subdue large areas of Arabia and leave a religious and political legacy that continues today in modern day Saudi Arabia. Although popularly called the Wahhabi movement after Muhammad ibn Abd al-Wahhab, one of its founders, its own self-designation was the "Unitarians," the *muwahiddun*, those who practice and uphold monotheism, who worship the one true God.

Abd al-Wahhab, the jurist and theologian, was dismayed by the condition of this society, which he saw as having degenerated to a condition little better than pre-Islamic Arabia, the *jahiliyya* period of ignorance of Islam. He was appalled by popular religious practices, such as the veneration of Sufi saints in their tombs, which he believed compromised the unity or oneness of God and that of the Islamic community in Arabia. Abd al-Wahhab condemned these and other Sufi practices as pagan superstitions, idolatry, using the term *bida*, which means deviation from true Islam; it's almost the equivalent of heresy in Christianity.

Abd al-Wahhab called for a rigorous purification of Islam, a return to fundamentals. The Wahhabi movement waged a rigorous holy war to subdue and once again unite the tribes of Arabia. The warrior missionaries were called the brotherhood, the *ikhwan*. Muslims who disagreed with them were declared enemies of God who must be fought. In contrast to the Mahdist, and other revivalist movements, the Wahhabi chose to completely suppress rather than merely reform Sufism. They destroyed not only Sufi shrines but also other sacred tombs and shrines, including the tombs of the Prophet and his companions in the Tomb of Hussein, a major Shii holy shrine in place of pilgrimage. This act has affected Wahhabi/Shii relations to this day. It influenced Ayatollah Khomeini's call for the overthrow of the House of Saud, the rulers of Saudi Arabia, and conflict between the Sunni majority and Shii minority within Saudi Arabia. Some have claimed that Wahhabi influenced the Taliban's destruction of Buddhist monuments in Afghanistan.

In contrast to the Wahhabi movement, the Mahdi of the Sudan, like other African revivalists, was a charismatic Sufi leader, who initiated a reformist religio-political movement. Muhammad Ahmad, who lived from 1848 to 1885, the founder of the Mahdiyya Sufi order, proclaimed himself Mahdi, the "divinely guided one" in 1881. Thus, he went beyond most other revivalist reformers who claimed the right to interpret Islam, and instead claimed to be a divinely appointed and inspired representative of God. The Mahdi established an Islamic community, uniting his followers and justified waging holy war against other Muslims; in this case, Sudan's Ottoman Muslim rulers. He declared them, "infidels who disobeyed the command of His messenger and His Prophet, ruled in a manner not in accord with what God had said, altered the Shariah of our master, Muhammad, the messenger of God, and blasphemed against the faith of God."

Sufism was reformed; alcohol, prostitution, gambling, and music were outlawed as foreign Ottoman Egyptian, un-Islamic practices that had corrupted society. From 1885 to 1889, after the Mahdist forces overcame Egyptian forces, and Islamic state was established in Khartoum. The Mahdi had supreme power as God's representative and the Shariah was its law.

Now, a transition took place in the late 19th and 20th centuries. Here, Islamic modernism of the 19th and 20th centuries comes as a response both to the continued internal weaknesses, but also very much to the external political and religiocultural threat of European colonialism. Like many parts of the world, Muslim societies fell victim to European imperialism. When Europe overpowered North Africa, the Middle East, South and Southeast Asia in the 19th century, and reduced most Muslim societies to colonies, many Muslims experienced these defeats as a religious, as well as political and cultural crisis. The Muslim world lost its political and cultural sovereignty to Christian Europe, symbolizing the decline of Muslim power and the apparent loss of divine favor and guidance.

Colonialism brought European armies and Christian missionaries. Europe legitimated its colonization of large areas of the underdeveloped Muslim world culturally. The French spoke of their "mission to civilize," the British of the "white man's burden." Missionaries accompanied the armies of bureaucrats, soldiers, traders, and teachers to spread the message of Western Christian religious and cultural superiority.

Muslim response to Christian Europe's political and religious penetration and dominance varied significantly, ranging from resistance or warfare, *jihad*, in defense of Islam, to accommodation, if not outright, assimilation of Western values. The result of Western imperialism from Muslims was a period of self-criticism and reflection on the causes of decline. Responses spanned the spectrum. Secularists blamed an outmoded tradition of Islam and advocated, instead, a separation of religion and politics, and the establishment of a Western-modeled modern nation-state building, from political institutions and the military, to education and law.

Conservative religious leaders, on the other hand, including most of the *ulama*, attributed Muslim impotence to divergence from Islam. They variously advocated non-cooperation or rejection of the West, believing that Western Christian ideas and values were dangerous to Muslim faith and culture. They believed that any form of cultural or political accommodation of Western culture was tantamount to betrayal, surrender, if you will, treason. Some concluded that Muslims who no longer lived under Islamic rule and Islamic territory ought to consider themselves in a land of warfare. They advanced either armed struggle, *jihad*, or emigration, *hijra*, to an Islamic territory. This was what they advised.

Islamic modernists, on the other hand, sought to respond to rather than react against the challenge of Western imperialism. They proclaimed the need for Islamic reform through a process of reinterpretation and selective adaptation, Islamization of Western ideas and technology. Like their 18th century predecessors, Islamic modernists also blamed the internal decline of Muslim societies for their loss of power back when this inability to respond effectively to European colonialism. They particularly blamed the blind and unquestioned clinging to the "past tradition," *taqlid*, which some had regarded as a virtue, following tradition. They now denounced it as a blind clinging to tradition, and a problem.

Modernists stressed the dynamism, flexibility, and adaptability that characterized the early development of Islam, leading to achievements in law, education, and the sciences, as we saw earlier in this course. Islamic modernism sought to reinterpret Islam, to demonstrate its compatibility with modern Western science and thought, and to resist European colonialism and meet the changing circumstances of Muslim life through religious, legal, educational, political, and social reforms. Major reform movements sprang up in the Middle East and South Asia, providing the legacy to reformers and revolutionaries in the 20th and 21st centuries.

In the Middle East, Jamal al-Din al-Afghani, who lived from 1838 to 1897, called for religious, scientific, and political reforms in order to defend Islam's strength in the Muslim community and ultimately regain independence from the West. He was both a political activist and, if you will, intellectual leader. Afghani's disciple or protégé, Muhammad Abduh, who lived from 1849 to 1905, was one of the great religious reformers of modern Islam, whose influence extended literally from North Africa to Southeast Asia. Muhammad Abdud, a prominent member of the *ulama*, and in late life a Grand Mufti of Egypt, chief religious leader, focused on religious, educational, and social reform rather than politics.

As had his predecessors, he blamed Muslim decline on the prevalence of un-Islamic popular religious practices, Sufi passivity and fatalism, and the rigid scholasticism of the traditionalist *ulama*, who had forbidden fresh religious interpretation. Abduh taught that Islam and science and reason were compatible, making it permissible for Muslims to selectively appropriate aspects of Western civilization that were not contrary to Islam. He provided an Islamic rationale for the selective integration of Islam with modern ideas and institutions.

Abduh's most prominent contribution was the distinction between Islam's fundamentals, which do not change. These were limited to matters of worship, for example, the Five Pillars. Then there were those which were subject to change as social and historical conditions warranted. These included issues related to social affairs, such as, penal, commercial, and family laws. Abduh was a strong supporter of women's rights.

Across the world in the Indian subcontinent, Sir Sayyid Ahmad Khan, who lived from 1817 to 1898, called for a modern, rational reinterpretation of Islam based upon the acceptance of the best that Western thought had to offer. Ahmad Kahn responded to the fall of the Mughal Empire in 1857 and British concerns about Muslim loyalty. He advocated a bold reinterpretation of Islam that called for the acceptance of the best that Western thought had to offer. In contrast to Afghani and other Middle Eastern reformers, and even some in South Asia, he preached an acceptance of the political reality of British rule, and restricted his Islamic concerns to the Muslims of India, since he believed that political resistance and appeals to pan-Islam were impractical.

Ahmad Kahn promoted the exercise of *ijtihad*, reinterpretation, as a means of boldly interpreting or reinterpreting Islam in light of its revealed sources, rather than simply using reason to get back to the original interpretations of Islam. His method departed from 18th-century practices, pre-modern 18th-century practices, due to his extensive use of reason, the degree to which he reinterpreted Islam, and his borrowing from the West. He taught that Islam was the religion of reason and nature, so that Islam was in total harmony with the laws of nature, and therefore, compatible with modern scientific thought.

He allowed reason to prevail over the text of the Quran. He called for metaphorical or allegorical rather than literal interpretation of passages that contained miraculous or supernatural language. Khan was particularly supportive of educational reforms that would allow for the development of the new generation of Muslim leaders, equipped to face the challenges and demands of modernity in the West.

A later reformer in South Asia, Muhammad Iqbal, who lived from 1875 to 1938, perhaps the most important Indian reformer and poet of the 20th century, was educated in Britain and Germany. He emphasized the dynamism and creativity of Islam, arguing for a reconstruction of religious thought. Iqbal combined an early Islamic education with advanced degrees from Cambridge and Munich in law and philosophy; from the best law school he earned his law degree and also then a Ph.D. from Germany. This education helped him to recognize the decay and decline of the Muslim community and formulate his process of reform.

During Iqbal's lifetime, the critical question of Muslim communal identity was viewed through the lens of the need for independence and national identity apart from British; the Brits had ruled in India and were ruling. The major question was whether Muslims should join with Hindus in a broad Indian independence movement, seeking the creation of a single secular nation-state in which Muslims would form a permanent minority, or if Muslims should insist upon their own separate state, in which they would be the majority.

Iqbal believed in the importance of the Muslim community living as a religiopolitical state, in which Islamic law must reign supreme, since he believed that Islamic law served as both a political and a moral force for Muslims. He did not recognize any separation of the spiritual and temporal, and is regarded by some as one of the fathers of modern day Pakistan, along with Ali Jinnah.

Like other Islamic modernists, Iqbal distinguished between the eternal, immutable principles of Islam, and those that were the product of human interpretation, and thus, subject to change. He therefore, extended and redefined *ijtihad*, independent reasoning, and *ijma,* consensus, to allow or legitimate modern legislative assemblies or parliaments to provide consensus for the Muslim community. Rather than the *ulama* providing this, he advocated that parliament could do this in the modern state.

He also believed that legislators should seek the advice of experts, including religious scholars, from both traditional and modern disciplines prior to passing legislation. Iqbal was especially important for his Islamization of Western concepts, like democracy and parliamentary government. He did not believe that he was creating an Islamic rationale for copying Western values; rather, he believed that these values were inherent to Islam and the Muslim historical experience. Thus, Iqbal rejected nationalism as a Western tool for dismembering the Muslim world; instead, he emphasized the idea of an Islamic community that transcended ethnic, racial, and national ties.

While talking a pan-Islamic language, however, he also realized in the short term the need for nation-states, and so supported the foundation of Pakistan as an Islamic republic. Although Islamic modernism existed in different places in context, Islamic modernists shared some common teachings and understandings. First of all, the modernists rejected an unquestioned return or dependence on past solutions in favor of accepting and incorporating change, and proclaimed that Islam was the religion of reason, science, and nature. They reclaimed the progressive, creative past of Islam, the Golden Age as it were, whose political and cultural florescence demonstrated Islam's ability to produce great empires and civilizations. They stressed that stagnation and decline were caused by blind imitation of the past, *taqlid*. The continued survival and revitalization of the Muslim community required a bold reinterpretation, *ijtihad*, of Islam's religious sources, of Islam's religious tradition.

Modernists criticized the popular religious practices of Sufism as responsible for un-Islamic and even superstitious practices that were a major source of decline. Islamic modernism had both positive and negative results; it appealed to only a small elite group of intellectuals, and never developed into a popular mass movement that could implement change at a national or regional level. Modernists did not provide a systematic, comprehensive theology or program for legal reform, nor establish effective organizations to continue and implement ideas, once the original charismatic leaders passed from the scene.

However, it had a long-term influence by emphasizing pride in an Islamic heritage and the dynamic, progressive, rational character of Islam; helping new Muslim generations to see change as an opportunity rather than a threat, and providing the vocabulary for new Islamic discourse for change and development. Modernists inspired educational reform and national independence movements rooted in religion that harnessed Islam for mass mobilization. Islamic modernism, then, produced a legacy of reinterpretation that often produced a synthesis of traditional concepts and modern thought to relate Muslim faith and religious tradition to modern realities.

At the same time, however, we see the emergence of modern Islamic revivalist movements, what some call fundamentalist movements. Some Muslims rejected both conservative and modernist positions, in favor of Islamic organizations and an Islamic ideology that combined religious activism and religious ideology. They thought that the conservatives or *ulama* were too rigid. They thought that Islamic modernists tended in keying to the Western interpreting Islam, to be Westernizers of Islam, in a sense, to produce a kind of protestant Islam or protestantization of Islam.

There were two major groups that had enduring influence on the Muslim Brotherhood in Egypt and the Jamaat-i Islami, The Islamic Society or Group, of the Indian subcontinent; they were a prominent example to modern revivalists or neo-revivalist Islamic organizations that linked religion to activism, political and social activism. Both movements emerged in the shadow of British colonialism in the mid 20th century, in societies where anti-colonial national independence movements were active.

Their leaders, the Muslim Brotherhood's Hasan al-Banna, 1906 to 1949, and the Jamaat's Mawlana Abu al-Ala Mawdudi, who lived from 1903 to 1979, respectively, were pious Muslims whose upbringing and educations exposed them to Islamic education, but also to Islamic modernist thought and Western learning.

Both leaders combined religion and activism. They shared a revivalist ideology and established activist organizations that remain vibrant today and have served as an example to others throughout much of the Muslim world. They are the trailblazers in many ways. Both movements were organized via, and garnered their ideological outlooks from the example of Muhammad and his first Islamic religiosocial reformation or revolution to the neo-revivalist movements of the 17th and 18th centuries. They established communities of true believers as they saw it, who were committed to the struggle to transform society.

Rather than leaving their societies, they organized their followers into an Islamically-oriented community in order to form a dynamic nucleus of leaders capable of transforming society from within. Each formed an ideological fraternity that developed a well-knit, socioreligious organization with a network of branches and cells. Members were trained and reinforced in their faith and commitment to create a more Islamically-oriented state in society.

Members underwent a period of training and ideological indoctrination that emphasized religious knowledge and moral fitness and concentrated on moral and social programs.

All of this was done out of a belief that the unity of the brotherhood of believers must replace the religious, political, and socioeconomic factions that divided and weakened the Muslim community. These societies supported religious instruction, youth work, schools, hospitals, religious publications, and social welfare projects in order to create a new generation of leaders, a new social order, and a more morally-oriented and stronger Muslim society.

The actual means of carrying out their visions varied. The Muslim Brotherhood grew rapidly as a mass movement, expanding to include members of the lower and middle classes in both rural and urban areas. The Jamaat, on the other hand, remained the more elitist movement, particularly focused on developing a new core of well-educated and Islamically-committed leaders, an alternative elite. The Muslim Brotherhood's dissatisfaction with the Egyptian government's failure to establish an Islamic state escalated into violence and the assassination of its founder, Hasan al-Banna, culminating in repression of the brotherhood, and a long series of confrontations between the brotherhood and government. Imprisonments, proscriptions, and executions followed.

The Jamaat served as an opposition party within South Asia, particularly within Pakistan, but also in India and other parts of South Asia, working through elections and in the system, and through political action, although some of its leaders from time to time, including its founder Mawdudi, were imprisoned.

Both the brotherhood and the Jamaat became models that inspired similar movements across the Muslim world. Their founders became the ideologues of contemporary Islamic movements, the people to be read and remembered. They influenced both mainstream and extremist movements. Both gained populous support when they addressed issues that directly concerned the cross section of society: Colonialism, dependence on the West, religious identity and re-appropriation of it issues of poverty, illiteracy, economic exploitation, education, healthcare, involvement with the material world, and the pursuit of social justice.

Political and social activism were critical components of the neo-revivalist message. They did not simply propagate religion, but called upon Muslims to become better and more involved in society. And indeed, it is these revivalist movements, as typified and in a sense represented by the Muslim Brotherhood and the Jamaat-i Islami that, as I said earlier, provide the model across the Muslim world.

Muslim Brotherhoods sprang up in Egypt, in Jordan, in Syria, throughout much of the Arab world, and influenced movements in South and Southeast Asia. The Jamaat-i Islami and its branches could be found in Pakistan and Bangladesh, in India, in Afghanistan.

The influence of the of the writings of Hasan al-Banna and Mawlana Mawdudi can be found when we look in the late 20th and 21st centuries across the Muslim world, translated with modern communications, modern printing press, modern technology, translated and disseminated literally from one part of the Muslim world to the other, from urban areas to rural areas. They have had an impact, then, on local and national Islamic organizations and societies as they developed, both in terms of their ideology as well as their actual organization and structure.

These new movements in countries responding to their local or national governments were borrowing from others, appropriating, and then building on them. As we turn now to the remainder of the course, we will see the impact of these movements from the mid- to late-20th century, and their significant impact in the late 20th and early 21st centuries.

The Contemporary Resurgence of Islam
Lecture 8

In the last decades of the 20ᵗʰ century, the Muslim world experienced the impact of another revival or resurgence of Islam in personal and in public life.

In the last decades of the 20ᵗʰ century, a series of political events and economic realities led to the desire of many Muslims to achieve greater authenticity and self-definition through a revival of Islam. This revival was reflected both in private life (greater mosque attendance and concern with Islamic dress and values) and in public life through political and social activism. While reformist movements have worked within mainstream society for change, extremists have resorted to violence and terrorism to achieve their goals. On the personal level, many Muslims have become more religiously observant, finding in Islam a sense of identity, meaning, and guidance.

In the public sphere, new Islamic governments or republics have been established in Iran, Sudan, and Afghanistan. Rulers, political parties, and opposition movements have appealed to Islam. Mainstream Islamic activists head governments and serve in cabinets, in elected parliaments, and as senior officials of professional associations of doctors, lawyers, engineers, and professors. At the same time, radical Islamic organizations have engaged in violence and terrorism to topple governments or to achieve related goals.

The causes and conditions that led to the contemporary resurgence of Islam are many. During the 20ᵗʰ century, Islamic empires and sultanates were obliterated and replaced by modern nation-states. Many countries in the Middle East were quite literally newly created, "mapped out" by European colonial powers (Britain and France) after World War I. Between World War I and World War II, most of newly created states won their independence from European colonial rulers. However, both the national boundaries of many modern states and their rulers, many of whom were placed on their thrones by Britain or France, such as in Jordan, Syria, and Iraq, were artificial creations. Moreover, European education, culture, and values permeated the urban areas and strongly influenced the elites in most states and societies. As a result, issues of government legitimacy, as well as national and religio-cultural identity, remained unresolved. Rulers rooted their legitimacy in an authoritarian state whose stability was due more to foreign (Western or Soviet) support, coupled with strong military-security apparatus, rather than an indigenous culture, political participation, and electoral politics.

Once these modern nation-states were created in the Muslim world, it was expected that they would generally follow a "modern," that is, Western, secular path of development. Although the majority populations in these countries were Muslim, they adopted Western-inspired institutions: parliaments, political party systems, legal codes, educational systems and curricula, banks, and insurance companies. However, the majority of countries, such as Egypt, Syria, Iran, Malaysia, and Indonesia, created what may be called Muslim states, in which the majority populations were Muslim, but despite some religious prescriptions, adopted Western-inspired institutions. Throughout much of the 20th century, progress and prosperity

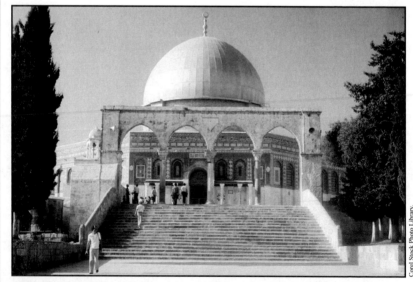

Corel Stock Photo Library.

When Muslim armies took Jerusalem without resistance in 635, they restored and rebuilt the temple. First they built a large mosque, the al-Aqsa, and then a shrine, the Dome of the Rock.

in Muslim societies depended on the degree to which Muslims and their societies were "modern"; this also meant conforming to "Western" and "secular" values.

Based on these criteria, Turkey, Tunisia, Egypt, Lebanon, and Iran were often seen as among the more modern, advanced, and "enlightened," that is, Westernized and secular, countries. Saudi Arabia, the states of the Persian Gulf, Afghanistan, Bangladesh, and Pakistan were generally regarded as more traditional, religious, and thus, "backward."

The failure of "modernity" in the 1960s and 1970s shattered the hopes and dreams of many who believed that national independence and Western-oriented development would usher in strong states and prosperous societies. A series of wars and riots during the 1960s and 1970s revealed the pitfalls and failures of many states and societies. Such catalytic events triggered a soul-searching reassessment among many Muslims focused on the reliance on Western models. Perhaps the most significant symbolic event, which sparked Muslim disillusionment and dissatisfaction, was the 1967 Arab-Israeli war, which came to be called the Six Day War. Because of its role in Islamic tradition, the loss of Jerusalem in the 1967 war was a traumatic experience, not only for Arab Muslims and Arab Christians alike, but also for Muslims worldwide, who all revere Jerusalem as a site of central religious significance.

The realities of Muslim societies (poverty, illiteracy, failed economies, high unemployment, and malapportionment of wealth) raised profound questions of national identity and political legitimacy and of religious faith and meaning. The signs of profound change would not become fully evident and appreciated in the West until a decade later, with the Iranian Revolution of 1978–1979.

Disillusionment and dissatisfaction with modernity were accompanied by an Islamic revival, marked by a quest for self-identity and greater authenticity, as many reaffirmed the importance of Islam and Islamic values in their personal and social lives. Islamic ideology, discourse, and politics reemerged as a major force in the development of the Muslim world, a force that both Muslim and Western governments have had to accommodate or contend with for several decades. Several phenomena may be identified as common to the contemporary Muslim experience: An identity crisis precipitated by a sense of utter impotence and loss of self-esteem. Disillusionment with the West (with its models of development and with the West as an ally) and with the failure of many governments to respond adequately to the political and socio-economic needs of their societies. A quest for greater authenticity, that is, to reappropriate a greater sense of indigenous identity, history, and values. Newfound sense of pride and power, which resulted from the Arab-Israeli war and oil embargo of 1973, the success of the Afghan *mujahideen* in their war against Soviet occupation of Afghanistan, and the global impact of Iran's Islamic revolution of 1978–1979. For many, these were signs of a resurgence of Islam and God's help to those who fought against overwhelming odds in the name of Islam.

> **By the late 1980s and early 1990s, it was clear that Islamists had moved from the periphery to mainstream politics and society.**

Although a tremendous diversity existed in the religious worldview and politics of Islamic activism from country to country, nevertheless, Islamic activists did share the following beliefs: Islam, a comprehensive way of life, is and must be integral to politics and society. The failures of Muslim societies were caused by departing from the path of Islam and depending on Western secularism, which separated religion and politics. Muslims must return to the Quran and the example of the Prophet Muhammad, specifically by reintroducing Islamic rather than Western laws. Modern development must be guided by Islamic values rather than the Westernization and secularization of society.

Islamic symbols, slogans, ideology, leaders, and organizations became prominent fixtures in Muslim politics. Libya's Muammar Qaddafi, Pakistan's General Zia ul-Haq, Egypt's Anwar Sadat, and Sudan's Jafar Numayri appealed to Islam to enhance their legitimacy and authority and to mobilize popular support.

At the same time, Islamic movements and organizations sprang up across the Muslim world. Opposition movements appealed to Islam: the Ayatollah Khomeini in 1979, militants who seized the Grand Mosque in 1979, religious extremists who assassinated Anwar Sadat in 1981, Afghan freedom fighters in the late 1970s and early 1980s. Other Islamic movements and organizations throughout the 1980s created or extended their influence over religious, educational, social, cultural, professional, and financial institutions. The leadership of most Islamic organizations (particularly Sunni groups) was and remains lay rather than clerical. Islamists have earned degrees in modern science, medicine, law, engineering, computer science, and education. Although the majority of Islamic organizations worked within the system, a minority of radical extremists insisted that violence and revolution were the only way to liberate society.

By the late 1980s and early 1990s, it was clear that Islamists had moved from the periphery to mainstream politics and society; a "quiet [nonviolent] revolution" had institutionalized Islamic revivalism and activism in mainstream society. Islamically inspired social and political activism produced schools, clinics, hospitals, day care, legal aid, youth centers, private (as opposed to government-controlled) mosques, and financial institutions, such as Islamic banks and insurance companies. Islamic candidates participated in local and national electoral politics and assumed positions of leadership in professional associations and trade unions. An alternative elite emerged in every sector of society, with a modern education but Islamically (rather than secularly) oriented.

Perhaps nowhere was the impact of the Islamic revival experienced more visibly than in political elections. As a legacy of pre-modern Muslim history and colonialism, the majority of governments in the Muslim world are authoritarian, but during the late 1980s, in response to mass demonstrations, elections were held in a number of countries and Islamic organizations emerged as the major political opposition. By the mid-1990s, Islamic activists could be found in the cabinets and parliaments of many countries and the leadership of professional organizations (doctors, lawyers, engineers). At the same time, radical extremist groups, such as like Egypt's Gamaa Islamiyya (Islamic Group), attacked Christian churches, businesses, tourists, and security forces.

Other extremists were convicted in America and Europe for terrorist acts, such as the bombing of New York's World Trade Center in 1993, of the American barracks in Saudi Arabia in 1995, and of American embassies in Africa in 1998, leading some governments and analysts to identify "Islamic fundamentalism" as a major threat to global stability. ∎

Suggested Reading

John L. Esposito, "Contemporary Islam: Reformation or Revolution?," *The Oxford History of Islam*.

————, *Unholy War: Terror in the Name of Islam*, chapter 4.

John O. Voll, *Islam: Continuity and Change in the Muslim World*, chapters 6–7.

Questions to Consider

1. What were the major catalysts for contemporary Islamic revivalism?

2. Compare and contrast the worldviews and strategies of mainstream and extremists movements.

The Contemporary Resurgence of Islam
Lecture 8—Transcript

In our last class, we talked about the rise of pre-modern and modern reform movements in Islam, as well as the emergence of Islamic revivalist movements, that is, modern Islamic activist movements like the Muslim Brotherhood and the Jamaat-i Islami. In the last decades of the 20th century, the Muslim world experienced the impact of another revival or resurgence of Islam in personal and in public life.

On the personal level, many Muslims have become more religiously observant, finding in Islam a sense of identity, meaning, and guidance, with greater emphasis on Islamic life and values, and religious observances such as prayer and fasting, and mosque attendance. There is also attention to Islamic forms of dress and family values.

In the public sphere, we've seen new Islamic governments or republics established in Iran, Sudan, and Afghanistan, with Muslim rulers, political parties, and opposition movements appealing to religion. Mainstream Islamic activists have headed governments, served in cabinets, and the elected parliaments, and as senior officials of professional associations of doctors, lawyers, engineers, and professors.

At the same time, radical Islamic organizations have engaged in violence and terrorism. The causes and conditions that led to the contemporary resurgence of Islam are many. We'll just summarize some as we go along. During the 20th century, Islamic empires and sultanates were replaced by modern nation-states. Many countries in the Middle East were quite literally mapped out by European colonial powers, Britain and France in particular, after World War I.

Between World War I and World War II, most of the newly created states won their independence from European colonial rulers: France, England, Holland, and Italy. Both the national boundaries of many modern states and their rulers, many of whom were placed on their thrones in Jordan, Syria, and Iraq, for example, by Britain and France, were artificial creations. Therefore, the problems with legitimacy continue.

Moreover, European education, culture, and values permeated the urban areas and strongly influenced the elites, in most cases, in societies. As a result, issues of governments' legitimacy, as well as national, religious, and cultural identify remained unresolved.

Rulers rooted their legitimacy in an authoritarian state, whose stability was to due more to foreign (Western or Soviet during the Cold War period) support, coupled with strong military-security apparatus, rather than indigenous culture, political participation, or electoral politics.

Indeed, in the Arab world, we refer to Arab countries as *muharabat* states, security states. Once these modern nation-states were created in the Muslim world, it was expected that they would generally follow a "modern," defined then as Western, secular path of development. Outwardly, this seemed to be the general case. While Saudi Arabia proclaimed an Islamic state based upon the Quran and Shariah law, most new nations adopted or adapted Western political, legal, social, economic, and educational institutions and values. In contrast to Saudi Arabia, Turkey was at the other end of the spectrum and positioned itself as a polar opposite state, defining itself as secular, as over and against religious, as completely secular.

Under the leadership of Mustafa Kemal Ataturk, Ataturk meaning the "father of the Turks," it supressed Islamic institutions, banned Islamic dress and law and transplanted Western secular laws and institutions to create its own version of a secular state. However, the majority of countries such as Egypt, Syria, Iraq, Malaysia, and Indonesia created what we might call "Muslim states." These are countries whose majority populations were Muslim, but who despite some religious prescriptions, adopted Western-inspired institutions: parliaments, political party systems or legal codes, educational systems and curricula, banks and insurance companies. Western dress, movies, and culture often became prominent and pervasive among the wealthy and powerful in urban centers.

Throughout much of the 20th century, progress and prosperity in Muslim societies were dependent upon the degree to which Muslims and their societies were regarded as "modern," conforming to "Western" and "secular" values. This understanding of modernity generally presupposed the Western secular bias or orientation. The degree of progress and success of individual cities and governments was often measured by conforming to Western standards and values. We judged people as being modern in terms of whether or not they wore Western dress, were speaking Western language, or earning a degree from a Western-oriented school, at home or preferably abroad. Were they working or living in office buildings, in homes reflecting Western architecture and furniture, and preferring Western music and movies?

Based on these criteria, Turkey, Tunisia, Egypt, Lebanon, Iraq and Iran were often seen among the more modern advanced and "enlightened," that is, Westernized and secular, countries. Saudi Arabia, states of the Persian Gulf, Afghanistan, Bangladesh, and Pakistan were generally regarded as more traditional, more religious, and in some sense, more "backward."

The 1960s and '70s, and the failures of modernity then, shattered the hopes and dreams of many who had believed the national independence in Western-oriented development would usher in strong states and prosperous societies. A series of events during the previous decade, the 1967 Arab-Israeli war, Malay-Chinese riots in Kuala Lumpur Malaysia in 1969, the Pakistan-Bangladesh civil war of 1971, the Lebanon civil war of the mid 1970s, and the Iranian Rrevolution of 1978 and '79 revealed the pitfalls and failures of many states and societies. Such catalytic events triggered a soul-searching reassessment among many Muslims who focused on the reliance on Western models of development in nation building, as well as personal life. There was a rethinking, in terms of what had gone wrong.

Perhaps the most significant symbolic event that sparked Muslim dissolutions and dissatisfaction was the 1967 Arab-Israeli war. Israel defeated the combined forces of Egypt, Syria, and Jordan in a preemptive strike, which the Israeli government justified as necessary to counter what was regarded as a planned Arab attack. The Arabs experienced a massive lost of territory: Sinai, Gaza, the West Bank and in particular Jerusalem, the third holiest city after Mecca and Medina of Islam. For different reasons, Muslims, like Christians for centuries, looked to Jerusalem, the city central to Muslim faith and identity, a place of religious shrines and pilgrimage.

The sacredness of Jerusalem comes from both its association with biblical prophets from David and Solomon to Jesus, as well as a miraculous event in Islamic belief, the Prophet Muhammad's "Night Journey," which we referred to earlier, and his Ascension. As we discussed, Muslim tradition teaches that one night in the year 620 when Muhammad prayed in the Kaaba, he was carried on a winged horse from Mecca to the Temple Mount in Jerusalem. There, Muhammad met with many of his prophetic predecessors: Adam, Abraham, Moses, John the Baptist, and Jesus preceded up the ladder that extended from the Temple Mount to the Throne of God.

When Muslim armies took Jerusalem without resistance in 635, they restored and rebuilt the temple are, what is called the "noble sanctuary," *al-haram al-sharif.* First they built a large mosque, the *al-Aqsa,* and then a magnificent shrine, the Dome of the Rock, on the site believed to be "the terminus of the Night Journey, and the biblical site of Abraham's sacrifice; and, the site also of Solomon's Temple." Historically, Jerusalem has been a point of contention from the Crusades, which were extensively called to liberate Jerusalem from Muslim control, to today with the ongoing Palestinian-Israeli conflict. The loss of Jerusalem in the 1967 war was a traumatic experience, not only for Palestinians and other Arabs, Muslim and Christian alike, but also for Muslims worldwide.

"All revere Jerusalem," which means, "al-quds," Arabic for the "holy city" as a site of central religious significance. The loss of Jerusalem made Palestine and the Arab-Israeli conflict and the liberation of Jerusalem, not just, then, a Palestine or Arab, but also a transnational Islamic issue. Many ask what and why had things gone wrong? Why had Israel been able to defeat the combined Arab forces so quickly? Were the weakness and failure of Muslim societies due to their faith? Was Islam incompatible with modernity, and thus the cause of Arab backwardness and impotence? Had God abandoned the Muslims?

These were questions that had been raised before. Indeed, at times they're even raised now. As we have seen, from the 17th to the 19th centuries, Muslim societies faced internal, and then external threats: the internal breakdown of societies, closely followed by the onslaught external threat of European colonialism extending into the 20th century. However, the failures they now faced occurred during a period of independence and Muslim self-rule. The realities of Muslim societies—poverty, illiteracy, failed economies, high unemployment, and mal-distribution of wealth—not in all but in many societies raised profound questions about national identities and political legitimacy. What were the rulers doing? They also questioned religious faith and meaning.

The failures of the modern experiment in these newly independent countries led many to turn to a more authentic, indigenous, alternative to nationalism and socialism. Despite significant differences, Islam became a rallying cry and a symbol for political organization and mass mobilization worldwide. The signs of profound change would not become fully evident and appreciated in the West until a decade later with the Iranian Revolution in 1978 and 1979.

Disillusionment with modernity and Western models of development were accompanied by an Islamic revival, marked by a quest for identity and greater authenticity as many reaffirmed the importance of Islam and Islamic values in their personal and social lives. Along with the reemphasis on religious identity and practice, prayer, fasting, dress, and values came an equally visible reemergence of Islam in politics and society; this was made by governments, as well as Islamic political and social movements. Islamic ideology and discourse in politics reemerged as a major force in the development of the Muslim world, a force that both Muslim and Western governments have had to accommodate or contend with for several decades.

Several phenomena may be identified as common to the contemporary Muslim experience. First—an identity crisis, precipitated by a sense of utter impotence and loss of self-esteem.

Second—disillusionment with the West, with its models of development and with the West as an ally, and with the failure of many governments to respond adequately to the political and socioeconomic needs of their societies.

Third—a quest for greater authenticity; that is, to re-appropriate a greater sense of indigenous identity, history, and values, which inalterably is connected to a sense of Islamic past, history, faith and values.

Fourth—a newfound sense of pride and power, which resulted from the Arab-Israeli war and òil embargo of 1973, the success of the Afghan *mujahideen* in their war against Soviet occupation of Afghanistan, and the global impact of Iran's Islamic revolution of 1978 and 1979. For many, these were signs of the resurgence of Islam and of God's help to those who, as in Afghanistan and Iraq, fought against overwhelming odds in the name of Islam.

After centuries of being in decline and at the other end of the stick, there was a sense of a re-appropriating of a glorious past, or at least its potential. Although a tremendous diversity existed in the religious worldview and politics of Islamic activism, from country to country, nevertheless Islamic activists did share the following beliefs. Islam, a comprehensive way of life, is and must be integral to politics and society. The failures in Muslim societies were caused by departing from the path of Islam and depending on Western secularism that separated religion and politics.

Muslims, therefore, must return to the Quran and the example of the Prophet Muhammad, specifically by reintroducing Islamic rather than Western laws. This would bring about again Muslim power. Modern development must be guided by Islamic values, rather than blindly depending on the Westernization and secularization of society. Islamic symbols, slogans, ideology, leaders, and organizations became prominent fixtures in Muslim politics.

Rulers like Libya's Muammar Qaddafi, Pakistan's General Zia ul-Haq, Egypt's Anwar Sadat, Sudan's Jafar Numayri appealed to Islam to enhance their legitimacy and authority and to mobilize popular support.

At the same time, Islamic movements and organizations sprang up across the Muslim world. Opposition movements appealed to Islam: the Ayatollah Khomeini and Iran's Revolution, militants seized the Grand Mosque in Saudi Arabia in 1979, Buddhist extremists assassinated Anwar Sadat in 1981, and Afghan freedom fighters in the late 1970s and early 1980s.

Other Islamic movements and organizations throughout the 1980s created or extended their influence over religious, educational, social, cultural, professional, schools, and financial institutions. The leadership of most Islamic organizations, particularly Sunni groups, was and remains lay rather than clerical. Islamists have earned degrees in modern science, medicine, law, engineering, computer science, and education.

While the majority of the Islamic organizations had worked within the system, a minority of radical extremists have insisted that violence and armed revolution was the only way, and is the only way, to liberate their societies. The most recent example is bin Laden and al-Qaeda.

By the late 1980s and early 1990s, it was clear that Islamists had moved from the periphery to mainstream politics in society. They were not just extremist, but indeed that a quiet nonviolent revolution had institutionalized Islamic revivalism and activism in mainstream society. Islamically-inspired social and political activism produced schools, clinics, hospital, daycare, legal aid, and youth centers. There were private, as opposed to government-controlled mosques and financial institutions, such as Islamic banks and insurance companies.

Islamic candidates and parties participated in local and national electoral politics, assumed positions of leadership, and became part of the professional associations of doctors, lawyers, engineers, and journalists, and trade unions.

A new alternative elite emerged in every sector of society, modern educated, but Islamically, rather than secularly, oriented. The quiet revolution could be seen clearly across the Muslim world. Perhaps nowhere was the impact of the Islamic revival experienced more visibly than in electoral politics in civil society.

By the late 1980s and early 1990s, it was increasingly clear that this quiet revolution had occurred in many societies. Islamic revivalism through social and political activism had become institutionalized in the mainstream, not just on the periphery. From Egypt to Tunisia, Islam played a more visible and important role in social, economic and political life. Islamically-inspired social and political activism produced, yes, the schools, clinics, hospitals, mosques and financial institutions, but it also would produce a wave of activists who would participate in elections, and in effect, would come to power. I think that becomes very important. This becomes a kind of critical transition point, because of that new alternative elite, and let me underscore this. The old elite, and its an elite that continues in so many societies and is often dominant, is a more secular, modern educated elite. But, the new alternative elite is modern educated but more Islamically-oriented. They are now, in a sense, a counter elite, to be found among doctors, engineers, lawyers, business people, university professors, and military officers.

They're in the mainstream, but they are a threat, if you will, to the establishment, to the secular elite because they are an alternative, and to many governments. Perhaps nowhere was this experienced more than in political elections. The majority of governments, secular and religious, in the Muslim world have been authoritarian. It is a legacy of pre-modern Muslim history, as well as European colonial rule. And post-independence governments have not fostered the growth of participation or democratic governments and institutions and values, but rather have been concerned with clinging to power, these security states.

Despite this fact, during the late 1980s, in response to food riots, economic breakdowns, protest and mass demonstrations over the economic failures of governments, elections were held in a number of countries: Jordan, Tunisia, Algeria, and Egypt. Islamic organizations such as the Muslim Brotherhoods of Jordan and Egypt, Tunisia's Nahda or Renaissance Party, and Algeria's Islamic Salvation Front, the FIS, participated. They stunned many. They emerged as the major political opposition. Indeed in Algeria, the Islamic Salvation Front swept not only the municipal, but later parliamentary elections, and thus was poised to come to power through the electoral process, through ballots, not bullets.

Power was being taken through ballots, not bullets. However, the specter of Islamists coming to power triggered a backlash. The Algerian military intervened, and canceled the election victory of the Islamic Salvation Front. They imprisoned and outlawed the FIS and installed a new government. This set in motion a spiral of violence and counter-violence that polarized Algerian society and produced the civil war costing more than a hundred thousand lives.

By the mid 1990s, Islamic activists could be found in the cabinets and parliaments of many countries and in the leadership of many professional organizations.

In Turkey, the most secular of Muslim states, the Islamist Welfare Party swept mayoral elections, and in 1995 elected its first Islamist prime minister, Dr. Erbakan. The Turkish military claimed that it could save Turkish secularism. Eventually, it pressured Erbakan to resign, and influenced the outlawing of the welfare and the imprisonment of some of its leaders. By the mid-1990s, Islamic activists could be found as people who had been or were in the executive. Erbakan in Turkey, Anwar Ibrahim, the Deputy Prime Minister of Malaysia, and the first President, eventually, of Indonesia, Abdurrahman Wahid, as well as in cabinets and parliaments of many countries.

At the same time, radical extremist groups continued to use violence and terror to destabilize Muslim governments and attack American and Western interests. Egypt's Islamic Jihad and Gama Islamiya, the Islamic Group, attacked Christian churches and businesses, and slaughtered tourists and government officials. Other extremists were convicted in American and Europe for the bombing of New York's World Trade Center in 1993, and plotting to attack major American sites. Osama bin Laden and al-Qaeda emerged as a major supporter of global terrorism, in a series of attacks against American military barracks and ships; these they either conducted or approved of in Saudi Arabia, in Yemen and against American embassies in Africa in 1998. This left some governments and analysts to identify "Islamic fundamentalism" wholesale as a major threat to global stability, and not to distinguish between mainstream and extremists.

This is a critical and important issue. We'll see this played out in our later lectures. What I've tried to talk about in this session is the fact that in the late 1980s and 1990s, we see that Islamic activist groups, what are popularly called "Islamic fundamentalism groups" or "Islamic fundamentalism." Some refer to it as "political Islam." Some refer to it as "Islamism" or refer to it as "Islamist groups."

Be that as it may, these Islamic activist groups have often been put under one umbrella, been seen monolithically as simply militant groups. When in fact, if we look at the facts on the ground, we see that yes, a minority have been and continue to be extremist who threaten, I might note, first and foremost until recently, their own societies, their own governments, and their own people. Secondarily, those outside Western governments that support governments that are regarded in the region as authoritarian. Therefore, if you are against the Egyptian government or the Saudi government, your first goal if you're an extremist is your ruler. But, secondarily, you'll go against those governments who are seen as politically, economically, or militarily supporting the regime to the extent that they provide military arms. These military arms are seen as not just being used out there against outside enemy, but being used by military and security forces at home.

What we see in the 80s and 90s, however, is clear evidence that a majority of Islamic activist groups are not simply restricted to the marginalized, to the few, to the alienated on the periphery of society, but are mainstream, function in mainstream society, and function nonviolently in mainstream society. They in fact come to constitute this alternative elite. They're comprised not just of the poor and the dispossessed, the disenfranchised, but turn out to be the middle class, even from the upper class. They draw people who are prominent businessmen, lawyers, judges, and people who run banks and institutions.

This becomes a crux to understanding the dynamics of the late 20th century and the early 21st century. Because as Islamic activist groups emerged in the post Cold War as mainstream, and stunned both their governments and Western governments when elections were held— remember, as I pointed out in today's class, these were authoritarian governments, most of which had never held elections and certainly didn't intend to implement a democratic form of government—because when they were stunned and saw that these Islamic groups could run—even though the state often controlled access to the media, the state often could intimidate those who could vote for Islamist parties—when they saw that they emerged as an opposition, even a minority opposition, shortly afterwards, they shut down their systems, often charging that they had discovered all these groups were in fact wolves in sheep's clothing, and that they were really extremists who were just acting like democrats.

Western governments were also stunned by these elections. All remember after the Iranian Revolution had been looking for and worried about other Irans. That dominated the 1980s, the fear of having to deal with "other" Irans.

Remember that Ayatollah Khomeini called for other Irans, other Iranian revolutions. He encouraged the governments of the Gulf to be overthrown; he encouraged people to rise up. There were disturbances in Saudi Arabia, and in the oil field areas of Saudi Arabia, the majority of Shii, even though Saudi Arabia's majority population is Sunni. There had been disturbances in countries like Bahrain in Iraq and Kuwait. Thus, the fear of the 1980s, and the expectation, was that Islamic fundamentalism meant Iranian style radicalism, and that one had to watch for other Irans.

Then one suddenly discovered in the late 1980s and 1990s that alongside extremist groups, you had mainstream groups. These mainstream groups could actually, if the people were given a chance, win; this went against the wisdom spouted by both governments in the region and by Western governments who always said, no, these people are extremist and if they ever had to run, the populations would reject them.

The clearest and most stunning case of this was Algeria, because Algeria had been a one-party governed state, secular, kind of elite, dominated strong militarian police, with a strong women's movement. The idea that Islamists could sweep mayoral elections, and after its leaders were imprisoned, could run in parliamentary elections, and still sweep those parliamentary elections defied the mind. As my mother would say, it boggled the mind. The idea that you could also see, in a place like Jordan, a dominate number of people in parliament turn out to be Islamists in terms of elections; and Islamists move into the cabinet. Later, as I said, you might see an Islamist emerge as the prime minister in Turkey. Turkey, the one government, one modern nation-state set up as an absolutely secular state? It's beyond belief.

We may also see others emerge as Deputy Prime Minister of Malaysia, or the fist president of Indonesia. Western governments had to grapple with that themselves, and in some ways the debate among scholars as to how to understand this phenomenon.

Some still prefer to see all Islamic movements, also called "fundamentalists" or "Islamists" movements, and some world leaders as a threat. They prefer to see this as a kind of monolithic threat. Many others say you have to distinguish between the majority mainstream—that participate within society, have demonstrated that they will participate within society, and that will only turn to violence, in terms of this mainstream, when violence is used against them—one has to distinguish between these mainstream and the extremist. This is very difficult for many governments to deal with, certainly for Western governments who tend to think that modern governments ought to be secular, and to have their relationships with authoritarian regimes.

We may not like some of the authoritarian regimes that we deal with, but as during the Cold War, if they will deliver the goods when it comes to our political military or economic needs—access to oil—we're willing to work with them.

On the other hand, we fear religiously-oriented groups or parties: A—because, with our secular approach, we have a kind of almost secular fundamentalist reaction to any kind of religious party coming to power, but B—because we do feel that they will be more independent, if not anti-Western. They will be more independent; they will be less controllable.

This, then, becomes the crux of the issues that we will explore later in this course as we look at the continuation of, on the one hand, the push of Islamic activist groups, and on the other, the attempt by governments in the region, often with support from Western governments, to control this kind of development and movement. Indeed, with events like September 11, and figures and groups like Osama bin Laden and al-Qaeda, it raises yet again this fear and threat. Is the problem global terrorism, or is it Islam?

Islam at the Crossroads
Lecture 9

What are the relevant and acceptable interpretations of Islam for today's world?

L ike members of other faith communities, contemporary Muslims face the challenge of defining the role, meaning, and relevance of Islam in both private and public life. Often we focus on radicalism and extremism, but a deeper and more pervasive struggle exists. At the heart of this "struggle for the soul of Islam" between conservatives and reformers, mainstream Muslims and extremists, is the question of who should interpret Islam and how reform should be achieved. Its major issues include the relationship of religion to state and society, the role of Islamic law, the status of women and non-Muslims, the compatibility of Islam and democracy, and relations with the West.

While the revolution occurring in contemporary Islam is often seen through the lens of explosive headline events, of radicalism and extremism, the real revolution is the quiet revolution in Islamic discourse and activism. The Quran and Sunnah ("example") of the Prophet Muhammad remain normative for all Muslims, but questions of interpretation, authenticity, and application have become contentious. Muslim scholars distinguish the eternal, immutable principles and laws in the Quran from its human interpretation and application (*fiqh*) by early jurists, which are prescriptions that are responses to specific contexts. Some distinguish between the Meccan, the earlier and more religiously binding, and the Medinan chapters of the Quran, which are seen as primarily political, concerned with Muhammad's creation of the Medina state, and therefore, not universally binding. The distinction is often made in the classical division of law into a Muslim's duties to God (*ibadat*, or "worship") and duties to others (*muamalat*, "social obligations"), which are the product of reason and social custom, contingent upon historical and social circumstances. Many *ulama* continue to accept the authoritative traditions (*hadith*) of the Prophet, but other Muslim scholars distinguish between authoritative texts and those that are not authentic.

Legal reform remains a contested issue in many Muslim states that implemented Western-inspired legal codes. Governments imposed reforms from above through legislation. In more recent decades, the debate over the Shariah has become a contentious issue. Does Islamization of law mean the wholesale reintroduction of classical law as formulated in the early Islamic centuries? Or does it mean the development of new laws derived from the Quran and Sunnah of the Prophet and the inclusion of laws, whatever their source, that are not contrary to Islam? Who is to oversee this process: rulers, *ulama*, or parliaments?

> **Modern reformers get at the core issue, the relationship of the divine to the human in Islamic law.**

The reintroduction of Islamic law has been diverse, as Iran, Sudan, Afghanistan, Pakistan, and Saudi Arabia demonstrate. Reimplementation of *hudud* (Quranically prescribed crimes and punishments for alcohol consumption, theft, fornication, adultery, and false witness) often had a negative impact on women and minorities, raising serious questions about a setback in the gains made in many societies.

Four general Muslim orientations can be identified. Secularists believe religion is a personal matter and should be excluded from politics and public life. Conservatives (most of the *ulama* and their followers) emphasize following *taqlid* ("past tradition") and are wary of any change, which they regard as *bida* ("deviation"), the Christian equivalent of heresy.

Mainstream Islamic activists (who are lay, not clerical) respect the classical formulations of law but are not wedded to them, emphasizing a return to "fundamentals" (Quran and Sunnah) and reinterpreting (*ijtihad*) Islamic belief and institutions. Like the Muslim Brotherhood, their holistic understanding of Islam fosters social and political activism. Because they have difficulty distinguishing between the divine and human prescriptions of the tradition, they are slow to reformulate Islamic responses in such sensitive areas as Islamic law and the status of women and minorities.

Modern reformers get at the core issue, the relationship of the divine to the human in Islamic law, by distinguishing between the Shariah, God's divinely revealed law, and *fiqh* ("understanding"), human interpretation and application that is historically conditioned. They go further than fundamentalists in their acceptance of the degree and the extent to which enshrined classical formulations of Islamic law may be changed.

Islamic reform is evident in the current debate over key issues, such as the relationship of Islam to the state, political participation or democratization, reform of Islamic law, and promotion of religious and political pluralism. Muslim experiments run the gamut from conservative monarchies, such as in Saudi Arabia, to radical approaches in Libya, Sudan, and Iran; from Islamic social and political activism working within society (creating schools and hospitals, providing social services, participating in elections) in Egypt, Turkey, and Jordan to violent revolutions that try to topple governments and impose authoritarian versions of Islamic rule.

Two questions face Muslim communities as they define the relationship and relevance of Islam to their lives: Who has the authority to interpret Islam and what are the relevant and acceptable interpretations of Islam for today's world? As in the past, both the *ulama* and Muslim rulers continue to assert their right to protect, defend, and promote Islam. Many rulers, through cooptation and coercion, combine their obligation to protect and promote Islam with the state's power to influence, control, and promote an acceptable "brand" of Islam. The result is a broad range of interpretations, from conservative to revolutionary. Today, many argue that not rulers or clergy but the laity and parliaments should be major actors in the process of change. As in Christianity and Judaism, an educated laity has increasingly asserted its role in the community. Today, the main issue is: Should the process of renewal and reform be one of restoration or reinterpretation?

A primary example of Islamic reformism and its method today is the debate over Islam and democracy. Some Muslims maintain that Islam has its own system of government, that democracy is based on un-Islamic Western principles and values. Others reinterpret traditional Islamic concepts, such as consultation and consensus of the community, to support modern political participation, such as parliamentary elections.

The status of non-Muslims is another example of the current debate. Many want to reinstate the traditional doctrine of non-Muslims as "protected" (*dhimmi*) people. Ahead of its time in the past, today, this doctrine consigns non-Muslims to second-class citizenship in rights to vote and to hold senior government positions. Others advocate non-Muslims' rights to full and equal citizenship, fostering an egalitarian and pluralist society of Muslims and non-Muslims. The swelling numbers of Muslim refugees and the migration of many Muslims to Europe and America make minority rights and duties an ever-greater concern for Islamic jurisprudence.

Another result of contemporary Islamic revivalism has been a reexamination of the role of women in Islam and, at times, a bitter debate over their function in society. The resurgence of Islam has sometimes worsened rather than alleviated the situation of Muslim women. Women have often become a "quick fix" for those who wish to Islamize society. This has often meant dismissing modern reforms or paradigms as simply Westernization. On the other hand, Muslim women have also become catalysts for change, entering new professions, running for elective office, becoming students and scholars of Islam, and establishing women's professional organizations, journals, and magazines.

The Islamic revival produced a third alternative, both modern and rooted in Islamic faith, identity, and values. Distinguishing between Islam and patriarchy, between revelation and male interpretations in patriarchal settings, women are working to redefine their role in society. In many instances, this change has been symbolized by a return to Islamic dress or the donning of a headscarf, or *hijab*, combining social change with indigenous Islamic values and ideals. New experiments have resulted in more women "returning to the mosque," forming their own prayer and Quran study groups. Women as individuals and organizations are writing and speaking out for themselves on women's issues ranging from dress to education, employment, and political participation.

In contrast to Judaism and Christianity, Muslims, under European colonial dominance and rule, have had a few decades to accomplish what in the West took the Enlightenment, Reformation, Counter-Reformation, and French and American revolutions. Like believers in other faiths, the critical question today facing Islam and Muslim communities globally involves the relationship of faith and tradition to change in a rapidly changing and pluralistic world. As Fazlur Rahman has said, Islamic reform requires "first-class minds who can interpret the old in terms of the new as regards substance and turn the new into the service of the old as regards ideals" (Rahman, p. 139). ∎

Suggested Reading

Akbar Ahmed, *Islam Today*, chapter 4.

John L. Esposito, *Unholy War: Terror in the Name of Islam*, chapter 4.

Questions to Consider

1. How have Muslims answered the question "Who has the authority to interpret Islam and what is the best method for reform?

2. What are some of the major debates and areas of reform in Muslim societies today?

Islam at the Crossroads
Lecture 9—Transcript

Islam and Muslims today, as in the past, are again at an important crossroads. Like members of other faith communities, contemporary Muslims face the challenge of defining the role, meaning and relevance of Islam in both private and public life. Although the media often focuses on radicalism and extremism, a deeper and more pervasive struggle exists. At the heart of this struggle for the soul of Islam, between conservatives and reformers, mainstream Muslims and extremists, is the question of who should interpret Islam and how reform should be achieved.

The struggle's major issues include the relationship of religion to state and society, the role of Islamic law, the status of women and non-Muslims, the compatibility of Islam and democracy, and relations with the West.

Muslim attitudes towards change have varied. In the early centuries of expansion, conquest and settlement, Islam was interpreted and applied to provide a framework of faith, meaning, and guidance. Throughout the ages, believers, wherever they might be, spread across the world, and however different their cultural context, they found in Islam a core of belief in practice that provided a sense of unity and identity, of faith and purpose.

As Muhammad brought his reformist message to Arabia, at critical points in history, when the Islamic community has been threatened or in danger, great religious leaders and revivalist movements have responded to the religious, intellectual and political challenges of the community, spawning a variety of reformers and revivalist reformist movements.

The cry, "Islam in danger!" has served as a battle cry to rise to the religious and political defense of Islam. Just as Islam was used by early caliphs and Islamic revivalists and reformers and in the 20th century in anti-colonial and independence struggles, so too, in recent years Islam has been a source of inspiration and popular mobilization. This has occurred in Palestine, Afghanistan, Bosnia, Cashmere, Chechnya and other parts of the Muslim world.

Today, Islam continues to reflect that same unity and diversity, for although believers continue to affirm their belief in God, the Quran and the Prophet Muhammad, they differ in their understanding and interpretation of what that should mean. The political resurgence of Islam has been accompanied by affirming in which contending voices and paradigms have emerged. If modernization brought widespread political and economic reforms in the 20th century, the pace of religious reform lagged behind.

Change has been more visible at the top, for a small group of elites rather than for the masses of Muslims in the Muslim world today. The political and economic failures of Muslim societies in the 1970s and 1980s have contributed to an Islamic revival that has challenged political and religious establishments alike, and called for an Islamic solution, the implementation of an Islamic alternative in personal and community life, in faith and politics. This call has divided as much as united Muslims, precipitating discussion, debate and confrontation within Muslim societies, and at times between the Muslim world and the West. Key to this process has been the question of the meaning and relevance of Islam in today's world, something that all believers have faced and do face.

Contending voices, clerical and lay, government and opposition, secular and Islamically-oriented elites, and their interpretations of Islam press their claims and compete for authority and legitimacy. Like all the children of Abraham, Muslims today, in facing the challenges of secularism and materialism, a faith in social justice, continue to bear witness to the fact that monotheism does not mean "monolithic." As in the past, the unity of Islam, as in all faiths, embraced a diversity of interpretations and expressions, which became a source of dynamism and growth as well as of contention and conflict, both among believers and at times with other faith communities.

The challenge for all believers remains the rigorous pursuit of what the Quran calls the "straight path, the way of God, to whom belongs all that is in the heavens and all that is on the earth." Quran 42, verses 52 to 53. And they must do so in a world of diversity and difference. While the revolution occurring in contemporary Islam is often seen through the prism or lens of explosive headline events, of radicalism and extremism, the real revolution is that quiet revolution that I've talked about before, that quiet revolution in Islamic discourse and activism. The Quran, the Sunnah, example of the Prophet Muhammad, remain normative for all Muslims, but questions of interpretation, authenticity and application have become contentious items.

Muslim scholars distinguish the eternal immutable principles and laws in the Quran from its "human interpretation and application," *fiqh*, those interpretations by early jurists that were prescriptive responses to specific contexts. Some today distinguished between the Meccan, the earlier and more religiously minded and binding, and Medinan chapters of the Quran, that are seen as primarily political, concerned with Muhammad's creation of the state in Medina, and therefore not regarded by some as universally binding.

Many *ulama*, religious scholars, continue to accept the authoritative traditions, and *hadith* of the Prophet, but other Muslim scholars distinguish between authoritative texts and those that are not authentic. Although the example Sunnah of the Prophet Muhammad has always been normative in Islam from earliest times, Muslim scholars saw the need to critically examine and authenticate the enormous number of prophetic traditions or *hadith*, in order to distinguish between authoritative texts and pious fabrications.

In the 20th century, a sector of modern Western scholarship questioned the historicity and authenticity of the *hadith*. Many maintained that the bulk of prophetic traditions were written much later. However, most Muslim scholars and some Western non-Muslim scholars have taken exception with this sweeping position.

If many of the *ulama* continue to unquestioningly accept the authoritative collections of the past, other scholars have in fact become more critical in their approach and use of tradition literature. New approaches to the study and interpretation of Islam sacred sources have been accompanied by similar debates over the nature of Islamic law, the Shariah. As noted earlier, and certainly above in this lecture, many of the *ulama* continue to equate Shariah, God's law, with its exposition in legal manuals developed by the early law schools.

Other Muslims, from Islamic modernists like Muhammad Abduh, Ahmed Khan and Muhammad Iqbal, to Islamic revivalists and neo-modernists today have distinguished between those laws based on clear text of the Quran and *hadith*, and other laws that are the product of human interpretation and application, the product of reason and social custom. Some express this distinction as between the eternal law, Shariah, of God, and its human interpretation and application, *fiqh*, by the early jurists. The distinction is often articulated in terms of the classical division of law into a Muslim's duties or obligations to God and worship, and his or her duties to others, social obligations.

The former, worship, for example the performance of the Five Pillars of Islam, are seen as unchanging. The latter are contingent upon historical and social circumstances, and therefore open to change. Contemporary Muslim discussion and debate over the role of Islam in state and society reflect a broad array of questions, is there one classical model, or many possible models for the relationship of religion to political, social, and economic development.

If a new Islamic synthesis is to be achieved that provides continuity with past tradition, how will this be accomplished? Will it be imposed from above by rulers and/or the *ulama*, or legislated from below through a representative electoral process, through a parliamentary system of government, for example?

Legal reform remains a contested issue in many Muslim states that implemented Western-inspired legal codes. Governments impose reforms from above through legislation, and we discussed some of this in earlier lectures.

In more recent decades, the debate over the Shariah has become a contentious issue. Does Islamization of law mean the wholesale reintroduction of classical law as formulated in the early Islamic centuries, or does it mean the development of new laws derived from the Quran and Sunnah of the Prophet, but the inclusion of laws whatever their source, which are not contrary to Islam? Who is to oversee this process, rulers, the *ulama,* or parliaments?

The reintroduction of Islamic law has not followed a fixed pattern or a set interpretation. During the post-independence period significant change has occurred in many countries, broadening the educational and employment opportunities and enhancing the legal rights of Muslim women. Women became more visible in the professions, as teachers, lawyers, engineers, physicians, and in government.

Admittedly, these changes affected a small proportion of the population and varied from one country or region to another, influenced by religious and local traditions, economic and educational development, and government leadership. As Iran, Sudan, the Taliban's Afghanistan, Pakistan, and Saudi Arabia demonstrate, the implementation of Shariah or Islamic law has diverse and divergent implications, even among those countries dubbed conservative or fundamentalist or Islamic states.

Women in Saudi Arabia and the Taliban's Afghanistan could not vote or hold public office. In Pakistan and Iran, despite other strictures and problems, women vote, serve in parliaments and cabinets, teach in universities, and hold professional positions. Pakistan has had a woman as prime minister.

Islamization of law has underscored several areas that have proved particularly problematic. The *hudud*, Quranically prescribed crimes and punishments for alcohol consumption, theft, et cetera, the status of non-Muslims (*dhimmi*) and minorities, and the status of women are among those issues. All involve the question of change in Islamic law. Re-implementation of the *hudud* often has had a particularly negative impact on women and minorities, raising serious questions about a setback in the gains made in many societies.

While many conservatives and so-called fundamentalists call for the re-implementation of these punishments of amputation for theft, or stoning for adultery, other Muslims argue that these are no longer appropriate. Among those who advocate imposition of the *hudud*, some call for its immediate introduction, and others argue that punishment such as amputation for theft are contingent upon the creation of a just society, where people will not be driven to steal in order to survive.

Some critics charge that while appropriate relative to the time they were introduced, the *hudud* punishments are unnecessarily harsh in a modern context. If many Muslim rulers and governments try to avoid addressing the issue directly, Malaysia's prime minister Dr. Mahathir Mohamad directly criticized the conservatism of his country's *ulama*, their legal opinions, their *fatwas*, and religious courts. He refused to allow the Malaysian state of Kelantan, the only state controlled by PAS, an Islamic opposition political party, to implement the *hudud*.

Muslim orientations to change and reform vary significantly. To understand the different approaches to change—although categories are not clear-cut and overlap at times, and I want to emphasize—four general Muslim orientations can be identified. Secularists believe religion is a personal matter and should be excluded from politics and public life. Like their counterparts in the West, secularists believe religion is a personal matter, and should be excluded completely from politics and public life. Calling for the separation of religion and the state, they believe that Islam belongs in the mosque, not in politics as some would say, and that the mosque should solely be a place of prayer, not of political activism. Sometimes dismissed by their opponents as non-believers, most secularists counter that they are religious but believe that religion should be restricted to private life, to matters of prayer, fasting, and pilgrimage.

Conservatives emphasize following—the traditional notion of *taklid*, following the tradition, following past tradition—and are wary of any change or innovation that they regard as "deviation," *bida*. I remember I mentioned earlier that this term *bida*, "deviation," is somewhat similar to the Christian equivalent of heresy. Conservatives are represented by the majority though certainly not all of the *ulama* and their followers. They continue to assert the primacy and adequacy of centuries-old Islamic law, a law that was developed by their jurist predecessors in the early period of Islamic development and expansion. Conservatives are followers rather than activists, advocating the re-implementation of Islamic law through the adoption of past legal doctrine; they resist substantive change. They would tend to argue that since Islamic law is the divinely revealed path of God, it's not the law that must change or modernize, but society that must conform to God's law as formulated in past centuries.

Mainstream Islamic activists, often referred to as fundamentalists or Islamists, are in many ways similar to conservatives though more flexible. They too place a strong emphasis on the need for a return to Islam and the

Shariah. However, while they respect the classical formulations of law, in contrast to conservatives they are not wedded to them, emphasizing instead a return to fundamentals in order to move forward. In the name of a return to the "fundamental" sources of Islam, Quran, and Sunnah, they are prepared to interpret, *ijtihad*, and reformulate Islamic belief and institutions. Their leadership tends to be lay rather than clerical, like many Islamic revivalist organizations in the 20th century, such as the Muslim Brotherhood, their holistic or comprehensive understanding of Islam forces the social and political activism, often challenging the political and religious establishment.

Though their advocacy of reinterpretation and change takes them well beyond conservatives, in reality their Islamic discourse and ideology are less innovative than Islamic reformers or modernists. Thus, they have often proven less progressive, though not always, in particularly sensitive areas like Islamic law, the status of women, and minorities.

Islamic reformers, though they overlap at times with some mainstream fundamentalists or more progressive fundamentalists, are more liberal or open to substantive change and to borrowing from other cultures. Like fundamentalists, they root their reforms in normative Islamic sources, the Quran and Sunnah, and are not wedded to classical Islamic law. They distinguish, in other words, between the divine element in Islamic law, the formulation of Islamic law and the human interpretation. However, their approach to change is more substantive or fundamental, and they distinguish more sharply between substance and form, between the principles and values of Islam's immutable revelation, and the historically and socially conditioned practices and institutions that can, and should, they believe, be changed to meet contemporary conditions.

The heart of a modernist approach gets at the core issue in contemporary Islamic reformism, the relationship of the divine to the human in Islamic law. In the terminology of classical jurisprudence, they focus on the need to distinguish between the Shariah, God's divinely revealed law, and *fiqh*, human understanding and interpretation and application that is historically conditioned. These reformers go further than fundamentalists in their acceptance of the degree and extent to which enshrined classical formulations of law may be changed, and they place more emphasis on the finite nature of early doctrines or formulations. Just as jurists applied the principles and values of Islam to their societies in the past, they argue that again today a new reinterpretation or reconstruction of Islam is needed.

Many reformers, after an early traditional or Islamic education, have obtained degrees from major national and international universities in the Muslim world and in the West, combining an appreciation of Islam with modern disciplines and knowledge. Islamic reform is evident in the current debate over key issues, like the relationship of Islam to the state, political participation or democratization, reform of Islamic law, and promoting religious and political pluralism.

Muslim experiments have run the gamut, from conservative monarchies like Saudi Arabia, to more radical approaches in Libya, Sudan, and Iran, from mainstream Islamic social and political activism, working within society, creating schools, hospitals, providing social services, participating in elections across the Muslim world, Egypt, Turkey, and Indonesia, to violent revolutionaries who try to topple governments and impose authoritarian versions of Islamic rule.

Two essential questions face Muslim communities as they define the relationship and relevance of Islam to their lives, and I think Jews and Christians and other believers can associate with these generic questions. "Whose Islam?" and "What Islam?" "Whose Christianity?" and "What Christianity?" "Whose Judaism?" and "What Judaism?"

Whose Islam? Who has the authority to interpret Islam, and what are the relevant and acceptable interpretations of Islam for today's world? As in the past, both the *ulama*, the religious scholars of Islam, and Muslim rulers continue to assert their right to protect, defend, and interpret Islam. The *ulama* remain persistent in regarding themselves as the guardians of Islam, the conscience of the community, and its only qualified interpreters. They continue to write religious commentaries, run schools and universities, seminaries, and promote their ideas, not only through publications but also increasingly through the use of modern media and technology.

Many rulers through co-option and coercion combine their obligation to protect and promote Islam with the state's power to influence, control, and promote an acceptable brand of Islam, their brand of Islam. Governments control and distribute funds used to build mosques, pay the salaries of religious officials and functionaries, approve the topic or outline for the Friday mosque sermon, and appoint religious leaders and judges. Saudi Arabia, Libya, and Iran, among others, through the creation and funding of international Islamic organizations, promote not only Islam—building a mosque, schools, hospitals, sending *imams* to serve as mosque leaders and preachers, and distributing Qurans and Islamic publications—but also their brands or interpretations of Islam, internationally among Muslim communities, in the Muslim world, and in the West.

The result has been the promotion and propagation of a broad range of interpretations, from the conservative to the revolutionary. Today, there are many that argue that it is not rulers or the clergy, but the laity and/or parliaments that should be major actors in the process of change. As we have seen, the *ulama* have often come under criticism from diverse sectors of Muslim society, viewed as out of touch with the demands and realities of the modern world, and as a religious establishment too easily co-opted by governments, or too compliant.

At the same time, as in Christianity and Judaism, an educated laity has increasingly asserted its role in the community, while the *ulama* base their authority on their training in traditional Islamic disciplines: Quran, *hadith*, and Shariah studies.

The laity counter that they possess the expertise—legal, economic, and medical—necessary to address contemporary issues, and should be counted among the qualified experts, along with the *ulama*, because remember an *alim* means "a learned one." Indeed many in the laity have also now earned their degrees in Quran studies and Islamic studies.

Just as the vast majority of Islamic political and social organizations—such as the Muslim Brotherhood or the Jamaat-i Islami, the Islamic Salvation Front and Islamic parties in Turkey and Tunisia and in Southeast Asia—are lay rather than clerically led, so too, in the latter half of the 20th century, the authors of contemporary Islamic thought increasingly came to represent lay as well as clerical experts offering their interpretations of Islam on political, social, and economic issues. And that continues today in the 21st century.

Critical to what we're looking at today, is the question of restoration, or reformation? Broadly speaking, the question today is: Should the process of renewal and reform be one of restoration, looking to the past and restoring, or reinterpretation, the re-implementation of classical Islamic law, or a bold reformulation and reconstruction of Islam?

Some who call for a return to Islam simply mean reclaiming and implementing the traditional classical legal blueprint for Muslim society and all of its details, as some Christians and Jews simply want to appropriate the traditions of the past. Others argue that times have changed and that it is necessary to replace or supplement laws formulated centuries ago with fresh interpretations that respond more adequately to conditions today. They wish to return to the sources of Islam, to the principles and values of a Quran, and the Sunnah, example of the Prophet, upon which new laws and institutions can now be formulated. This discussion, debate, and, at times, battle can be seen across the Muslim world, from Egypt and Morocco, to Malaysia and Indonesia. It can be seen among Muslims in Europe and America within all Muslim communities.

What are some of the issues that emerge? Islam and democracy would be a primary example. Islamic reformism in the 21st century in particular, but it also occurred in the late 20th century, has struggled with the issue of democracy democratization.

Some Muslims maintain that Islam has its own system of government, that democracy is based on un-Islamic or Western principles and values. Others reinterpret traditional Islamic concepts, like consultation, consensus, and *ijtihad*, the interpretation, so consultation and consensus of the community to support modern political consultation, modern political participation such as parliamentary elections.

Another issue is the status of non-Muslims, and this is a major and current debate. Many want to reinstate traditional doctrines, such as the doctrine that non-Muslims are a "protected" people, *dhimmi*. While it was ahead of its time in the past, as we talked about earlier, today it would consign non-Muslims to a second-class form of citizenship in terms of rights to vote or to hold senior government positions. Others advocate non-Muslims' right to full and equal citizenship, fostering an egalitarian and pluralist society of Muslims and non-Muslims. The swelling numbers of Muslim refugees, and the migration of many Muslims to Europe and America make minority rights and duties an ever-greater concern for Islamic jurisprudence today.

Of course, there is the issue of women. One result of contemporary Islamic revivalism has been a reexamination of the role of women in Islam, and at times a bitter debate over their function in society. The resurgence of Islam has sometimes worsened rather than alleviated or improved the situation of Muslim women. Women have often been the "quick fix" for those who wish to Islamize a society; this has often meant dismissing modern reforms or paradigms as simply Westernization, and restoring the paradigms of the past.

On the other hand, Muslim women have also become catalysts for change, entering the professions, running for elective office, becoming students and scholars of Islam, and establishing women's professional organizations, journals, and magazines. We'll spend a good deal of time in a future lesson looking at the place and role of women within Islam and within Muslim societies, both past and present.

The contemporary Islamic revival produced a third alternative, both modern and rooted in Islamic faith, identity, and values. Distinguishing between Islam and patriarchy, between revelation and male interpretations in patriarchal settings, women are working to redefine their role in society, much, I must say, as their sisters in Judaism and Christianity have done before them and still do today.

In many instances this change has been symbolized by a return to Islamic dress, or the donning of a headscarf or *hijab*, combining social change with indigenous Islamic values and ideals. New experiments have resulted in more women "returning to the mosque," forming their own prayer and Quran study groups, and in some cases women praying behind other women who lead the prayer.

154

Women as individuals and organizations are writing and speaking out for themselves on women's issues, ranging from dress to education, employment and political participation. In contrast to Judaism and Christianity, Muslims under European colonial dominance and rule have had only a few decades since gaining independence, relatively speaking, four or five decades, to accomplish what the West needed and took centuries for in terms of the Enlightenment, the Reformation, the counter-Reformation, the French and American Revolutions, et cetera.

Like believers in other faiths, the critical question today facing Islam and Muslim communities globally involves the relationship of faith and tradition to change in a rapidly changing and pluralistic world. This remains the challenge, and it is a challenge that we'll be looking at and continuing to look at as we move through the rest of the course, as we look at the role of women, as we look at the question of Muslims in Europe and America, and finally as we talk about the future of Islam, as we look out, as it were, beyond the first part of the 21st century.

I think it's important to recall today the words of Fazlur Rahman, a prominent Muslim scholar in the 20th century who taught at the University of Chicago for many years. He commented in regard to Islamic reform; he said that Islamic reform requires "first-class minds who can interpret the old in terms of the new as regards substance, and turn the new into the service of the old as regards ideals." This, I think, in many ways, constitutes the marching orders for Muslims, who, like Jews and Christians, are challenged to move forward into the 21st century.

Women and Change in Islam
Lecture 10

The status of women in Islam is a hotly contested issue, both in the Muslim world and in the West.

For several decades, women in Muslim societies have been part of the dialectics of change, an erratic, vacillating, and contradictory process that creates many anomalies and contradictions. Evidence of women's status represents great diversity across the Muslim world. In some Muslim countries, women drive cars and ride motorcycles freely; hold professional positions in virtually every sector; serve as ambassadors, parliamentary members, judges; outnumber men at universities; and have the right to vote. In others, they need a male's permission to travel; cannot drive a car; are sexually segregated; must be completely covered in public; cannot vote; are restricted by "Islamic laws" that severely limit their rights in marriage, divorce, and inheritance; and face courts that condemn them to be stoned to death if found guilty of fornication or adultery.

Such contradictions are also evident in the issue of veiling. If many associate the veil with the oppression of women, others say veiling preserves women's dignity, freedom, and modesty. Since the 1970s, a significant number of "modern" women from Cairo to Jakarta have turned or returned to wearing Islamic dress. Such women are active agents for change. They believe they are better able to function as independent subjects, commanding respect as individuals, rather than sex objects. Islamic dress is also used as sign of protest and liberation. It has developed political overtones, becoming a source of national pride and resistance to Western cultural and political dominance and to authoritarian regimes.

Although women's status in Muslim countries has long been seen as evidence of "Islam's" oppression of women, the reality is far more complex. The revelation of Islam raised the status of women by prohibiting female infanticide, abolishing women's status as property, establishing women's legal capacity, granting women the right to receive their own dowry, changing marriage from a proprietary to a contractual relationship, and allowing women to retain control over their property and use their maiden names after marriage. The Quran also granted women financial maintenance from their husbands and controlled the husband's free ability to divorce.

The Quran declares that men and women are equal in the eyes of God; man and woman were created to be equal parts of a pair (51:49).

Men and women are equally responsible for adhering to the Five Pillars of Islam (9:71–72). Some modernist scholars argue on the basis of both content and chronology that this verse s the ideal vision of the relationship between men and women in Islam—one of equality and complementarity.

If this is the case, why are there problems with the status of women in Muslim countries? Most Islamic societies have been patriarchal, and women have long been considered to be the culture-bearers within these societies. The Quran, *hadith*, and Islamic law have long been interpreted by men in these patriarchal societies. Women, from the Prophet's wives to scholars and Sufi mystics, have exercised leadership at different points in history. Yet, in practice, patriarchy prevailed, as men functioned as the primary political, religious, and intellectual leaders and women were often marginalized in the mosque and public spaces. Reformers have argued that Quranic verses favoring men need reinterpretation in light of the new social, cultural, and economic realities in the 20th and 21st centuries.

Women, from the Prophet's wives to scholars and Sufi mystics, have exercised leadership at different points in history.

Quranic interpretation is at the center of many debates. One controversial verse is Quran 4:34, which says, "Men have responsibility for and priority over women, since God has given some of them advantages over others and because they should spend their wealth [for the support of women]." Contrary to many traditional interpretations, contemporary scholars have noted that the "priority" referred to in this verse is based on men's socioeconomic responsibilities for women. It does not say women are incapable of managing their own affairs. Nowhere does the Quran explicitly state that all men are superior to, preferred to, or better than all women. God's expressed preference for certain individuals in the Quran is based on their faith, not their gender.

Another controversial Quranic stipulation (2:282) is that two female witnesses are equal to one male witness. Over time, this was interpreted by male scholars to mean that a woman's testimony should always count for one-half of the value of a man's testimony. Contemporary reformers stress the socio-historical context in which the verse was revealed, a time when women were not active in business or finance and a woman's expertise in these fields would most likely have been less than a man's. Another interpretation argues that the requirement was based on the concern that male family members might pressure a woman into testifying in their favor. Others argue for women's free access to education, both secular and religious, so that they will automatically be equal to men in a business environment—something that is not prohibited by the Quran. In light of women's right to own property and make their own investments, they say, this interpretation reflects broader Quranic values.

Gender discrimination broadly exists in women's restricted divorce rights in contrast to men's extensive divorce and marriage rights in many regions. Reformers maintain that the Quran and *hadith* literature support contemporary reinterpretation and reform in divorce laws. They have also argued that Quranic verses prohibit polygamy and that the true Quranic ideal is monogamy. Particularly notable across the Muslim world in the latter half of the 20th century have been reforms in marriage and divorce laws, including the abolition or severe limitation of polygamy; expanded rights for women seeking divorce, including the right to financial compensation; expanded rights for women to participate in contracting their marriages; prohibition of child marriages; and expanded rights of women to have custody over their older children, but this process is not over.

The practice of separation has both religious and cultural origins. The Prophet's Medina did not practice sexual segregation, although the Quran advises Muhammad's wives to "stay in your homes," "not display your finery," and place a barrier between themselves and unrelated males. Modern reformers explain that these controversial verses specifically address only the wives of the Prophet and that, until the modern age, jurists relied primarily on prophetic traditions, as well as the belief that women are a source of temptation for men. However, ultraconservatives have maintained that these verses apply to all Muslim women. Opinions vary today about the necessity of separation of the sexes.

A new source of women's empowerment today has become their active participation in the mosque and their use of scripture and religion to reclaim their rights in Muslim societies. In political affairs, women independently pledged their oath of allegiance (*bayah*) to Muhammad, often without the knowledge or approval of male family members, and in many cases, distinguished women converted to Islam before the men in their families. In the centuries after the death of Muhammad, women prayed regularly with men in the mosque and played a significant role as transmitters of *hadith* (prophetic traditions) and in the development of Sufism (Islamic mysticism). Reformers today emphasize that just as women during the time of the Prophet prayed in the mosque, so too today, they actively exercise that right.

The contemporary reality in much of the Muslim world reflects deep divisions in the ongoing struggle over the status and rights of Muslim women between conservatives and "fundamentalists" versus a broad spectrum of reformers. As the examples of the Taliban's Afghanistan and courts in Nigeria and Pakistan reflect, patriarchal interpretations of the past and tribal custom have proven a formidable obstacle and a source of oppression and injustice. At the same time, in an increasingly modern, globalizing world, where two incomes are often necessary to maintain a household, Muslim women in many societies, from Egypt and Syria to Malaysia and Indonesia, have greater access to education and employment and are forging new paths for themselves and the next generation. ■

Akbar Ahmed, *Women and Gender in Islam*.

Yvonne Y. Haddad and John L. Esposito, *Islam, Gender and Social Change*.

Amina Wadud, *Quran and Women*.

Questions to Consider

1. What are the major obstacles that have contributed to the low status of women in many societies and that continue to impede progress today?

2. What are some of the major issues that women have confronted in redefining and reforming their status and roles?

Women and Change in Islam
Lecture 10—Transcript

The status of women in Islam is a hotly contested issue both in the Muslim world and in the West. Muslim women are often viewed through Western stereotypes or the policies of extremists, like the Taliban in Afghanistan. Gender in Islam remains a highly charged issue today at the popular level, as well as among scholars and religious leaders.

If some blame Islam for the oppression of women, others see it as a beacon of light in reform. Still others insist that the status and role of women in Muslim societies should be attributed primarily to socioeconomic forces, to patriarchy rather than religious belief. The explanations are as diverse as the Muslim world itself. Thus, charting the progress or regression of women, whether under secular or religious governments, is a tricky task.

While some claim that Islam oppresses women, others view Islam as a source of women's empowerment. The diversity of practice is reflected in dress, access to education, and professional positions, and the visibility and roles of women across time and space. The veil has become a particularly charged symbol, yet even the wearing of the veil has diverse meanings for the wearers and the observers. Increasingly, Muslim women today are struggling to forge new paths, reinterpreting the Quran and Muslim traditions, taking their place in education and the professions, and seeking to improve their status both within the family and as professionals.

For several decades, women in Muslim societies have been part of the dialectics of change, an erratic, vacillating, and contradictory process that creates many anomalies and contradictions. Evidence of women's status represents great diversity across the Muslim world.

In some Muslim countries women drive cars, ride motorcycles, hold professional positions in virtually every sector, serve as ambassadors, parliamentary members, and judges, outnumber men at universities, and have the right to vote. In others, they need a male's permission to travel, cannot drive a car, are sexually segregated, must be completely covered in public, cannot vote, are restricted by Islamic laws that severely limit their rights in marriage, divorce, and inheritance, and that condemn them to be stoned to death if found guilty of fornication or adultery.

The following examples give some sense of the complexity and anomalies of gender relations in the Muslim world, and here I'm going to refer to anomalies that existed recently. Some of them have passed recently from the scene, but they're all within the last couple of decades, and you'll note how some countries seem very progressive on many things but not on other things, and vice versa.

In Egypt, long regarded as, and indeed one of the most modernizing of Muslim states, women cannot serve as judges, yet they can be members of parliament, and they have been in the cabinet. Yet in Morocco, more than 20 percent of the judges are women. Women in Egypt and Malaysia have access to the best education, and hold responsible professional positions in virtually every sector. Yet, like women in many Muslim societies, they have needed a male relative's permission to travel.

Women in Saudi Arabia own much of the real estate in Riyadh and Jeddah, can own businesses, but cannot drive a car, and are sexually segregated and restricted to appropriate professions, much as women in the West have had to deal with that themselves. Certain professions such as teaching, nursing, for example, in the West have been seen in the past as more appropriate than being a corporate executive.

In nearby Kuwait, women function in society and hold responsible positions in many areas, but have not been able to get the vote. More recently, there has been a move to sexually segregate universities, that is, students in universities.

In Iran, which we think of often as a fundamentalist state, where women must wear the *chador* in public, women constitute the majority of students in universities, hold professional positions, and serve in Parliament. Moreover, the Islamic Republic of Iran has had a woman vice president. Though Pakistani women can vote, serve as ambassadors to the United States and even as prime minister, they, particularly the poor and powerless, also suffer under Islamic laws, or so-called Islamic laws, enacted by General Zia ul-Haq in the past, but still in force today.

In Afghanistan, the Taliban in the name of Islam required women to wear the *chador*, forced professional women to give up their jobs, and prohibited girls from attending school. Such contradictions are also evident in the issue of veiling. If many associate the veil with the oppression of women, others say veiling preserves women's dignity, freedom, and modesty.

The Islamic style of dress is known by many names, *hijab*, *burqa*, *chador*. Veiling ranges from wearing a headscarf to covering the entire body and face. A multitude of styles, colors, and fabrics are worn by Muslim women in countries extending from Morocco to Iran to Malaysia to Europe and the United States, because of diverse customs and interpretations of the Quranic verses. Veiling of women did not become widespread in early Islam until three or four generations after the death of Muhammad.

Veiling was originally a sign of honor and distinction, not oppression. During Muhammad's time, Muhammad's wives and upper-class women wore the veil as a symbol of their status. Generations later, Muslim women adopted the practice more widely. They were influenced by upper- and middle-class Persian and Byzantine women, who wore the veil as a sign of their rank to separate themselves, not from men but from the lower classes. The mingling of all classes at prayer and in the marketplace encouraged use of the veil among urban Muslim women.

Since the 1970s, a significant number of "modern" women from Cairo to Jakarta have turned, or returned, to wearing Islamic dress. Often, this is a voluntary movement led by young urban middle-class women who are well educated and work in every sector of society; ironically, they have often been the daughters of women a generation before who, as it were, threw off the veil in order to turn to and wear Western dress.

In many cases, the process is distinctly modern, with new fashions and styles encompassing new understandings of the status and role of women, fashions that are sold in boutiques. Such women are not passive victims of male-imposed mores, but active agents for change. Some who wear Islamic dress believe that they are able to function as active, self-directed, independent subjects, commanding respect, acknowledged and treated as persons rather than sex objects. Western and Muslim critics of Islamic dress, on the other hand, question those who say it is their free choice to wear the veil. They see such women as being under the sway of an oppressive patriarchal culture, or as just submitting to the dictates of their religion, or the particular brand of religion taught in their country or community.

They also say that after seeing the *hijab* used to control and segregate women, as in Afghanistan under the Taliban, the rest of the world perceives the veil as a symbol of conformity and confinement that reflects on any women who wear it. Some Muslims, however, contend that Western women only believe that they are free. They do not see how their culture exploits them when they choose to spend their countless hours on their appearance, wear uncomfortable, skin-tight clothes and dangerous high-heeled shoes, and allow themselves to be displayed as sexual objects to sell cars, shaving cream, and beer. These Muslims say that Westerners condemn the veil because they themselves are not free to choose.

Women who wear the scarf complain that, instead of asking what the *hijab* means to them, people simply assume that veiled women are oppressed. This assumption, they say, oppresses Muslim women more than any manner of dress ever could. Even if a woman wearing the veil is strong and intelligent, people who are reluctant to get to know her or invite her to participate in activities, automatically discount her value. They point out that women of many other cultures and religions, such as Russian women, Hindu women, Jewish women, Greek women, Catholic nuns, have worn head coverings. They ask why these women are not viewed as oppressed. If opponents assume that women of other cultures who cover their heads are liberated, why can't they imagine freedom for Muslim women, who wear a veil?

Muslim women often talk about what the *hijab* symbolizes to them: religious devotion, discipline, reflection, respect, freedom, and modernity, being valued for who they are rather than what they look like. Islamic dress is also used as a sign of protest and liberation. It has developed political overtones, becoming a source of national pride and resistance to Western cultural and political dominance, and authoritarian regimes. It existed from the Algerian independence movement in the 1960s to the Iranian Revolution in 1978-79 and beyond.

While women's status in Muslim countries has long been seen as evidence of "Islam's" oppression of women, the reality is far more complex. As we have seen before, the revelation of Islam raised the status of women by prohibiting female infanticide, abolishing women's status as property, establishing women's legal capacity, granting women the right to receive their own dowry, changing marriage from a proprietary to a contractual relationship, and allowing women to retain control over their property and, in many cultures, to use their maiden name after marriage.

The Quran also granted women financial maintenance from their husbands and control of the husband's free ability to divorce. Again, I must remind you that, over time, in many societies these rights were in fact ignored or circumvented.

The Quran declares that men and women are equal in the eyes of God. Men and women were created to be equal parts of a pair, the Quran states in chapter 55, verse 49. It describes the relationship between men and women as one of "love and mercy," chapter 30, verse 21. Men and women are to be like "members of one another," chapter 3, verse 195; like each other's garment, chapter 2, verse 187.

Men and women in Islam are equally responsible for adhering to the Five Pillars of Islam. This is stated clearly in the Quran: "The Believers, men and women, are protectors of one another; they enjoin what is just, and forbid what is evil; they observe regular prayers, pay *zakat*, and obey God and His Messenger. God will pour His mercy on them, for God is exalted in Power, Wise. God has promised the Believers, men and women, gardens under which rivers flow to dwell therein."

This verse draws added significance from the fact, as I pointed out in one of our first lectures, that it was the last Quran verse to be revealed that addressed relations between men and women. Thus, as we noted earlier, some scholars argue, on the basis of both content and chronology, that this verse outlines the ideal vision of the relationship between men and women in Islam, one of equality and complementarity. Needless to say, this is a contended issue within Islam and within Muslim communities but, if this is the case, why are there problems with the status of women in Muslim countries?

Most Muslim societies have been patriarchal, and women have long been considered to be the culture bearers within their societies. The Quran, *hadith*, traditions of the Prophet, and Islamic law have long been interpreted by men in these patriarchal societies. One need only think of the way in which the role of women in Christianity and Judaism, as in Hinduism and Buddhism, was affected by patriarchy and the fact that it was, as I like to put it, the "good ole boys" who did the reinterpreting, and often continue to, in some instances.

Women, from the Prophets' wives to scholars and Sufi mystics, have exercised leadership at different points in history, yet in practice, patriarchy prevailed, as men functioned as the primary political, religious, and intellectual leaders while women were often marginalized in the mosque and in public space.

Reformers have argued that traditional interpretations of Quranic verses favoring men need reinterpretation in light of the new social, cultural, and economic realities in the 20th and 21st centuries. Quranic interpretation is at the center of many debates. One controversial verse is Quran chapter 4, verse 34, which says, "Men have responsibility for and priority over women, since God has given some of them advantages over others, and because they should spend their wealth for the support of women."

Contrary to many traditional interpretations, contemporary scholars have noted that the priority referred to in this verse is based upon men's socioeconomic responsibilities for women. It does not say women are incapable of managing their own affairs. They further argue that nowhere in the Quran does it say explicitly that all men are superior to, preferred to, or better than all women. God's express preference for certain individuals in the Quran is based upon their faith, not their gender.

Another controversial Quranic stipulation can be found in chapter 2, verse 282. It states that two female witnesses are equal to one male witness, and this gets reasserted today in a number of modern Muslim states, though certainly not all. Over time, this was interpreted by male scholars to mean that a woman's testimony should always count for one-half of the value of a man's testimony.

Contemporary reformers stress the socio-historical context in which the verse was revealed, a time when women were not active in business or finance and a woman's expertise in these fields would most likely have been less than a man's. Others argue for women's free access to education, both secular and religious, so that they will be equal to men in the business environment, something that is not prohibited by the Quran. In light of women's right to own property and make their own investments, they say, this interpretation reflects broader Quranic values. Within a country like Saudi Arabia, which in many ways is seen very conservative, women do own significant pieces of property, and women do function, in a sexually segregated society, running their own corporations.

Quranic interpretation is at the center of reformism. Some note that the Quran itself specifically distinguishes between two types of verses, and we'll hear this time and time again: those that are universal principles and those that were responding to specific social and cultural contexts or questions, and were subject to interpretation. They believe that those verses that assign greater rights to men, such as verses found in chapter 2, verse 223, and chapter 2, verse 228, reflect a patriarchal context in which men were dominant, and solely responsible for supporting women.

Today, rather than being interpreted literally, reformers argue that these verses should be reformulated to reflect changing socioeconomic conditions, and the interests of public welfare. They further argue that gender equality is the intended order established by God, because God does not make distinctions based upon gender in matters of belief and morality. All are equally responsible in terms of belief and morality and in terms of modest dress, for example.

However, Muslims who advocate a literal interpretation of the Quran believe that the gender inequalities it prescribes apply to every time and place, as God's revealed social order. Biology is often used as a justification. Because only women can bear children, they argue, the man must provide for and maintain the family so that the woman can do her job of bearing and raising children. Gender inequality broadly exists in family law, in women's restricted divorce rights as they stand in contrast to men's extensive divorce and marriage rights in many regions, certainly in terms of modern standards.

Reformers attempt to address this by maintaining that the Quran and the *hadith* literature support contemporary reinterpretation and reform in divorce laws. Particularly notable since the latter half of the 20th century across the Muslim world have been several reforms in marriage and divorce laws, including the abolition or severe limitation of polygamy, expanded rights for women seeking divorce, including the right to financial compensation, expanded rights for women to participate in contracting their marriage, prohibitions with regard to child marriage, and expanding the rights of women to have custody over their older children.

This process remains contested and is rejected by more conservative Muslims, however. Look at gender segregation. The practice of separation has both religious and cultural origins. The Prophet's Medina did not practice sexual segregation. Although an integral part of the community because of their special status, Muhammad's wives were told by the Quran, "O wives of the Prophet! You are not like any other women. If you fear God, do not be complacent in speech, so that one in whose heart is a sickness may covet you, but speak honorably. Stay with dignity in your homes, and do not display your finery as the pagans of old did." Quran chapter 33, verses 32 to 33.

The Quran later tells Muhammad's wives to place a barrier between themselves and unrelated males. Muslim men are told, "And when you ask his wives for anything you want, ask them from before a screen." Here we're referring to Muhammad's wives. The Quran continues, "That makes for greater purity for your hearts and for theirs," chapter 33, verse 53.

There have been many debates about how these verses, concerned with modesty and segregation, should be interpreted with respect to Muslim women in general. Modern reformists have pointed out that they specifically address only the wives of the Prophet rather than all of womankind. They maintain that, until the modern age, jurists relied primarily on prophetic traditions, *hadith*, as well as the belief that women are a source of temptation for men, to support women's segregation.

In recent decades, more ultra-conservative fundamentalist Muslim leaders have maintained that the verses addressing the wives of the Prophet apply to all Muslim women, who are to emulate the behavior of Muhammad's wives.

Opinions today vary about the necessity of separation of the sexes. While many believe that the absolute separation of the sexes is unnecessary, many others believe that modesty requirements can be met through appropriate dress and through limiting interaction with unrelated males to conversations such as those concerning professional and educational matters, since many women attend both work and school in mixed company.

This holds true even in the religious realm, since women have come to play an important role in the mosques, where they not only attend services and pray with men, but also teach Quran classes, run independent auxiliaries, and run for and hold elected offices. Indeed, in several Muslim countries, Pakistan, Bangladesh, Turkey, and Indonesia, women have been prime ministers or presidents.

A new source of women's empowerment today has become their active participation in the mosque, and their use of scripture and religion to reclaim their rights in Muslim societies. Reformers today emphasize that, just as women during the time of the Prophet prayed in the mosque, so too today they actively exercise that right, and should exercise that right.

In the centuries after the death of Muhammad, women prayed regularly with men in the mosque and played a significant role as transmitters of *hadith,* prophetic traditions, and in the development of Sufism, Islamic mysticism.

Women in the early Muslim community, like Khadija, the wife of the Prophet, owned and sold property, engaged in commercial transactions, and were encouraged to seek and provide educational instruction.

Many women were instructed in religious matters in Muhammad's own home. Muhammad's daughter, Fatima, his only surviving child, played a prominent role in his community. She was the wife of the caliph, Ali, and the mother of *imams*, Hussein and Hassan. Seen as immaculate and sinless, the pattern for virtuous women, an object of prayer and petition, articles have been written comparing her, by the way, to the role of the Virgin Mary in Roman Catholicism. Like her son Hussein, she embodies a life of dedication, suffering, and compassion.

Muhammad's wife, Aishah, also played a unique role in the community as an acknowledged authority on history, medicine, poetry, and rhetoric, as well as one of the most important transmitters of *hadith*. In political affairs, women independently pledge their oath of allegiance to Muhammad; both in the time of Muhammad and also at the early Caliphs, you acknowledged the ruler by an oath of allegiance, *bayah*. They did this often without the knowledge or approval of male family members and, in many cases, distinguished women converted to Islam before the men in their family.

The second caliph, Umar Ibn al-Khattab, appointed women to serve as officials in the marketplace of Medina. The Hanbali School of Law, interestingly enough, often seen as one of the most conservative schools of law, supports the right of women to serve as judges, something in some modern Muslim countries that still hasn't been implemented, although in many others it has.

The Quran holds up the leadership of Bilqis, the Queen of Sheba, as a positive example in chapter 27, verses 23 to 44. Rather than focusing on gender, the Quranic account of this queen describes her ability to fulfill the requirements of her office, her purity of faith, her independent judgment, and her political skills, portraying a woman serving as an effective political leader. Gradually, however, women's religious role and practice, particularly their access to education and the mosque, was severely restricted. Male religious scholars cited a variety of reasons, from moral degeneration in society, to women's bringing temptation and social discord, in order to restrict both their presence in public life and their access to education into the mosque.

The contemporary reality in much of the Muslim world reflects deep divisions in the ongoing struggle over the status and rights of women between conservatives and so-called fundamentalists versus a broad spectrum of reformers. As the examples of the Taliban's Afghanistan and legal cases in Nigeria and Pakistan reflect, patriarchal interpretations of the past and tribal custom have proven a formidable obstacle, and a source of oppression and injustice.

At the same time, in an increasingly modern globalizing world, where two incomes are often necessary to maintain a household, Muslim women in many societies, from Egypt and Syria to Malaysia and Indonesia, have greater access to education and employment, and this trend is clearly one that's in place. However, the ability for this trend to develop will be affected not only by the impact, if you will, and the ongoing impact of patriarchy, but also, as is true of all religious traditions, the impact of the traditions of the past and the extent to which reform does occur or can occur.

A major obstacle will also remain economic development, which naturally has a significant effect on educational development. Lack of resources, economic resources, means often a lack of the proper schools, the proper curriculum, the ability to attract the right teachers, et cetera. Given the integral role of religion to Muslim societies, Islam's formative influence on gender relations in the past, and the impact of Islamic revivalism, religion continues to play a significant role as women forge new paths for themselves and future generations. As we've seen before, and as we shall see in our subsequent lecture, particularly in our final lecture on the future of Islam, this trajectory will continue, and part of the trajectory is not just a conflict between, if you will, modernizing reform-minded and conservative resistance to change.

The fact is, however, within those who are modern educated and reform minded, today we see both your more secular, Western-oriented women and your more Islamically-oriented women, and this can be seen most visibly in terms often of matters of dress. That is, you can have women in the workplace with the same educations or in government, some wearing what one might call modern Western dress and some wearing Islamic dress, as well as in the mosques and in other sectors of society.

In many ways, they reflect the broader dynamic that is playing out within Muslim societies today in terms of the issues of the relationship of Islam to modern reform, the relationship of past to present, and the ability to establish a continuity between the practice of today with the traditions of the past.

Islam in the West
Lecture 11

> **Muslims in Europe and America are a combination of immigrants and indigenous converts. They represent a cross-section of national, ethnic, and racial backgrounds and socioeconomic classes. They, like religious minorities before them, face issues of faith and identity, integration and assimilation.**

Muslims were present in America before the 19th century. The explorers, traders, and settlers who visited the New World from the time of Columbus included Moriscos (Spanish Muslims who hid their Muslim faith) who migrated to both Spanish and Portuguese settlements in America. Between 14 and 20 percent of the African slaves brought to America between the 16th and 19th centuries were Muslim, although they were forced to convert to Christianity. Indians and Arabs, who were not slaves, also immigrated during this period and maintained their spiritual, cultural, and social identity.

The numbers of Muslims in America increased in the late 19th century. Significant numbers of immigrants from the Arab world (Syria, Lebanon, and Jordan) settled in the Midwest and Canada as blue-collar workers and assimilated into American society. After World War II, large numbers of immigrants from Palestine, who had lost their homes after the creation of Israel in 1948, and elites from the Middle East and South Asia, seeking an education or professional advancement, came to America.

In recent decades, many students from the Muslim world have come to study in the United States, and many well-educated professionals and intellectuals have come from South and Southeast Asia, as well as from the Middle East, for political and economic reasons.

African-American Islam emerged in the early 20th century when a number of black Americans converted to Islam, the religion they believed was part of their original African identity and that they preferred over Christianity, which was seen as a religion of white supremacy and oppression. In the early 1930s, Wallace D. Fard Muhammad, called the Great Mahdi, drew on the Quran and the Bible to preach black liberation and build the Nation of Islam in the ghettos of Detroit.

When Fard mysteriously disappeared in 1934, Elijah Muhammad (1897–1975) took over and built the Nation of Islam, into an effective national movement whose members became known as "Black Muslims." Elijah Muhammad denounced white society's political and economic oppression of blacks and its results—self-hatred, poverty, and dependence—and taught self-improvement and empowerment. By the 1970s, his Nation of Islam had more than 100,000 members. Many Black Muslim movement beliefs differed from mainstream Islam, and the Nation did not follow the Five Pillars of Islam or observe major Muslim rituals.

Malcolm X, ex-smoker, ex-drinker, ex-Christian, and ex-slave gained prominence in the Nation of Islam. In 1964, he started his own organization and went on pilgrimage to Mecca, returning as El Hajj Malik El-Shabazz, a Muslim. On February 21, 1965, Malcolm X was assassinated as he spoke to an audience in New York City. Two members of the Nation of Islam were convicted of the murder.

In the 1960s, the sons of Elijah Muhammad challenged their father's teachings and strategies. Near the end of his life, Elijah Muhammad also made the pilgrimage to Mecca and began to modify some of his teachings. When Wallace D. Muhammad succeeded his father, he implemented major reforms to align the community with the global and American mainstream Islamic community. Media coverage of the Black Muslim movement often focuses on Louis Farrakhan, who led a minority of Nation members in protest against Warith's reforms. In recent years, Farrakhan has moved the Nation closer to more orthodox Islamic practices, maintaining a closer identity with mainstream Islam.

The problems the growing Muslim community faces in the United States start with the fact that only a few decades ago, Muslims were mostly invisible in the West. Their visibility then emerged by association with the "militant"

Nation of Islam or conflicts (Iranian Revolution, hijackings, hostage taking, and acts of terror in the Middle East and South Asia). Some saw these events as signs of an Islamic threat or a clash of civilizations, Islam versus the West. America's relationship with Muslims was seen in a context of conflict and confrontation.

Like many other immigrants of diverse religious and ethnic backgrounds, Muslims have been challenged to define their place in American and European society. Like Jewish law for Jews, Islamic law is central to a Muslim's life, covering religious requirements, dietary regulations, and family law. Ironically, many of the minorities who preceded them and "made it in America" do not identify with Muslims and fail to see the similarities between their own past and Muslims' current problems.

Often, Muslims fall outside the circle of American pluralism. However different previous religious and ethnic minorities, the vast majority were Judeo-Christian. Most regard Islam as foreign. Few think of it as an Abrahamic religion, part of a Judeo-Christian-Islamic tradition. In the absence of this knowledge and awareness, Islam is often seen through explosive "headline events," and thus, the hatred and violence of a minority of religious extremists obscure the faith of the mainstream majority.

In recent years, a major issue for Muslims has been the Americanization of the Muslim experience. Because *imams* coming from foreign countries are not always aware of or sensitive to the problems that American Muslims encounter, training of "native" *imams* has been seriously undertaken since the 1980s. Legal councils addressing life in America have been founded to respond to questions raised by communities here and Muslims participate in interfaith activities with Jews and Christians. Additionally, a host of national and international organizations have been created to monitor and promote Muslim causes and interests.

Despite problems, however, Muslims, long regarded as "other," are now part of the fabric of our society, as neighbors, coworkers, citizens, and believers. Muslims have increasingly become more integrated into the American political process, both as individuals and organizationally.

Estimates of the number of Muslims living in Western Europe range from 12 to 15 million. The ethnic diversity of Muslims in Europe represents most of the major ethnic groups of the Muslim world. Most numerous are Turks, Algerians, Moroccans, and Pakistanis. Because of this great diversity and despite a common religious bond, it is difficult to speak of a homogenous Muslim community in any individual country, let alone across Europe.

Muslims may be found in significant numbers in most Western European countries. The largest Muslim populations are in France, Germany, and the United Kingdom, followed by smaller communities in such countries as Belgium, Spain, the Netherlands, Sweden, Denmark, Norway, and Austria. Some estimates indicate that Muslims will outnumber non-Muslims in Europe by 2050. The major waves of Muslim migration to Europe came after World War II, in large part, the result of labor immigration and a vestigial colonial connection. When their countries achieved independence, many Muslims chose to emigrate. Professionals and skilled laborers from former European colonies in Africa, South Asia, and the Arab world sought a better life.

Some estimates indicate that Muslims will outnumber non-Muslims in Europe by 2050.

In the 1960s and 1970s, unskilled laborers flooded into a Europe whose growing economies were in need of cheap labor. From the 1970s onward, increasing numbers of Muslim students came to Europe, as they did to America, to study. Although many returned home, others, for political or economic reasons, chose to stay.

Britain's 1 to 2 million Muslims come primarily from the Indian subcontinent. In contrast to France and Germany, where most Muslims do not have the right to vote, most Muslims in Britain come from British Commonwealth countries and, thus, have enjoyed British citizenship and full participation in political life, as voters and as candidates; indeed, some have been elected to political office.

175

Assimilation has been particularly acute in France, where the government insists on full integration, rather than the multicultural approaches of Britain and America.

However different their experiences may be, Muslims in Europe and in America have common concerns about practicing their faith, retaining Islamic identity, and preserving family life and values. Specific concerns include taking time out from work to pray daily, to attend mosque on Friday, and to celebrate the two great Islamic holidays (Eid al-Adha and Eid al-Fitr); the availability of *halal* foods in schools and the military; and for those women who wish to do so, the right to wear a headscarf (*hijab*). Some request segregated athletics classes and are concerned about coeducation, sex education, homosexuality, and secularism in the schools.

Living as a minority in a dominant culture that is often ignorant about Islam, or even hostile to it, many Muslims experience a sense of marginalization, alienation, and powerlessness. Muslim experiences in Europe and America have been affected significantly by the actions of militants, especially since September 11, 2001, as well as by domestic issues. In France, Islamic terrorism has also led to doubts about Islam's compatibility with French culture and concerns that French Muslims could ever be loyal citizens. One of the most serious effects has been the increasing concern over the erosion of civil liberties for Muslim Americans.

Muslims are now part of the fabric of American and European societies. In the United States, a host of national and international organizations have been created to monitor and promote Muslim interests. Obviously, coexistence of Muslims and non-Muslims is here to stay. All are challenged to move beyond stereotypes and established patterns of behavior to a more inclusive and pluralistic vision informed by a multidimensional dialogue, to build a future based on mutual understanding and respect. ∎

Suggested Reading

Yvonne Y. Haddad, "The Globalization of Islam," *The Oxford History of Islam*, chapter 14.

Yvonne Y. Haddad and John L. Esposito, *Muslims on the Americanization Path?*

Jane Smith, *Islam in America*.

Shireen Hunter, *Islam: Europe's Second Religion*.

Questions to Consider

1. What are some of the challenges facing Muslims as religious minorities in the West?

2. Why and how did the Nation of Islam develop and how did it become integrated with the mainstream Islamic community?

Islam in the West
Lecture 11—Transcript

Although estimates of the number of American Muslims vary from four to twelve million, there are at least six million, making Islam the third largest religion after Christianity and Judaism in America. In Europe, the approximately 15 million Muslims make Islam the second largest religion. Many believe that in the first half of the 21st century, Islam will become the second largest religion in America. Thus, Islam is very much in the West.

Historically, Muslims were present in America before the 19th century. The explorers, traders, and settlers who visited the New World from the time of Columbus included Moriscos, Spanish Muslims who hid their Muslim faith. They migrated to both Spanish and Portuguese settlements in America. Between 14 and 20 percent of the African slaves brought to America between the 16th and the 19th centuries were Muslim, although they were forced to convert to Christianity.

Indians and Arabs who were not slaves also immigrated during this period, and maintained their spiritual, cultural, and social identity. The numbers of Muslims in America increased in the late 19th century. Significant numbers of immigrants from the Arab world, places like Syria, Lebanon, Jordan, settled in the Midwest and Canada as blue-collar workers, and assimilated into American society.

After World War II, large numbers of immigrants from Palestine who had lost their homes after the creation of the state of Israel in 1948, as well as elites from the Middle East, South Asia, and other places, came to America seeking higher education or professional advancement.

In recent decades, many students from the Muslim world have come to study, and many well-educated professionals and intellectuals have emigrated from South and Southeast Asia, as well as from the Middle East and parts of Africa, for political and economic reasons.

About two-thirds of the Muslims in America today are immigrants or the descendants of immigrants. The other third is indigenous, made up of

African-Americans, many African-American converts to Islam, along with smaller numbers, but a significant number of white American converts, and more recently Hispanic Muslims.

The largest Muslim communities in the United States are in cities, like Boston, New York, Detroit, Dearborn, Toledo, Chicago, Houston, and Los Angeles. As compared to 30 years ago, when I first began to study Islam and Islam was invisible on our landscape, in many of not only these major cities, but many rural areas, you will find mosques and Islamic centers today.

Like most Americans, Muslims in America are diverse. We sometimes forget this. We'll say are there 6 or 8 million Muslims, and the presumption will be that they are all religiously observant, for example; whereas, we don't make that same presumption when we talk about the numbers of Jews or Christians. Muslims in America are diverse. They're secular and religious, observant and nonobservant, liberal, conservative, fundamentalists, Democrat, and Republican.

African-American Islam emerged in the early 20th century when a number of black Americans converted to Islam. The religion, they believe, was part of their original African identity, preferred over Christianity, which was seen as a religion of white supremacy and oppression. It was the slaveholder's religion, as it were. In the early 1930s, Wallace D. Fard Muhammad, called the Great Mahdi, drew on the Quran and the Bible to preach black liberation, and to build the Nation of Islam in the ghettos of Detroit.

When he mysteriously disappeared in 1934, Elijah Muhammad, who lived from 1897 to 1975, took over and built what was called the "Nation of Islam" into an effective national movement, whose members became known as "Black Muslims." Elijah Muhammad denounced white society's political and economic oppression of blacks and its results of self-hatred, poverty, and dependency, and taught self-improvement and empowerment.

By the 1970s, his Nation of Islam had more than 100,000 members. Many Black Muslim movement beliefs at that time differed from mainstream Islam. The nation, for example, did not follow the Five Pillars of Islam or observe major Muslim rituals.

A number of basic beliefs in the Black Muslim movement differed significantly from mainstream Islam: black separatism, remember the notion of the *ummah*, the community of Muslims transcends race, tribe, and nation. However, Elijah Muhammad announced that Wallace D. Fard was Allah, which would go directly against mainstream Islamic thought. This also meant that God was a black man, and that he, Elijah Muhammad, not the Prophet Muhammad, was the last messenger of God. The nation taught black supremacy and black separatism, not Islam's brotherhood, which transcends, as I said earlier, racial, tribal, and ethnic differences.

A prominent figure and most charismatic leader emerged, Malcolm X. He took the "X," meaning, ex-smoker, ex-drinker, ex-Christian, and ex-slave. Malcolm gained prominence in the Nation of Islam. However, in 1964, he started his own organization and went on pilgrimage to Mecca, returning as El-Hajj Malik El-Shabazz, a mainstream Muslim. On February 21st, 1965, Malcolm X was assassinated as he spoke to an audience in New York City. Two members of the Nation of Islam were convicted of the murder.

In the 1960s, the sons of Elijah Muhammad challenged their father's teachings and strategies. Near the end of his life, Elijah Muhammad also, himself, made the pilgrimage to Mecca and began to modify some of his teachings. One of his sons, Wallace D. Muhammad, succeeded his father as supreme minister of the Nation of Islam, and implemented major reforms. He revised doctrines and organizational structure so that they conformed to the teachings of orthodox, or again mainstream, Sunni Islam. Wallace Fard was thus identified now as the "founder of the Nation, and Elijah Muhammad as the leader who brought black Americans to his interpretation of Islam.

Wallace Muhammad made the pilgrimage to Mecca and encouraged his followers to study Arabic in order to better understand Islam. Temples, the Nation of Islam called its places of meeting or worship "temples," were renamed "mosques." Their leaders were now called *imams*, leaders, not the *imam* in the sense of the *imam* in Shii Islam, but the generic term *imam*, which just means leader, and is used in Islam for a religious leader; he is particularly one who leads the prayer, and often is the person who, for example, runs or supervises the mosque. Anyone who leads the prayer could be called the *imam*, the leader of the prayer. Thus, they came to be called *imams* rather than ministers.

The community observed the Five Pillars of Islam in union with the worldwide Islamic community to which they now belonged. Black separatist doctrines were dropped, as the nation's community began to participate within the American political process. Finally, the equality of male and female members was reaffirmed, and women were given more responsible positions in the ministry of the community.

While the Nation continued to work for social and economic change, business ventures were cut back, and religious identity and mission were given greater priority. At the end of the 1970s, Wallace transferred organizational leadership to an elected council of six *imams*, or leaders, and focused on his own role as primarily a religious and spiritual leader.

In the mid 1980s, signaling his and the nation's new religious identity and mission, Wallace changed his name to Warith Deen Muhammad and renamed the community the American Muslim Mission, integrating it within the global mainstream Islamic community, and within the American Muslim community, remembering that community is made up of both immigrant and indigenous. Media coverage of the Black Muslim movement often focuses on Louis Farrakhan, who led a minority of Nation members in protest against Warith's reforms.

In recent years Farrakhan, who then became the leader of and retained the notion of the Nation of Islam with many of the trappings, leaders called ministers, et cetera, Farrakhan, himself, moved away from some of his earlier black separatist doctrines, or claimed to move away, along with his anti-Semitic statements, and has moved the nation closer to more orthodox Islamic practices, maintaining a desire for a closer identity with mainstream Islam.

The problems the growing Muslim community faces in America start with the fact that only a few decades ago, Muslims were mostly invisible in the West. Their visibility then emerged by association, often with the militant Nation of Islam, or with conflicts such as the Iranian Revolution, hijackings, and hostage taking in the Middle East and South Asia. Some saw these events as signs of an Islamic threat or a clash of civilization, Islam versus the West.

America's relationship with Muslims has been seen within a context of conflicting confrontation. Islam has been viewed as a foreign religion, distinct from the Judeo-Christian tradition, rather than the notion of children of Abraham. This reinforced the sense of "us-and-them." Subsequent attacks against America and Americans in Somalia, Saudi Arabia, and Africa in the late 1990s, and most recently in New York and Washington on September 11, have led many to regard Islam and Muslims with fear and distress.

They judge Islam as inherently violent and militant, religiously and culturally. This has an impact on the status and role of Muslims. Like many other immigrants of diverse religious and ethnic backgrounds, Muslims have been challenged to define their place in American and European society. Like Jews and Catholics before them, they struggle with assimilation, integration, multiculturalism, intermarriage, gender relations, worship, and education, a whole host of issues.

Some struggle with the English language, as new immigrants do, as well as with the tasks of holding on to their native or homeland cultures. How much of the old culture should one hold on to? Many face religious and ethnic discrimination in the workplace and in society.

Like Jewish law for Jews, as I noted earlier, Islamic law is central to a Muslim's life, covering religious requirements, dietary regulations, and family law. Thus, for Muslims living as minorities in America and Europe, the question is: How does one then bring this along and fit it into the new environment, into the new culture, into the new society?

Ironically, many of the non-Muslim minorities who preceded them and made it in America do not identify with Muslims, and fail to see the similarities between their own past and Muslims' current problems. It was disheartening to me at one point to see, after September 11, the owner of a gas station who, from his name looked like he was Italian-American, saying, "Send them all back to where they came from." I kept thinking that, being Italian-American, this guy is probably is second generation, and suddenly he acts as if he was always here, as if he were a native American Indian or had come over on the Mayflower, and had suddenly fallen into an "us-and-them" mentality.

Oftentimes, Muslims fall outside the circle, therefore, of American pluralism that is the comfortable circle, because they are not part of the Judeo-Christian or even, in a sense, the secular culture. However different previous religious and ethnic minorities, the vast majority were Judeo-Christian. Most regard Islam or have regarded Islam as foreign. Few have thought of it as an Abrahamic religion, as part of a Judeo-Christian-Islamic tradition.

In the absence of this knowledge and awareness, Islam is often seen through explosive headline events. And thus, as I've said before, the hatred and violence of a minority of religious extremists obscure the faith of the mainstream majority. In recent years a major issue for Muslims has been the Americanization of the Muslim experience, because *imams* coming from foreign countries are not always aware of or sensitive to the problems that American Muslims encounter.

The training of "native" *imams* or indigenous *imams* has been seriously undertaken since the 1980s. Legal councils addressing the issues of life in America have been founded to respond to questions raised by communities here in America, rather than always relying on scholars overseas to provide the norm, or to interpret the norm for today, although that continues to exist as well. Muslims do participate today, increasingly, in interfaith activities with Jews and Christians, at the local, national, and the international levels. A host of national and international organizations have been created to monitor and promote Muslim causes and Muslim interests, much as other ethnic and religious groups have done the same before them.

Despite problems, however, Muslims long regarded as "other" are now part of the fabric of our society, as neighbors, as coworkers, as citizens, and as co-believers. I often give the example that one point my wife had an accident. We needed to rush her to the hospital in Georgetown; fortunately it proved not to be super-serious, but the first physicians that we encountered at Georgetown Hospital were a Saudi resident, and an Iranian American. The first two physicians were from the Muslim world, indicating the beginning of that change. Muslims have increasingly become more integrated into the American political process, both as individuals and organizationally.

Now, the situation in Western Europe is somewhat the same, somewhat different. Estimates of the number of Muslims living in Western Europe range from 12 to 15 million, but I'll work with the 15-million figure. The ethnic diversity of Muslims in Europe represents most of the major ethnic groups of the Muslim world.

Remember that a key factor here, too, is that Europe was a major colonial power, and so many people from the colonies then have come to European countries after independence had been established. Most numerous are the Turks, Algerians, Moroccans, and Pakistanis. Because of this great diversity, despite a common religious bond, it is difficult to speak of the homogenous Muslim community in any individual country, let alone across Europe. Muslims may be found in significant numbers in most Western European countries. The largest Muslim populations are in France, approximately five million. Germany has approximately 3.2 million, and the United Kingdom, two million. There are also smaller communities established in such countries as Belgium, Spain, the Netherlands, Sweden, Denmark, Norway, and Austria.

Some estimates indicate that Muslims will outnumber non-Muslims in Europe by the year 2050. This is a contentious point, but it's out there. In many of the major European cities, however, given the low birth rates of an indigenous, non-Muslim population, Muslim schoolchildren will be in the majority within the next decade.

The major waves of Muslim migration to Europe came after World War II, due in large part to labor immigration and an vestigial colonial connection. When their countries achieved independence, some, many depending on what country and the conditions there, Muslims chose to emigrate. Professionals and skilled laborers from former European colonies in Africa, South Asia, and the Arab world sought a better life.

A significant difference between the European and the American experience could be seen in the 1960s and 1970s, and it affects the extent to which the majority of Muslims in Europe, in fact, come from an unskilled laborer background rather than a professional one. In the 1960s and 1970s, unskilled laborers flooded into a Europe, whose growing economies were in need of cheap labor and welcomed it.

From the 1970s onward, increasing numbers of Muslim students came to Europe, as they did to America, to study as well. While many returned home, others, for political, and very much economic reasons, chose to stay. France has the largest Muslim population in Europe, totaling five million; including more than 35 thousand converts, this group accounts for almost 10 percent of the population. Most Muslims in France come from North Africa.

Britain's two million Muslims come primarily from the Indian subcontinent, but increasingly from other parts of the world, from the Middle East, and from North Africa. By contrast, in Germany, where citizenship and the right to vote are more difficult to obtain, most Muslims in Britain, for example, come from British Commonwealth countries, and thus, were able to enjoy British citizenship and full participation in political life, as voters and as candidates. Indeed, some have been elected to political office, and are members of the House of Lords in Parliament.

The issue of assimilation has been particularly acute in France, where after a long battle, the government has taken a firm stand on full integration, rather than using the multicultural approaches of Britain and America. In a celebrated case, France outlawed the wearing of a headscarf, or *hijab*, by female students. Both France's Ministry of Education, and its teachers' unions were united in claiming that the *hijab* violated France's secular constitution and traditions. They made no such argument with regard to Jewish students wearing the *yamaka* or Christians wearing a Christian chains or pendants. After several years of bitter debate, the French Constitutional Council ruled in October 1996 that despite the education ministry's ban, students could not be expelled, as indeed they had been, for wearing headscarves if no proselytizing occurred.

At the heart of the French debate has been a tendency to see Islam as a foreign religion, placing it over and against its Judeo-Christian and very strong secular tradition, that is, France's secular tradition. While the government has insisted upon a process of acculturation that left little room for a multicultural approach, many Muslims have argued that they should be allowed to develop a distinct, French Muslim identity that blends established French principles and values with their Islamic faith and values.

However different their experiences may be, Muslims in Europe and America have common concerns about practicing their faith, retaining Islamic identity, and preserving family life and values. Specific concerns include taking time out from work to pray daily, to attend mosque on Friday, and to celebrate religious feasts, particularly the great *eids* or festivals, the Eid al-Adha and the Eid al-Fitr, to ensure the availability of *halal* food, that is, food that is carefully prepared or correctly slaughtered, analogous to kosher food within Judaism. The availability of *halal* food or foods in schools, in the military, or in prisons, is increasingly being addressed.

The same is true for those women who wish the right to wear a headscarf, or *hijab*. In addition, the issue of a beard has come up with regard to some police forces and in other kinds of positions in these societies. Some have requested segregated athletics classes, are concerned about coeducation, sex education, and secularism in the school. Some of these issues are not very different from those of many conservative Christians and Jews. I use the term "conservative" here in the broader sense.

Others have supported the development of Islamic schools as a way to address these issues. As Catholics and Jews in the past have developed religious schools, so it is with Islamic schools. Many, like a growing number of non-Muslim Americans, have turned to home schooling, teaching their children at home.

Living as a minority in a dominant culture that is often ignorant about Islam or even hostile to it, many Muslims experience at times a sense of marginalization, alienation, and powerlessness. That's not to say that for many, many there isn't the sense of fitting in, of being able to move forward, or of being accepted. For a minority, however, these problems exist.

Some Muslims are further marked as different by their manner of dress. As I said before, women who wear veils and men who wear beards, skullcaps, or turbans are sometimes singled out for harassment. Think of the Sikh cabdriver, a non-Muslim, who was murdered post-September 11; whoever did it apparently thought that somehow he was a Muslim, because he saw a turban. This has increasingly been the case since September 11, 2001. Muslim experiences in Europe and American have been affected significantly by the actions of these militants, as well as by domestic issues.

For example, in France, Jean-Marie Le Pen's right-wing National Front targeted Muslims as the reason for its growing unemployment problem, though they had been welcomed during the period of economic expansion as a cheap foreign labor force. They became a convenient scapegoat, charged with stealing French jobs. Le Pen advocated the forced expulsion of three million immigrants, as well as urging that priority be given to native French in jobs, housing, and welfare benefits.

At the same time, many North Africans from Morocco, Tunisia, and Algeria have entered France legally and illegally. The civil war in Algeria that we've talked about before caused many more Algerians to flee to France, swelling the ranks of its sizeable North African population.

After the Islamic Salvation Front swept the municipal and parliamentary elections in Algeria in the early 1990s, the military had stepped in, seized power, canceled the second round of parliamentary elections, and denied the FIS their parliamentary victory, charging that Islamics were out to use elections to highjack democracy. In the ensuing spiral of violence and counter-violence, which claimed more than 100,000 lives, moderates became radicalized; not all, but some. New extremist groups like the Armed Islamic Group rose up, as well as extremist groups within the military, called the eradicateurs.

Bombings in Paris have been attributed to Algeria's radical Armed Islamic Group, and post September 11 concerns about al-Qaeda and the arrests of suspected terrorists had contributed to questions about Islam's compatibility with French culture, its Judeo-Christian or secular life/world, and whether Muslims could be true and loyal citizens of France.

In America, the World Trade Center bombing of 1993, and the subsequent conviction of Shaykh Omar Abdur Rahman and others for plotting other attacks in major urban areas like New York, had raised serious questions about domestic terrorists. The attacks of September 11, revelations about the presence of many of the attackers in America—the fact that they lived in America and also visited and lived in Europe—the use of legislation—like the Secret Evidence and Patriot Acts, and its continued use—along with new measures being proposed for the Congress, and actions being proposed and taken by the FBI and other agencies—such as raising issues about the monitoring not of some mosques but all mosques, or the question whether all Muslims should be monitored, the issue of profiling, indiscriminate profiling—have raised substantial questions both within the Muslim community, but also among non-Muslims about the future of civil liberties for Muslim Americans. Similar questions have been raised within Europe.

As we look at the Muslim experience in the West, in America and Europe, we can make some observations. Despite problems, Muslims, long regarded as "other," are seen increasingly now as being part of the fabric of American and European societies by many in our societies. In America, they are increasingly regarded by most as neighbors, coworkers, citizens, and believers.

We still have major problems, however. Some of the e-mails and letters that I get from some people who claim to be Christians or say that they belong to Christian groups, or the statements made by people like Pat Robertson and Franklin Graham, statements that Islam is an evil religion, and the failure to distinguish between Muslim extremists and mainstream Islam create enormous problems for Muslims, and, I think, enormous problems within our own non-Muslim society.

Muslims have increasingly, though, become more integrated into the American political process, both as individuals and organizationally. A host of national and international organizations have been created to monitor and promote Muslim causes and interests. Among the more prominent are the American Muslim Council, the AMC; the Council for American Islamic Relations, CAIR; the Muslim Public Affairs Council, MPAC; and the Center for the Study of Islamic Democracy, CSID. We at the Center for Muslim-

Christian Understanding in Georgetown ran a major project called *Muslims in the American Public Square*, studying these issues in this role.

However, issues of coexistence continue. First and foremost, there is the need to distinguish between the faith and practice of the majority of Muslims, and the actions of a minority of religious extremists. Muslims and non-Muslims in the West face a common challenge of pluralism and tolerance. Too often in the past, tolerance has meant suffering the existence of others, while regarding them as inferior. Today, all are challenged to embrace a modern form of pluralism and tolerance, based upon mutual understanding and respect. To affirm the truth of one's own religion or worldview does not exclude the ability to acknowledge principles and values shared by others. Recognition of significant religious differences can still be accompanied by respect for the rights of others to hold different religious beliefs.

The Future of Islam
Lecture 12

> For Muslims, the 21st century will be a time not only for self-reflection, self-criticism, and internal reform, both religiously and politically, but also a time for educating, engaging in dialogue with, and finding new ways in which to work with and within the West and global civilization.

In the 21st century, Islam remains the fastest growing religion in many parts of the world and a significant factor in international politics. Thus, as we have seen, expanding our understanding of this global religion is important. Our past lessons have focused on the dynamism and creativity that exists in the history and development of Islam. Although a dynamic faith and source for the development of vast empires and rich civilizations in the past, in recent centuries, Islam seemed stagnant, passive, of marginal concern, and in decline, doomed to be overtaken by modernization and development. In the latter half of the 20th century, an Islamic resurgence, as we have seen, has challenged all expectations and predictions. However, this revitalization of Islam in Muslim life and society, which sometimes seems to be a radical revolution, is both a challenge and a threat to Muslim societies and the West.

Despite its emergence as the second and third largest religion in Europe and America in the late 20th century, for many majority non-Muslim populations, the religion of Islam is still regarded as foreign to their Judeo-Christian and secular backgrounds. In recent centuries, Islam has been associated with underdevelopment, authoritarian regimes, religious extremism, and terrorism. Ethnic and cultural differences and the Taliban, Osama bin Laden, and al-Qaeda have raised the specter of a particularly violence-prone religion.

A Judeo-Christian-Islamic tradition actually exists. As we have seen, despite significant differences, Islam shares many important similarities and linkages with the worldviews of Judaism and Christianity, from its belief in one God and acceptance of biblical prophets and revelation to moral responsibility and accountability. However, relations among the children of Abraham have, from the seventh century to the present, been characterized as much by competition and conflict as by coexistence and cooperation. The impact of European colonialism, secular paths of modernization and Westernization chosen by many Muslim states, and the nature of authoritarian regimes and their consequent hold on tradition have stifled the pace of Islamic reform.

Contemporary Islamic revivalism emerged in the latter half of the 20th century as a response in personal and public life to the failures of Muslim states and the excesses of Westernization. Religion became the dominant language and symbolism of political discourse in many Muslim societies. The impact of Islamic revivalism in its violent revolutionary forms, from Egypt and Iran to Afghanistan and Pakistan, has strengthened militant interpretations of Islam and proven a major obstacle to Islamic reform. Militants have not only imposed their brand of Islam but also silenced alternative voices.

The struggle for an Islamic reformation in the 21st century is a battle in which lines are increasingly drawn between conservatives, fundamentalists, and reformers. Muslim understanding and interpretation of Islam, along with attitudes toward change and modernization, reflect a broad religious diversity.

Secularists, in light of the chaos and carnage caused by militants and Muslim extremists, reemphasize the idea that the future development of Muslim societies is contingent on the separation of religion and politics. Many argue that after the death of Muhammad, religion, though used by rulers, was in fact, separate from the state. Conservatives and traditionalists reaffirm the continued relevance of Islamic faith and traditions amidst rapid, predominantly Western-oriented change, whose secularism and material excesses they reject.

Liberal reformers, an extension of early Islamic modernists, advocate an Islamic reformation, a fresh reinterpretation or reconstruction of religious thought, and the transformation of Muslim societies based on a selective synthesis of aspects of Islamic, Western, and other cultures.

Islamic activists, commonly referred to as fundamentalists or Islamists, maintain that reform is possible by returning to the sources of Islam, the Quran and Sunnah of the Prophet, to revitalize and reform Muslim societies. They are more critical of any form of dependency on or significant influence by the West. They are particularly sensitive to the penetration of Western culture and values. Islamic movements and organizations span the spectrum, from mainstream organizations that operate within society to extremists who rely on violence and terrorism.

As with other religions, central to contemporary Islamic reform are issues of authority: the authority of scripture, tradition, and the *ulama*. Tradition plays a major role in all the world's religions and is especially sacrosanct in Islam, a primary source of Islamic law and of Muslim faith and belief.

Although the authority of the Quran remains paramount for all observant Muslims, reminiscent of biblical criticism, some scholars (more non-Muslim than Muslim) have raised substantive questions about the historicity of the Quran, Muhammad, and much of early Islamic history. However, the majority of scholars, while affirming the need for ongoing reassessment of scholarship in light of new information, would continue to affirm the essential historicity of the Prophet and the text of the Quran.

Because Islam is the youngest of the Abrahamic faiths, its historical issues are far less complicated than historical questions regarding early biblical prophets, such as Moses, David, and Saul. Non-Muslim and some Muslim scholars have also questioned the authenticity of many prophetic traditions. Although some have questioned the authenticity of the bulk of the *hadith*, most have not. Wherever one stands on this issue, at the very least, the *hadith* are important because they present a glimpse of the early social history of the Muslim community: its issues, concerns, and responses.

The voices of change are not restricted to the *ulama*, the traditional standard bearers of Islam. Increasingly, reformers are lay men and women with modern education and Islamic orientation, who assert their competence to address issues as diverse as bioethics and medical ethics (birth control, abortion, cloning), gender, violence and religious extremism, democratization, and pluralism.

At the end of the 20th century, the future of Islam in the 21st century held the hope of a new millennium of globalization and opportunity. For many Muslims, there were dreams of peace in Palestine, increased democratization and greater freedom in Muslim countries, and the growth and empowerment of Muslims in America and Europe, where Islam had emerged as a major religious presence. However, the lives, expectations, and dreams of many were shattered with the September 11, 2001, terrorist attacks against the World Trade Center and the Pentagon. These attacks reinforced the voices of a clash of civilizations between peoples with diametrically opposed principles, values, and interests. Within a matter of hours, a handful of terrorists transformed the 21st century from a century of great expectations to a world dominated by an American-led war against global terrorism. It reinforced the image of Islam and Muslims as a religion and a people to be feared and fought.

Historically, religion has been and continues to be used and misused. Although religion is a source of transcendence, it has also had its dark side. Judaism, Christianity, and Islam, all of which teach peace, the value of human life, morals, and accountability, have been used to legitimate holy wars and the slaughter of innocent people, past and present.

Islam and Muslims continue to be plagued by questions in the wake of the impact of religious extremism in the Muslim world and the West. Among them are: Is Islam a particularly violence-prone religion, one that educates and motivates terrorists who attack the West? Religion has been used by diverse governments and groups, secular and religious, mainstream and extremist, to legitimate their policies or anti-Westernism. For example, more secular Arab socialist regimes in Egypt, Libya, Syria, and Iraq in the 1960s and early 1970s and Pakistan's Zulfikar Ali Bhutto used Islam to legitimate their versions of socialism and to criticize Western capitalism. In the 1980s, self-styled Islamic governments in Iran, Afghanistan, Pakistan, and Sudan also appealed to Islam. Although many Islamic political and social organizations have worked within the system, extremists have appealed to religion to legitimate their acts of violence and terror.

The extent to which extremists have hijacked Islam was signaled tragically by the September 11, 2001, attacks masterminded by Osama bin Laden and al-Qaeda. The hijacking of religion by extremists is not limited to Islam but is found in the history of most religious traditions. Extremists have used Christianity to justify slavery, the Klu Klux Clan, the decades-long war between Catholics and Protestants in Northern Ireland, Serbian genocide in Bosnia, and the destruction of abortion clinics. Jewish extremists have claimed religious legitimacy in the assassination of Israel's Prime Minister Rabin or slaughtering Muslims at Friday prayer in the Hebron mosque, built on a site sacred to Muslims and Jews.

Terrorists, including bin Laden and others, go beyond classical Islam's criteria for a just *jihad* and recognize no limits but their own, using any weapons or means. They reject Islamic law's regulations regarding the goals and means of a valid *jihad* (that violence must be proportional and that only the necessary amount of force should be used to repel the enemy), that innocent civilians should not be targeted, and that *jihad* must be declared by the ruler or head of state. Today, individuals and groups, religious and lay, seize the right to declare and legitimate unholy wars in the name of Islam.

On the other hand, many Islamic scholars and religious leaders across the Muslim world, such as the Islamic Research Council at al-Azhar University, regarded by many as the highest moral authority in Islam, have made strong, authoritative declarations against bin Laden's initiatives.

What does Islam have to do with the fact that many Muslim countries are authoritarian, limit free speech, and have weak civil societies? The sources of authoritarianism have less to do with religion and more to do with the legacy of European colonialism and the nature of most modern Muslim states. On achieving independence in the mid-20th century, governments were led by rulers who were kings, military or ex-military, who turned to authoritarian rule and security forces to remain in power and to ensure the stability and security of their governments. Many of these governments have had close ties with America and European powers, from Egypt, the Shah's Iran, and Saudi Arabia to Pakistan and Suharto's Indonesia.

Is Islam incompatible with democracy, pluralism, and human rights? In recent decades, Islam has been cited by a broad range of Muslims who believe it is incompatible with democracy, from the conservative monarchy of King Fahd of Saudi Arabia to radical extremist organizations. At the same time, reformers have reinterpreted traditional Islamic beliefs and concepts (*ijtihad, shura, ijma, maslaha*) to support modern notions of popular political participation, pluralism, and human rights.

Is Islam incompatible with capitalism? Historically, Islam is a religion that grew up in a commercially oriented society and has been intertwined with commerce and trade. The Prophet Muhammad was a successful businessman, as were many early Muslim leaders and scholars. The great mosques of Islam, such as the Umayyad Mosque in Damascus, have extensive bazaars adjacent, selling every imaginable product. Private property has always been recognized in Islam. Many of the *ulama* come from business- and land-owning families. In practice, capitalism has not been a religious stumbling block. Unfettered capitalism and conspicuous consumption that are insensitive to issues of social justice do present a problem for the religiously minded.

Is Islam incompatible with capitalism?

Many in the Muslim world, like many in other parts of the world, are concerned about the dark side of capitalism. Others fear a globalization that will lead to greater Western economic penetration in Muslim countries and the result, continued Muslim dependence on the West. Perhaps the best response to those asking if Islam and capitalism are compatible is to look at the lives of millions of Muslims who live and work in our midst in America and Europe who have come here to enjoy the freedom and opportunities offered by our economic and political systems.

Is Islam a particularly misogynist religion? One of the major criticisms of Islam and Muslim societies involves the status and treatment of women.

After September 11, 2001, the plight of women under the Taliban, as well as their sisters in Saudi Arabia, Pakistan, and elsewhere, resulted in a powerful critique of Islam and a clarion call for change. Increasingly, women are challenging the patriarchy of their Islamic tradition in mosques and societies, from Egypt and Iran to America, as they seek to carve out new paths in their quest for empowerment and liberation.

The debate over the *hijab* ("headscarf") rages from Muslim Turkey and Tunisia to secular France and America. Critics continue to see the *hijab* as a symbol of oppression and subservience to a male-dominated culture. Yet increasing numbers of women see the *hijab* as a symbol of freedom, as well as a bridge between their religious tradition and the realities of modern life. ■

Suggested Reading

Akbar Ahmed, *Islam Today.*

John L. Esposito, *Islam: The Straight Path*, chapters 5–6.

———, "Contemporary Islam: Reformation or Revolution?" *The Oxford History of Islam*, chapter 15.

Yvonne Y. Haddad and John L. Esposito, *Muslims on the Americanization Path?*

Questions to Consider

1. What are the differing ways in which Muslims have responded to modern reform?

2. Identify and discuss two major issues faced by contemporary Muslims

The Future of Islam
Lecture 12—Transcript

At the close of the 20th century, it appeared that the future of Islam could be one of new opportunities for peace, democracy, expanded human and women's rights, political and social economic empowerment, an increasing acceptance in Western societies of this notion of a Judeo-Christian-Islamic tradition, and of the presence of Muslims in our societies as fully equal partners, as it were.

September 11, and the hijacking of Islam by militant extremists, shattered the hopes and the dreams of many Muslims throughout the world as they found themselves facing a new millennium, one in which the old stereotypes of Islam, and of Muslims as a violent religion and people to be feared and fought, returned to center stage.

Thus, the 21st century for Muslims will be a time not only for self-reflection, self-criticism and internal reform, both religiously and politically, but also a time for educating, dialoguing with, and finding new ways in which to work with and within the West and global civilization.

In the 21st century, Islam remains the fastest growing religion in many parts of the world, and a significant factor in international politics. Thus, as we have seen, expanding our understanding of this global religion is important, if not critical. Our past lessons have focused on the dynamism and creativity that exists in the history and development of Islam.

Let's think about it for a second. Muhammad's life and message brought religious and social reform to Arabia, and in subsequent centuries Islam spread its faith, empire, and civilization. Islamic law, theology, and mysticism articulated the message and mission of Islam. Caliphs and sultans legitimated their rule and imperial designs in the name of religion. A world-class civilization emerged, encompassing philosophy, science, mathematics, medicine, art, and architecture.

A rich legacy from Islamic civilization was appropriated by the West, or re-appropriated, by a West that was emerging from a long dormant period of the Dark Ages. Although a dynamic faith in source for the development of vast regimes and rich civilizations in the past, in recent centuries Islam seemed stagnant, passive, of marginal concern, and in decline, doomed to be overtaken by modernization and development.

In the latter half of the 20th century, an Islamic resurgence, as we have seen, has challenged all expectations and predictions. However, this revitalization of Islam in Muslim life and society that sometimes seems to be a radical revolution, is both a challenge and sometimes a threat to Muslim societies and the West. Despite its emergence as the second- and third-largest religion in Europe and America in the late 20th century, for many majority non-Muslim populations, the religion of Islam is still regarded as foreign to their Judeo-Christian and secular backgrounds.

In recent centuries, as we've noted a number of times in this course, Islam has been associated with underdevelopment, authoritarian regimes, religious extremism, and terrorism, and that includes today. Ethnic and cultural differences, the Taliban, Osama bin Laden, and al-Qaeda have raised the specter of a particularly violence-prone religion and raised many issues about that.

Yet, the Judeo-Christian-Islamic tradition actually exists, as we have seen. Despite significant differences, Islam shares many important similarities and linkages with the worldviews of Judaism and Christianity, from its belief in one God, its absolute monotheism, and acceptance of biblical prophets and revelation, to moral responsibility and accountability.

However, relations among the children of Abraham have, from the seventh century to the present, been characterized both by competition and conflict as well as by coexistence and cooperation. The impact of European colonialism, secular paths of modernization and Westernization chosen by many Muslim states, the nature of authoritarian regimes, and consequent hold of tradition, have stifled at times the pace of Islamic reform.

Contemporary Islamic revivalism emerged in the latter half of the 20th century in many ways as a response in personal and public life to the failures of Muslim states and the excesses of Westernization, or at the least the perceived excesses of Westernization. Religion became the dominant language and symbolism of political discourse in many Muslim societies, and remains so today. The impact of Islamic revivalism in its violent revolutionary forms, from Egypt and Iran to Afghanistan and Pakistan, has strengthened militant interpretations of Islam, and proven a major obstacle to Islamic reform.

In some Muslim societies reformers are caught between a rock and a hard place, whether they are secular or religious reformers—between authoritarian regimes that will imprison and perhaps execute you, certainly torture you, on the one hand, and a minority of extremists that will kill you if they don't like what you're saying, on the other. Militants have not only imposed their brand of Islam, but have also silenced alternative voices. The struggle for the soul of Islam is being waged across the Muslim world and within Muslim societies.

While many Muslims wish to simply return to and re-appropriate an often romanticized and in some cases "re-imagined" past, others look to the past for inspiration in order to reinterpret, reform, and propel Islam further down the road in the 21st century. The struggle for an Islamic reformation in the 21st century is a battle in which lines are increasingly drawn between conservatives, fundamentalists, and reformers.

Muslim understanding and interpretation of Islam, attitudes towards change, and modernization reflect a broad religious diversity. We've talked about a few lessons ago, but at this juncture, as we look to the future of Islam, it's important to remember where we are today.

Secularists, in light of the chaos and carnage at times caused by militants and Muslim extremists, reemphasize that the future development of Muslim societies is contingent upon the separation of religion and politics. Many argue that after the death of Muhammad, religion, though used by rulers, was in fact separate from the state. Conservatives and traditionalists reaffirm the continued relevance of Islamic faith and traditions amidst rapid, predominantly Western-oriented change, whose secularism and material excesses they reject.

Islamic reformers, an extension of early Islamic modernists, advocate an Islamic reformation. They don't always use this language, but they advocate a broad process of reform, a fresh re-interpretation or reconstruction of religious thought, and the transformation of Muslim societies based upon a selective, and this word is important, a selective synthesis of aspects of Islamic and Western, as well as other cultures.

Islamic activists, those who apply political and social activism, commonly referred to as fundamentalists or Islamists, maintain that reform is possible by returning to the sources of Islam, the Quran and Sunnah, example of the Prophet, to revitalize and reform Muslim societies. They are more critical of any form of dependency on, or significant influence by the West; this is what they would see as Westernization. Some call it "West-toxification," or "Westermania."

They are particularly sensitive to the penetration of Western culture and values, which of course go to the heart of the people's identity and faith, any people's identity and faith. Islamic movements and organizations span the spectrum, from mainstream organizations, that operate within society as we've seen, to extremists who rely on violence and terrorism.

What we see today are challenges to the authority of the past, as with other religions central to contemporary Islamic reform are issues of authority, the authority of scripture, or more particularly how scripture and tradition are to be understood and interpreted, the authority of the *ulama*, the religious scholars.

Tradition plays a major role in all the world's religions and is especially sacrosanct in Islam, a primary source of Islamic law, and in Muslim faith and belief. Think about the role of the traditions of the Prophet, for example. While the authority of the Quran remains paramount for all observant Muslims, for all the Quran is the final and complete Word of God, although they may differ in terms of their interpretation. While it remains paramount, reminiscent of biblical criticism, not exactly the same, but reminiscent of it, some scholars, more non-Muslim than Muslim, have raised substantive questions about the historicity of the Quran, Muhammad, and much of early Islamic history. However, the majority of scholars, while affirming the need for ongoing reassessment of scholarship in light of new information, would continue to affirm the essential historicity of the Prophet in the text of the Quran. Because Islam is the youngest of the Abrahamic faiths in terms of the establishment of the community, its historical issues are far less complicated than historical questions regarding, for example, early biblical prophets like Moses, David, and Saul.

Non-Muslim and some Muslim scholars have also questioned the authenticity of many prophetic traditions. While some have questioned the authenticity of the bulk of the *hadith*, most have not. Wherever one stands on this issue, at the very least the *hadith* are important, for they represent a glimpse of the early social history of the Muslim community, its issues, concerns, and responses.

The voices of change are not restricted to the *ulama*, the traditional standard bearers of Islam. Increasingly, reformers are modernly educated and Islamically-oriented lay men and women, who assert their competence to address issues as diverse as bioethics and medical ethics, birth control, abortion, cloning, gender relations, violence and religious extremism, democratization, and pluralism.

At the end of the 20th century, the future of Islam in the 21st century held the hope of a new millennium of globalization and opportunity. For many Muslims, certainly as a result of the early part of the 1990s, the Oslo Accords, there were dreams of peace in Palestine, increased democratization, and greater freedom in Muslim countries, as well as the growth and empowerment of Muslims in America and Europe, where Islam had emerged as a major religious presence.

However, the lives, expectations, and dreams of many were shattered with the September 11 terrorist attacks against the World Trade Center and the Pentagon. I in fact at that time was writing a book called *The Future Of Islam*, which I had to put on the backburner and instead address the issues of September 11 in a book called *Unholy War: Terror In The Name Of Islam,* and then one called *What Everyone Needs To Know About Islam.* It's only now, and even tentatively, that I've returned to dealing with the subject of the future of Islam.

September 11 reinforced the voices of a clash of civilizations between peoples, so some said, who were diametrically opposed, and who had diametrically opposed principles, values, and interests.

How many of us remember after September 11, when people said "Why did this happen?" The answer was "I don't know," or "It's just a clash, they're completely different than we are." "They don't like our democracy, our freedoms, our secularism, or our capitalism." Within a matter of hours, a handful of terrorists transformed the 21st century from a century of great expectations to a world dominated by an American-led war against global terrorism. It reinforced the image of Islam and Muslims as a religion and a people to be feared and fought.

Historically, religion has been and continues to be used and misused or abused. This is true for all religions. While religion is a source of transcendence, with a transcending God, and a means of people being able to transcend themselves, historically it has also had its dark side, and we've looked at part of that dark side.

Religions like Judaism, Christianity, and Islam that teach peace, the value of human life, and moral accountability and responsibility have been used to legitimate, as we've seen in the past and in recent times, holy wars, crusades, and the slaughter of innocent people, whether we're talking about times past or more recently.

Islam and Muslims continue to be plagued by questions in the wake of the impact of religious extremism, in the Muslim world and the West. Among them are: "Is Islam a particular violence-prone religion, one that educates and motivates terrorists to attack the West?" Religion has been used by diverse governments and groups—secular and religious, mainstream and extremist—to legitimate their policies and/or anti-Westernism.

For example, more secular Arab socialist regimes of Egypt, Libya, Syria, and Iraq in the 1960s and early 1970s, and Pakistan's Zulfikar Ali Bhutto, the father of Benazir Bhutto, used Islam to legitimate their socialisms and to criticize Western capitalism, as well as to often criticize the conservative monarchies of the gulf.

In the 1980s self-styled Islamic governments in Iran, Afghanistan, Pakistan, and Sudan also appealed to Islam. Now while many Islamic political and social organizations have worked, as we've seen within the political and social system, extremists have also appealed to religion to legitimate their acts of violence and terror, to hijack their religion. For surely, whether they be Jews, Christians, or Muslims, when they use their faith to engage in clear acts of terrorism, they're hijacking the heartland of their religious tradition.

The extent to which extremists have hijacked Islam was signaled tragically by September 11, 2001, by the attacks masterminded by Osama bin Laden and al-Qaeda. The hijacking of religion by extremists is not limited to Islam, but as we've seen earlier in this course, it is found in the history of most religious traditions. Extremists have used Christianity to justify slavery, the Ku Klux Klan, the decades-long war between Catholics and Protestants in Northern Ireland, Serbian genocide in Bosnia, and the blowing up of abortion clinics.

Jewish extremists have claimed religious legitimacy in the assassination of Israel's Prime Minister Rabin, and the slaughtering of Muslims at Friday prayer in the Hebron mosques in the 1990s, a mosque built on a site sacred to Muslims and Jews.

Terrorists like bin Laden and others go beyond classical Islam's criteria for a just *jihad*, and recognize no limits but their own. Employing any weapons or means, they reject Islamic law's regulations regarding the goals and means of a valid *jihad*—that violence must be proportional: that only the necessary amount of force should be used to repel the enemy: that innocent civilians, non-combatants, should not be targeted: and that *jihad* must be declared by the ruler or head of state, by a legitimate authority. Instead, someone like Osama bin Laden gives his own *fatwa*, even though formally he's not a *mufti*, with his own interpretation.

Today, individuals and groups, religious and lay, seize the right to declare and legitimate unholy wars in the name of Islam. On the other hand, many Islamic scholars and religious leaders across the Muslim world, such as the Islamic Research Council at al-Azhar University in Cairo, regarded by many as the highest moral authority in Islam, have made strong authoritative declarations against bin Laden's initiatives, such as the following: "Islam provides clear rules and ethical norms that forbid the killing of non-combatants, as well as women, children, and the elderly, and also forbids the pursuit of the enemy in defeat, the execution of those who surrender, the infliction of harm on prisoners of war, and the destruction of property that is not being used in the hostilities."

What does Islam have to do with the fact that many Muslim countries are authoritarian, limit free speech, and have weak civil societies? The sources of authoritarianism have less to do with religion and more to do with the legacy of European colonialism and the nature of most modern Muslim states.

Parenthetically, let's recall that while we think of Judaism and Christianity as accepting modern democracy, and representing or reinforcing modern democracies today, in pre-modern times they reinforced and supported divine right kingdoms and feudal systems.

Upon achieving independence in the mid-20th century, Muslim governments were led by rulers who were kings, military or ex-military, who turned to authoritarian rule and security forces to remain in power, not elections, and to assure the stability and security of their own governments. Many of these governments have had close ties with American and European powers, from Egypt, the Shahs of Iran, Saudi Arabia, and Pakistan, to Suharto's Indonesia.

Is Islam incompatible with democracy, pluralism, and human rights? Islam in recent decades has been cited by a broad range of Muslims who believe that it's incompatible with democracy, from the conservative monarchy of King Fahd of Saudi Arabia, who believes that it is not in line with Islamic traditions, to radical extremist organizations.

At the same time, reformers have reinterpreted traditional Islamic beliefs and concepts: *ijtihad*, the right to reinterpret; *shura*, consultation; *ijma*, consensus, and *maslaha*, the public's general welfare, to support modern notions of popular political participation, pluralism, and human rights.

Is Islam incompatible with capitalism? Historically Islam is a religion that grew up in a commercially-oriented society, and has been intertwined with commerce and trade. The Prophet Muhammad, remember, was a successful businessman, as were many early Muslim leaders and scholars. The great mosques of Islam, such as Ummayad Mosque in Damascus, have extensive bazaars adjacent, selling every imaginable product. Among the major missionaries were the early traders and merchants who brought Islam to many parts of the world. Private property has always been recognized in Islam.

Many of the *ulama*, the religious scholars, have been or come from business and landowning families, or marry into such families. In practice, capitalism has not been a religious stumbling block, although unfettered capitalism, capitalism without limits, and conspicuous consumption and that is insensitive to issues of social justice, do present a problem for religiously-minded Muslims, as it does for religiously-minded Jews, Christians, and others.

Many in the Muslim world, like many in other parts of the world, are concerned about the dark side of capitalism and the possible abuses of the free market economy, including the seeming lack of concern for the poorer and weaker sectors of society. Others fear a globalization that will lead to greater Western economic penetration in Muslim countries and the result, continued Muslim dependence on the West, and particularly a globalization that will lead through international communications, to a greater cultural penetration of the West. Even the French are concerned about globalization and communications, and its impact on French culture.

Perhaps the best response to those asking if Islam and capitalism are compatible is to look at the lives of hundreds of millions of Muslims, who live and work in our midst in America, and Europe, but also those in the Muslim world. Look at those in particular who've come to Europe and America. Why have they done so? To enjoy the freedom and opportunities offered by our economic and political system, freedoms that they would want for their original countries.

Is Islam a particularly misogynist religion? One of the major criticisms of Islam and Muslim societies involves the status and treatment of women, and we've talked about that a number of times. After September 11, the plight of women under the Taliban as well as their sisters in a number of other Muslim countries, some of those cited Saudi Arabia or Pakistan and elsewhere, have resulted in a powerful critique of Islam, and a clarion call for change from some.

Muslims in the 21st century do grapple with gender issues, often torn between advocates of sexual segregation and reformers who seek to redefine the roles of men and women. Increasingly, women are challenging the patriarchy of their Islamic tradition in mosques and societies, from Egypt and Iran to America, as they seek to carve out new paths in their quest for empowerment and liberation. As we've seen the debate over the *hijab*, the headscarf, rages on, not only in France but in Muslim Turkey, where women who go to university have not been able to wear a headscarf; they've been turned away. The same has happened at medical schools.

They are also not allowed to enter the parliament; women parliamentarians had been denied the right to enter the parliament and be sworn in if they wear a headscarf. Thus, that debate rages from Muslim Turkey and Tunisia, to secular France and America. Critics continue to see the *hijab* as a symbol of oppression, of subservience to a male-dominated culture. Yet increasing numbers of women see the *hijab* as a symbol of freedom, as well as a bridge between their religious tradition and the realities of modern life; thus, for example, many young women in America and Europe whose parents may not have worn the *hijab* are taking the *hijab*, and we see them in our major universities, in our schools, in our societies.

A primary area of substantial change is the status of Muslim minorities. There are more Muslim minority communities globally than at any time in history. In contrast to the past, most are permanent communities, whose members have settled in other countries and will not be returning to their countries of birth. Substantial numbers of Muslims today live in a secular Europe and America, where they seek to preserve their faith and identity while accommodating life in Western societies. As with religious and ethnic groups before them, the Jews, the Catholics, and a variety of ethnic groups, they have had to struggle with a cross-section of issues, among them the question of integration or assimilation, the extent to which their religion is compatible with living in a secular society, how to deal with and resolve conflicts between their Islamic and Western values, and how to raise the next generation to be modern Americans while still retaining their religious, and indeed, their cultural heritage.

Post-September 11 has made the processes of adaptation and change more difficult, as Muslims face those who charge that Islam is incompatible with, or a threat to, Western societies. It's compounded by legislation and policies that threaten the civil liberties of Muslims in America and in Europe.

The agenda facing Islam in the 21st century is daunting. Unlike Judaism and Christianity, which had centuries to undergo their own processes of modern reform, Muslim societies have had a far more telescoped, narrower window, narrower timeframe, to do so. And they do so while responding not only to the realities within their societies and communities, but also to a Western-dominated world, an era of globalization. This isn't like early Islam, when Muslims were in charge and expanding, and therefore could borrow or not borrow. They were in charge of the process of change; they were the masters.

The process of Islamic reform, as reform in Christianity and Judaism is at times, is a religious battlefield. The Christian reformation included bitter and divisive theological debates and religious wars between Catholics and Lutherans, et cetera.

The theological and legal differences are reflected in the many Christian denominations. They're also reflected in Judaism, in the range of orientations, including orthodox, conservative, reform and reconstructionist Jews.

Islam today is at a crossroads. Mainstream Muslims, from conservative, to fundamentalist, to liberal reformers argue and debate. Radical fundamentalists or extremists often engage in a holy war that pits Muslim against Muslim, as well as Muslim against non-Muslim.

Despite setbacks for more than 14 centuries, Islam has proven vibrant and dynamic, growing spectacularly as a faith and empire. From the time of the Prophet Muhammad, Islam's message and way of life has attracted followers of every race and culture, adapting to diverse cultures from Africa to Asia, from Europe to America. Unity of faith has been accompanied by a diversity of expressions.

In the 21st century, Islam, the second largest and among the fastest-growing of the world's religions faces yet another watershed, as believers struggle to implement their faith and practice within the realities of contemporary life. Given the realities of recent history, and the nature of many Muslim societies, the challenges are many. The struggle for reform will be religious, intellectual, spiritual, and moral, but it must be a more rapid and widespread program of Islamic renewal, that not only builds on past reformers, but also more forcefully follows the lead of enlightened religious leaders and intellectuals. Today, it must more forcefully and effectively engage in wide-ranging processes of reinterpretation and reform.

Like those who have gone before, today's Muslims are guided by their belief in one true God, the Quran, and the example of the Prophet Muhammad, as they too seek to follow the straight path, the way of God to whom belongs all that is in the heavens and all that is in the earth, as the Quran in chapter 42, verses 52 to 53 states.

Timeline

c. 570 .... Birth of Muhammad.

610 .... Muhammad receives call to prophethood with first revelation of the Quran.

620 .... Muhammad's night journey to Jerusalem.

622 .... *Hijra* of Muhammad and early Muslim community to Medina from Mecca; first year of the Muslim lunar calendar.

624 .... Battle of Badr, in which Muslims are outnumbered but victorious over Meccans.

627 .... Battle of the Trench; Muhammad and Muslims victorious over Meccans.

632 .... Death of Muhammad.

632–661 .... Reign of four Rightly-Guided Caliphs, formative period for Sunnis.

638 .... Muslims conquer Jerusalem.

661–750 .... Umayyad caliphate.

680 .... Martyrdom of Husayn and followers in Karbala; beginning of Shii paradigm of protest, suffering, and injustice.

8th–9th centuries .... Major Sunni law schools founded.

750–1258	Abbasid caliphate, high point of Islamic civilization, patronage of art and culture, development of Islamic law, and rising trade, agriculture, industry, and commerce.
874	Twelfth Shii *imam* disappears/goes into occultation, ending direct rule of Shii *imams.*
1058–1111	Abu Hamid al-Ghazali, synthesizer of Islamic law, theology, and mysticism.
1095–1453	Crusades.
1099	Christian Crusaders capture Jerusalem and establish Latin Kingdom.
12th century	Rise of Sufi orders.
1187	Saladin recovers Jerusalem for Muslims.
1281–1924	Ottoman Empire.
1501–1722	Safavid Empire (Iran).
1526–1857	Mughal Empire (South Asia).
18th century	Major period of Islamic revivalism and reform, in which Islam is posited as a means for socio-moral reconstruction of society.
1703–1792	Muhammad Ibn Abd al-Wahhab, founder of Wahhabi movement.

19th century .... Islamic modernism develops in response to European imperial expansion in Muslim world.

1817–1898 .... Sayyid Ahmad Khan, Indian religious and educational reformer.

1838–1897 .... Jamal al-Din al-Afghani, father of Islamic modernism.

1848–1885 .... Muhammad Ahmad, Mahdi of Sudan and founder of Islamic state.

1849–1905 .... Muhammad Abduh, co-founder of Salafiyyah movement and major architect of Islamic modernism.

1865–1935 .... Rashid Rida, cofounder of Salafiyyah movement in Egypt and Islamic modernist movements.

1877–1938 .... Muhammad Iqbal, ideologue for foundation of Pakistan as homeland for Indian Muslims.

1897–1975 .... Elijah Muhammad, leader of the Nation of Islam in the United States.

1903–1979 .... Mawlana Mawdudi, founder of Jamaat-i Islami in Pakistan.

1906–1949 .... Hasan al-Banna, founder of Muslim Brotherhood in Egypt.

1906–1966...................................... Sayyid Qutb, radical and militant
Islamic scholar and activist calling for
violence as a means of restoring and
implementing Islam in the
public sphere.

1928... Muslim Brotherhood founded in Egypt.

1941... Jamaat-i Islami founded in Pakistan.

1947... Foundation of Pakistan as homeland
for Muslims.

1956... Pakistan becomes Islamic republic.

1967... Arab-Israeli war sparks Islamic revival.

1973... Second Arab-Israeli war—"Operation
Badr"—results in recovery of some
Egyptian territory; first Arab oil
embargo against West places Arabs as
world economic power.

1978–1979...................................... Iranian Revolution and foundation
of Islamic Republic of Iran under the
leadership of Ayatollah Khomeini;
seizure of the Grand Mosque in Mecca
by Islamic militants.

1981... Assassination of Egyptian president
Anwar al-Sadat by Muslim extremists.

1988... Benazir Bhutto elected prime minister
of Pakistan, making her the first elected
female Muslim head of state.

1990.. Islamic Salvation Front (FIS) wins
major victory in Algerian elections
against the secular FLN.

1992.. After FIS victory in parliamentary
elections, the military stages a coup
to prevent FIS from coming to power,
sparking a 10-year civil war in which
100,000 die.

1994.. Baruch Goldstein (Jewish settler) kills
29 Muslim worshippers at the Mosque
of the Patriarch in Hebron, sparking
Palestinian-Israeli and Jewish-Muslim
violence and HAMAS suicide bomber
attacks against Jewish civilians in
Israel; Taliban fundamentalists gain
power in Afghanistan.

1997.. Mohammad Khatami elected president
of Iran on a platform to bring greater
reforms (political participation, rule of
law, civil society, and human rights) to
Iranian society.

2000.. Warith Deen Muhammad, head of
American Muslim Mission, offers
prayer at opening of U.S. Congress.

2001.. U.S. Postal Service issues stamp
commemorating Muslim holidays of
Id al-Fitr and Id al-Adha, representing
Islam's place as part of the American
landscape; attacks against the World
Trade Center and Pentagon by terrorists
in the name of Islam.

Glossary

Abrahamic tradition: Belief in Abraham as the first monotheist and common religious ancestor of Muslims, Christians, and Jews.

Allah: God.

caliph: Sunni political successor to Muhammad.

Eid al-Adha: "Feast of the Sacrifice," major Muslim holiday. Occurs toward the end of the *hajj*.

Eid al-Fitr: "Feast of the Breaking of the Fast," major Muslim holiday. Occurs at the end of the month of Ramadan.

fatwa: Legal opinion given by an expert in Islamic law.

fiqh: Islamic jurisprudence.

Five Pillars: Five requirements of faith for all Muslims, which are making the declaration of faith, engaging in prayer five times daily, tithing, fasting during the month of Ramadan, and making the pilgrimage to Mecca at least once in a lifetime.

hadith: Accounts of the sayings and deeds of Muhammad, considered, along with the Quran, to be divine and authoritative revelation.

hajj: Pilgrimage to Mecca to be made once in a lifetime by every Muslim.

halal: Food prepared in accordance with Islamic law.

hijab: Headscarf or veil worn by Muslim women.

hudud: Literally, "limits". Refers to crimes specified by the Quran and carrying harsh penalties.

ijma: Consensus or agreement of the community, a source of Islamic law.

ijtihad: Independent reasoning.

imam: Shii political and religious successor to Muhammad.

Islam: "Submission" to God's will.

jihad: "Struggle" or "exertion." Can refer to internal struggle of Muslims to live a moral life or external struggle for social justice or defense of Muslim community.

Kaaba: Cube-shaped structure that is the object of the *hajj* pilgrimage to Mecca.

minaret: Tower of a mosque from which the call to prayer is issued.

mosque: Muslim house of worship.

muezzin: Person issuing the call to prayer.

mufti: Person issuing a legal opinion (*fatwa*).

mujtahid: Person carrying out independent interpretation of Islamic law (*ijtihad*).

Muslim: One who submits to God, or follows Islam.

qiyas: Juristic reasoning by analogy, a source of Islamic law.

Quran: Divine revelation of Islam.

Ramadan: Month of fasting for Muslims.

salat: Prayer or worship five times a day.

shahadah: Declaration or witnessing that "There is no god but the God and Muhammad is His Messenger."

Shariah: Islamic law.

Shii: "Partisan"; one who believes that succession to leadership of the Muslim community should be hereditary.

Sufi: Muslim mystic.

Sunnah: Example of Muhammad, largely recorded in the *hadith*.

Sunni: "One adhering to the Sunnah"; one who believes that leadership of the Muslim community should be based on merit.

taqlid: Imitation of the past, particularly with respect to the interpretation of Islamic law.

tawhid: Unity of God, absolute monotheism.

ulama: Religious scholars.

ummah: Transnational Muslim community.

zakat: Tithing, which includes a percentage of a person's total wealth (not just income) given for the poor.

Biographical Notes

Ali ibn Abu Talib (r. 656–660): Cousin and son-in-law of Muhammad, husband of Fatima, and father of Hasan and Husayn. Fourth caliph of Sunni Islam and the first *imam* of Shii tradition. Ali was also the first male convert to Islam. His rule as caliph was marked by political crisis and civil strife, ending with his assassination.

Aisha: Muhammad's multitalented and influential wife, daughter of the first Sunni caliph, Abu Bakr. Recognized as an important source of knowledge of history, *hadith*, medicine, and rhetoric. Led her troops against those of Ali in the first inter-Muslim conflict.

Muhammad Abduh (1849–1905): Important Egyptian Islamic scholar, theologian, jurist, journalist, reformer, and activist who is widely considered to be the architect of Islamic modernism. Taught that Islam and modernity are compatible and that revelation and reason, correctly perceived, are inherently harmonious. Used his position as Grand Mufti to implement educational, legal, and social reforms. The bitter opposition he experienced from academic and legal foes reflected the range of his influence and vision for a renewed Islam. His ideas opened up a fresh viewpoint and a reformist movement but left many issues unresolved.

Jamal al-Din al-Afghani (1838–1897): "Father" of 19th-century Islamic modernism. Influential writer and political activist who emphasized the need for Muslim solidarity in the face of Western Christian imperialism. Taught the compatibility of Islam and science and encouraged the pursuit of scientific and technical education, self-improvement, and reform. Reinterpreting Islam in a modernist, pragmatic direction, Afghani was one of first Muslim activists to promote Islam as a primarily political program.

Abu Bakr (r. 632–634): First Sunni caliph (successor) and father of Muhammad's wife Aisha. Sunnis believe that he was elected to the caliphate by leaders of the early Muslim community after Muhammad's death. Abu Bakr unified Arabia by asserting his legitimacy on the basis of consultation.

Hasan al-Banna (1906–1949): Founder of Muslim Brotherhood in Egypt as a movement for political and religious activism. Taught that Islam is a comprehensive way of life. Sought the establishment of an Islamic state in which the Quran would serve as the constitution and Islamic law would be implemented. Advocated major principles of Islamic social justice that should be carried out by state institutions. Actively involved in a political underground that overthrew the Egyptian monarchy. Al-Banna was assassinated by Egyptian secret police in 1949 because of his opposition to the government.

Fatimah: The daughter and only child of Muhammad to survive into adulthood, Fatimah was the wife of Ali and mother of Hasan and Husayn. Shiis trace the lineage of the *imams* through her. Popularly believed to be the perfect example of Muslim womanhood and motherhood. Shiis further believe that she was sinless and immaculate. Known for her compassion for people and dedication to Islam. Comparable to the Christian Virgin Mary as a woman of sorrow.

Hussein (626–680): Grandson of Muhammad, son of Ali and Fatima, and third Shii *imam*. His quest to claim his position as *imam* led to his martyrdom, along with that of many of his followers, in military conflict with the Umayyad caliph, Yazid. Husayn's martyrdom established the Shii paradigm of suffering and oppression of their righteous community. Martyrdom has been interpreted in the contemporary era as a religious obligation of political resistance, revolution, and struggle for social justice. Husayn's martyrdom is ritually reenacted annually by Shiis during the Ashura observance, much like the crucifixion of Jesus in the Christian tradition.

Al-Ghazali, Abu Hamid (1058–1111): Major Muslim scholar, theologian, and philosopher. Popularly considered one of the great revivers of Islam. Al Ghazali synthesized theology, Islamic law, and mysticism by emphasizing Islam's rationalism, as tempered by direct personal religious experience and interior devotion. He secured a place for Sufism within Islamic orthodoxy while rejecting an overly rationalist approach to Islamic law and theology.

Muhammad Ibn Abd al-Wahhab (1703–1792): Founder and ideologue of the Wahhabi movement. His strict adherence to *tawhid* ("absolute monotheism") was symbolized by his support for the destruction of objects of popular veneration, including tombs and monuments. The Wahhabis became famous for their suppression of Sufism and opposition to Shiism. Some believe Wahhabism's influence is apparent today in the Taliban's destruction of Buddhist statues in Afghanistan.

Muhammad Ahmad (1848–1885): Self-proclaimed Mahdi and founder of an Islamic state in Sudan who claimed to be God's divinely appointed representative. An opponent of alcohol, gambling, prostitution, and music as un-Islamic, foreign (Ottoman Egyptian) practices that had corrupted Sudanese society, he called for holy war against other Muslims who rejected his teachings.

Muhammad Iqbal (1877–1938): Ideologue for the foundation of Pakistan as a homeland for Indian Muslims, as well as a religious and political leader and writer, professor, poet, and lawyer. Iqbal emphasized themes of the necessity of Muslim self-determination, national liberation of Muslims from India and Hindu rule, and Muslim nationalism. He taught the compatibility of Islam and science and encouraged Muslims to embrace and learn modern technology and science in order to improve their lives and development. Iqbal called for the reconstruction of religious thought in Islam.

Khadija: First and only wife of Muhammad for the 24 years of their marriage, which ended with her death. She met Muhammad when she hired him to oversee her caravan trade. Khadija was the first convert to Islam and Muhammad's major supporter and encourager.

Mawlana Mawdudi (1903–1979): Ideologue and founder of Pakistani Jamaat-i Islami. A revivalist who called for purification and restoration of Islam to rejuvenate Muslim culture and society, Mawdudi campaigned for an Islamic state in Pakistan to establish Islamic society and order from the top down, although he discouraged the use of violence. He taught that education was a keystone of Islamic activism and that social activism was a necessary component of the practice of Islam.

Muhammad (c. 570–632): Prophet of Islam who received the revelation of the Quran. Muhammad served as the religio-political leader, social activist and reformer, judge, arbiter, lawgiver, and military leader of the early Muslim community. Muslims believe that he represents the perfect example of humanity because of his perfect adherence to the teachings of the Quran in both words and deeds. Records of his sayings and actions (*hadith*) are a source of scripture for Muslims.

Saladin: Leader of Muslim forces during the Crusades and one of the greatest Muslim military heroes, Saladin was responsible for the recovery of Jerusalem for Muslim rule. Renowned for his merciful treatment of prisoners, faithfulness to his word, and the fact that he allowed prisoners to practice their own religion, he was often contrasted by Muslims with the Christian hero Richard the Lionheart, who accepted the surrender of Acre, promising amnesty to its inhabitants but then slaughtering all, including women and children.

Umar ibn al-Khattab (r. 634–44 C.E.): Second Sunni caliph and companion of Muhammad. A great military leader who oversaw the major expansion of the Islamic Empire, he established many of the fundamental institutions of the classical Islamic state. Al-Khattab instituted practices of appointing an "election committee" to select his successor and allowing conquered people to continue to practice their own religions, as long as they recognized Muslim hegemony and paid a poll tax.

Uthman (r. 644–656): Third Sunni caliph and companion of Muhammad. Collection and preservation of the Quran as it is known today was completed under his reign. Uthman was believed to be personally pious but lacked the character to prevent his relatives from amassing political power. Discontent with his reign ended in his murder by opponents.

Bibliography

Akbar Ahmed, *Islam Today*, 2nd ed. (London: Tauris, 2002). A useful introduction to contemporary Islam by a prominent Muslim anthropologist, emphasizing history, culture, and society.

Leila Ahmed, *Women and Gender in Islam* (New Haven: Yale University Press, 1993). A comprehensive and well-written historical introduction to women in Islam from the origins of the Muslim community to the present.

Karen Armstrong, *Muhammad: A Biography of the Prophet* (San Francisco: Harper, 1993). An engaging biography and introduction to the Prophet Muhammad and his role in the development of Islam and the Muslim community.

Jonathan Bloom and Sheila Blair, *Islam: A Thousand Years of Faith and Power* (New York: TV Books, 2000). A superb introduction to the first millennium of Islam, complements their video, "The Empire of Islam"

John L. Esposito, *Islam: The Straight Path*, 3rd ed. (New York: Oxford University Press, 1998). An introduction to the religion of Islam and its historical development from its origins to the present.

———, ed., *The Oxford Dictionary of Islam* (New York: Oxford University Press, 2003). Focusing on the modern period, the more than 2000 entries in this dictionary focus on the religion of Islam and its impact on history, politics, and society.

———, ed., *The Oxford History of Islam* (New York: Oxford University Press, 1999). A comprehensive and richly illustrated introduction to Islamic history (faith, law, science, art, and philosophy).

———, *The Islamic Threat: Myth or Reality?* (New York: Oxford University Press, 1999). A study of historical encounters between Islam and the West

that focuses on contemporary Muslim politics and the future of Muslim-Christian relations.

————, *Unholy War: Terror in the Name of Islam* (New York: Oxford University Press, 2002). A response to the World Trade Center and Pentagon attacks of September 11, 2001, that analyzes the history and sources of religious extremism, the rise of Osama bin Laden and al-Qaeda, and their relationship to mainstream Islam.

————, *What Everyone Needs to Know about Islam* (New York: Oxford University Press, 2002). A brief introduction to Islam in a question-answer format that focuses on questions and issues raised after September 11, 2001.

————, *World Religions Today*, "The Many Faces of the Muslim Experience" (New York: Oxford University Press, 2001). An introduction to the world's major religions that is unique in its approach. To demonstrate the status and vitality of these religious traditions today, the treatment of each religion begins with the present, then connects current realities to past history and tradition.

Yvonne Y. Haddad and John L. Esposito, *Islam, Gender and Social Change* (New York: Oxford University Press, 1998). A collection of case studies from across the Muslim world that reveal the diverse roles of Islam in gender relations and social change.

————, *Muslims on the Americanization Path?* (New York: Oxford University Press, 2000). Case studies of the many challenges Muslims in America and Canada face, with substantial coverage of the origins and development of African American Islam.

Shireen Hunter, *Islam, Europe's Second Religion* (Westport, CT: Praeger, 2002). An excellent collection of studies on Islam in Europe with country case studies.

Martin Lings, *What Is Sufism?* (Cambridge, UK: Islamic Texts Society, 1999). An introduction to Sufism, its doctrine, and method; clear, sensitive, and insightful.

Seyyed Hossein Nasr, *The Heart of Islam* (San Francisco: Harper San Francisco, 2002). A major scholar, reflecting on the essence of Islam, presents the core spiritual and social values of Islam. Relating them to their counterparts in the Jewish and Christian traditions, he discusses the common ground of the Abrahamic faiths.

Fazlur Rahman, *Islam and Modernity* (Chicago: University of Chicago Press, 1982). A prominent 20th-century Muslim scholar's analysis of the religious and intellectual challenges facing the Muslim community.

Jane Smith, *Islam in America* (New York: Columbia University Press, 1999). A clear, straightforward introduction to the diversity of the Muslim-American experience.

John O. Voll, *Islam: Continuity and Change in the Muslim World* (Syracuse, NY: Syracuse University Press, 1994). A masterful study of the role of Islam in modern history, distinctive for its comprehensive geographic coverage.

Amina Wadud, *Quran and Woman* (New York: Oxford University Press, 1999). A fine study of women in the Quran, written from a woman's perspective, that focuses on the issue of gender equality in the Quran.

John Alden Williams, *The Word of Islam* (Austin, TX: University of Texas Press, 1994). A wide-ranging anthology of texts from the Quran, collections of *hadith*, legal manuals, and other sources.

Michael Wolfe, *Hadj: An American's Pilgrimage to Mecca* (New York: Atlantic Monthly Press, 1993). A compelling description of an American convert's experience of the pilgrimage, with extensive description and engaging human encounters.

Website:

http://www.islam-online.net/english/index.shtml

Notes

Notes